3—

Sportometrics

Number Eleven:
Texas A & M University Economics Series

Sportometrics

Edited by Brian L. Goff and Robert D. Tollison

TEXAS A&M UNIVERSITY PRESS, COLLEGE STATION

Kenneth Lehn, "Property Rights, Risk Sharing, and Player Disability in Major League Baseball, *Journal of Law and Economics* 25 (Oct. 1982): 343–66; Robert E. McCormick and Robert D. Tollison, "Crime on the Court," *Journal of Political Economy* 92, no. 2 (Apr. 1984): 223–35; Thomas A. Zak et al., "Production Efficiency: The Case of Professional Basketball," *Journal of Business* 52, no. 3 (July 1979): 379–92; Robert E. McCormick and Maurice Tinsley, "Athletics versus Academics? Evidence from SAT Scores," *Journal of Political Economy* 95, no. 5 (Oct. 1987): 1103–16; and Richard A. Zuber et al., "Beating the Spread: Testing the Efficiency of the Gambling Market for National Football League Games," *Journal of Political Economy* 93, no. 4 (Aug. 1985): 800–806, all copyright © by the University of Chicago and reprinted with permission. Robert C. Clement and Robert E. McCormick, "Coaching Team Production," *Economic Inquiry* 27 (Apr. 1989): 287–304; and Kenneth Lehn, "Information Asymmetries in Baseball's Free Agent Market," *Economic Inquiry* 22, no. 1 (Jan. 1984): 37–44, are reprinted with permission from the Western Economic Association International. Philip K. Porter and Gerald W. Scully, "Measuring Managerial Efficiency: The Case of Baseball," *Southern Economic Journal* 48, no. 3 (Jan. 1982): 642–50, is reprinted with permission from the Southern Economic Association. A. A. Fleisher et al., "Crime or Punishment? Enforcement of the NCAA Football Cartel," *Journal of Economic Behavior and Organization* 10 (1988): 433–51, is reprinted with permission from Elsevier Science Publishers. Rex L. Cottle, "Economics of the Professional Golfers' Association Tour," is reprinted from *Social Science Quarterly* 62, no. 4 (Dec. 1981), by permission of the University of Texas Press. Robert E. McCormick and Robert D. Tollison, "Crime and Income Distribution in a Basketball Economy," *International Review of Law and Economics* 6, no. 1 (June 1986): 115–24, copyright © by Butterworth and Company Ltd.

Library of Congress Cataloging-in-Publication Data

Sportometrics / edited by Brian L. Goff and Robert D. Tollison. — 1st ed.
    p.   cm. — (Texas A&M University economics series ; no. 11)
   Includes bibliographical references.
   ISBN 0-89096-425-4 (alk. paper)
   1. Sports—Economic aspects. I. Goff, Brian L. II. Tollison, Robert D. III. Series.
GV716.S64   1990
338.4'7796—dc20   89-49065
                                                         CIP

Contents

VIII. Sports and Income Distribution

IX. Conclusion

Preface

Traditionally, the application of economics to sports consisted of analyses of the antitrust implications of sports leagues or of the labor contracts negotiated with players. This book is different, fundamentally so. The basic point of the papers in this volume is to analyze individual behavior in the setting of sports competition in terms of the economic paradigm of choice within constraints. In other words, the athlete is modeled as an economic entity rather than simply as an athlete. This is useful from a number of points of view, as discussed more fully in the volume; but, essentially, it is useful in showing the power of economics to illuminate individual behavior and institutions in a new setting. This is justification enough for the book in our view.

A number of the essays that appear in this volume have previously appeared in print, and the publishers have granted permission for us to reprint them. Also, we wish to express our gratitude to the authors of all the essays, for allowing us to present their work in this volume.

Brian L. Goff
Robert D. Tollison

1   Introduction

Brian L. Goff and Robert D. Tollison

Sports as Economics

I.   Introduction

There is a scholarly literature that deals with the economics of sports
leagues.[1] Historically, this work has been guided by concerns about the
antitrust status of sports leagues and their associated practices, such as the
player draft. This is a valuable literature, providing, for example, insightful hypotheses about such matters as the Coase theorem, monopsony
power, leagues as single entities, and many other issues relevant for public
policy and the antitrust laws.

This collection of papers seeks to reverse the metaphor. Rather than the
"economics of sports," we introduce the idea of "sports as economics."
Rather than studying sports as an industry, we examine the play of sports
as an expression of rational human action subject to the relevant constraints. In other words, the economic paradigm of Rational Economic
Man can be applied to explain the activities of participants in sporting
events. At a simple level this expansion of economics is important in its
own right, showing the explanatory power of economic science. But, as we
shall see, we also can find scaled-down models of behavior in many other
parts of the economy on the playing field, and hence we can use sporting
competitions as a means to test economic hypotheses of more general
applicability.

We claim that our perspective is unique and rapidly developing—hence,
the reason for pursuing a collection of papers on the subject. The application of economic analysis to the organization, behavior, and outcomes
in the world of sports represents a developing subfield within economics.
The name *sportometrics* tentatively describes this new area. The common
thread of this research is the development and testing of economic hypotheses using sports data as a laboratory. In many cases these hypotheses deal
with matters beyond the playing field, addressing broader issues such as

income distribution, the theory of the firm, the nature of team production processes, industry structure problems and many other topics.

Our purpose in this collection of papers is twofold. First, we want to take the first steps toward systematizing the contributions to this area of research. We have arranged the papers to highlight the common areas of interest among the different authors. Second, in showing the broad and related applications in this subfield, we desire to increase the awareness and usefulness of this research. Our approach is simple: sports teaches us about the expanse of the economic paradigm, it involves very basic, ubiquitous human behavior, and it provides a reliable pool of data and experience with which to develop and test hypotheses of general interest.

This introductory chapter develops the following propositions in detail. First, the view of sports as economics acknowledges the far-reaching applicability of economic tools of analysis. In this regard sportometrics can be seen as a part of a much larger movement in economics that has expanded the use of economic tools to explain nonmarket behavior in such areas as politics, the family, and crime. Second, sporting events provide insight into how closely monitored competition within well-defined rules works. As we shall see, we can learn things about competitive processes in general from observing and analyzing competition on the playing field. Moreover, such "play" constitutes a significant part of human activity. To analyze the economics of play, then, is to analyze an important aspect of the human experience. Third, sport provides a useful and clean laboratory for an economist inclined toward empirical work. General hypotheses can be offered and tested on data that are relatively free of reporting error, especially when compared with the usual data sets employed by economists.

II.   Economic Imperialism and Sports Behavior

Without beating the drum too loudly, we think that it is a useful exercise to show the power of rationality in explaining human behavior. In the present case, we take the relevant locus for this exercise to be the playing field. A small group of economists have started to view sports as an arena in which athletes behave according to incentives and constraints. We have tagged this developing area with the title *sportometrics*. The common thread of this research consists in the idea that sporting events are economic environments. This approach allows for the development and testing of economic hypotheses using sports data as a laboratory.

In this regard sportometrics is simply following the trend in economics. Economic analysis has demonstrated that few, if any, settings are devoid of economic behavior. The prices that drive behavior may be shadow prices rather than explicit ones, and the production function may include inputs beyond those that can be purchased in the market. Nonetheless, the focal variables of economic analysis (product prices, opportunity costs, input prices, and property rights) drive the relevant behavior of important actors.

Even without the diversity of topics and applications within sports data, analysis of sports behavior for its own sake is interesting and useful. Demand curves are demand curves whether they model consumer behavior in automobile markets or the behavior of a coach or referee in monitoring player performance. Even casual observation makes clear that sports is big business across the world. People pay to see sports and are keen analysts of sporting outcomes, and sportometrics is a natural outgrowth of this preference.

III. Sports as Play

Play is a basic human behavior. Whether tossing a ball, assigning fictional domestic roles, or finding hidden participants, children begin to engage in competitive situations called "play" at very early ages.[2] Although a distinction sometimes is drawn between play and competition, to an economist the behavioral patterns do not necessarily warrant such a distinction. Play most often is a form of competition. Many times the games appear frivolous to adults; appearances, however, are deceiving. Sometimes the games include small or large degrees of cooperation between some or all players. Occasionally, the game is against oneself or the clock. In every case incentives (real or imagined) are set up, constraints are declared, and outcomes are generated. In this respect the study of play and economics are nearly identical.

From an economist's perspective the difference between play by children and play by adults rests on the magnitude of incentives and costs. Indeed, almost all behavioral situations involve play. For example, in business situations metaphors involving play are used extensively. Workers compete for higher-paying positions; groups of individuals form teams (firms) and vie against other teams for consumers' dollars. In politics individuals and semicooperative groups (parties) struggle against each other for votes and sometimes trade votes; they engage in "political games." Even within the household setting, spouse, sibling, and parent-children relationships are structured around the incentive-constraint domain of play.

Certainly, sporting events qualify as play. In fact, usage so closely associates these things that the previous sentence might read: play qualifies as play. To some, play is frivolous; sports is play; therefore, research on sports is frivolous. The importance of play as fundamental economic behavior changes this perspective. The fact that athletic events present very pure forms of play strengthens the case for economic research into sports rather than rendering such work less interesting. Sports becomes an arena of pure economic activity. Incentives and constraints are spelled out clearly; players act as rational economic agents; sporting events and seasons can be seen as the operation of miniature economies; and so on.

This description of play and its relationship to sports and economic research does not minimize psychological approaches to play. The most fundamental questions about why children and adults choose some games versus others is of interest, but is not our basic concern in this volume. We leave questions such as why children like toy guns more than dolls (or vice versa) to other research programs. For whatever reasons individuals demand or supply play, and sporting venues provide clear examples of this behavior.

IV.   Sports as an Economics Lab

Sporting events take place in a controlled environment, and generate outcomes that come very close to holding "other things equal." In other words, athletic fields supply real-world laboratories for testing economic theories. The data supplied in these labs have some advantages over the data normally used in economic research.

In sporting events the relevant variables are measured with great accuracy. Rushing yardage for an NFL running back, goals scored by a NHL forward, or shots blocked by an NBA center all measure the desired statistics with very little error. In contrast, economists frequently test hypotheses with data sets that suffer severely from "errors in variables" problems. For example, national income data and other aggregate variables used in macroeconomics, though improved, still have many conceded shortcomings. The underground economy, international trade, and imputed capital values introduce fairly large discrepancies into the data. The CPI faces the constant problem of changes in relative demand for the constituent bundle of goods. The same point holds for many microeconomic data sets such as crime statistics, which are notorious for reporting biases. In general, most sports variables can be measured more closely than many commonly used economic variables.

Of course, a home run in Fenway Park in Boston is not necessarily the same thing as a home run in Busch Stadium in St. Louis. However, even in this case, the statistic can be adjusted because of the accuracy of field and fence dimensions. Many other sports statistics must be adjusted before use, especially in a long time series. Definitions of variables like assists or steals may change in practice, variance in athletic abilities may fall, and so on. In most cases, however, the relevant adjustment statistics can be obtained.

In this regard sports research mimics experimental economics.[3] Whether of the animal (pigeons or rats), the human laboratory, or the computer-simulation type, experimental economics attempts to test economic hypotheses in controlled environments. The advantages of this growing branch of economics is the ability to avoid some of the data pitfalls of econometric research. The economist can perform controlled experiments similar to those performed by the physical and life scientists. Sports data afford a similar opportunity. Although the laboratory is a playing field, the data generated are very "clean." Most external influences are regularly controlled by the rules of the game.

The primary difference between experimental economics and sportometrics is simply that one uses data from playing fields rather than from cages, classrooms, or computers. Of course, the economist cannot design the play on the field around personal research interests, and this is a relative disadvantage of sports behavior research. This loss in control, however, is partly offset by the gain found in using data drawn from actual economic settings. Play on the field "means" something. Sports-generated data thus have one major advantage over much of the experimental data. Experimental data with small groups of people or animals in contrived settings can suffer from the so-called uncertainty principle. In short, this problem arises when outcomes are changed because of the observation of the experimental objects. In the sports case, the objects of observation are large in number (for an entire league), and they are concerned primarily with large financial incentives rather than with an experiment. The participants compete in actual contests but in a very controlled environment.

Aside from measurement errors, economic research sometimes has the "omitted variables" problem; that is, some significant regressors are not included in the estimation. The reasons for this condition vary. Sometimes, economists must conjecture about control variables. Or, perhaps, the proper control variables are known conceptually, but the variables are unobtainable or very costly to measure. Economists can obtain data on GNP and inflation relatively costlessly. However, many interesting hypotheses must be left untested or tested with incomplete data sets and "proxy" variables. Using sports data does not completely solve the omitted variables problem; however, it does reduce it. Almost all sports leagues are prolific data collectors, and one can measure most aspects of sports performance directly at relatively low cost.

In addition to the reliability of sports data, this laboratory contains other advantages. Primarily, the data are applicable to a wide variety of economic hypotheses. Obviously, the statistics in this area can handle a sports-specific model. As the papers in this volume indicate, however, the range of potential analysis extends much wider than sports as such. Questions about competitive versus monopolistic structure can be examined. The data can test models of monopsonistic versus competitive labor markets. Collusion among teams in their "purchase" of players at the collegiate level provides a rich source of information on the behavior of cartels. Between the sports boundary lines "criminal" behavior takes place that is analogous to such behavior beyond those boundaries. Various hypotheses concerning the supply of labor under varying incentives and organizational structures can be addressed.

We mention these cases as examples. Economic analysis has only scratched the surface of the topics that can be studied with sports data. Health and injury hypotheses have been developed. The data offer lessons on value-maximizing rules for a sports league or "constitutional economics." Labor supply under different incentive schemes is observable. In short, sports data are available, accurate, and nearly as broad in scope as economics itself.

V.   Overview

Part II contains three papers that in one way or another deal with the role of individual incentives in sports performance. Higgins and Tollison offer an explanation of the supply of effort in track events. They develop a theory in terms of contest analysis, and test it on data from the modern Olympic Games and the Kentucky Derby. Runners, even in the 100-meter dash, balance costs and benefits at the margin. Kenneth Lehn applies the concept of property rights to the modern baseball labor market. In the wake of free-agency court rulings in baseball, Lehn examines the incentives and performance of players signed to multiyear contracts. As to be expected, incentives matter, and player performance recedes under such a change in property rights. In other words, the nature of what is produced is related to the contractual nexus between players and owners in professional sports. The paper by McCormick and Tollison is about college basketball. They examine the impact of the addition of the third official in college basketball on basketball crime (fouls). They find massive rationality on the court, a lower crime rate, and apparently a better-played game (i.e., a game that has more economic value).

Part III uses sportometrics to better understand the management of team production processes. Clement and McCormick use data on the play and coaching of college basketball to study the role of the manager. They find strong evidence that a manager is the agent of the workers in a team production process and that pairing playing time with observable performance leads to better basketball management (more wins). Porter and Scully devise a means to measure managerial efficiency. They use data from major league baseball to derive something akin to a marginal revenue product function of a manager. Some major league managers in their sample are worth several extra wins to a team over the course of a season. Zak, Huang, and Siegfried estimate a production function for professional basketball teams. Besides indicating the determinants of team performance, they estimate the relative efficiency of different teams. The principles of production theory apply to the world of sports.

Part IV presents papers that deal with issues of the structure of competition. Goff, Shughart, and Tollison show that the competitive structure of sports at the high school level in a state can have a significant impact on the future basketball performance of players from different states. The paper, in essence, tests a survivorship hypothesis. Players from open competition states are better adapted for future survival (i.e., they have longer careers, all else equal) as NBA players than players from classified or cartelized states. Laband investigates how the structure of the competitive process in golf and tennis affects serial correlation (repetitiveness) among winners. The operative difference between the structure of competition in the two sports is that between open versus match play, and structure clearly determines outcomes to an important extent in the two sports. Tennis exhibits a great deal of serial correlation in winners, whereas golf does not.

Part V considers some implications of organizational economics in the context of sports data. Fleisher et al. examine how the NCAA enforces its college player monopsony. Essentially, they argue that the NCAA uses indirect evidence based on the variability of team won-loss records to infer cartel violations. Teams that start to improve on the playing field are turned in and penalized, returning their performance to its historical norm. Fleisher, Goff, and Tollison examine the pattern of NCAA voting on academic standards, arguing that such voting reflects an effort by schools with higher standards to maintain parity on the playing field. In two papers McCormick and Tinsley examine the relationship between student body quality, academic contributions and success on the playing field. Contrary to conventional wisdom in academia, they find that these three things go in the same direction, other things the same.

Part VI presents tests of the famous efficient markets hypothesis using betting market data for the NBA and NFL. Dobra, Cargill, and Meyer basically cannot refute the efficient markets hypothesis using data on betting on NBA games. Zuber, Gandar, and Bowers, on the other hand, fail to support the hypothesis in NFL betting markets. Though they reach contradictory results, these papers illustrate how a major economic idea can be tested at relatively low cost in unique market settings.

Part VII addresses issues of labor supply. Lehn considers the advantage that present versus potential employers have in the estimation of worker marginal products. Using the experience of professional baseball players for his data base, he finds that owners adjust to expectations of free agent performance. Laband and Lentz examine the economics of occupational following (father-son) in major league baseball. Cottle, looking at the monopolistic behavior of the PGA tour, describes how the PGA works as an (unstable) cartel of professional golfers.

In Part VII, McCormick and Tollison illustrate how a basketball economy mimics the actual economy in terms of an income distribution experiment. Moreover, they examine the relationship between crime (fouls) and this distribution and find that a more equal distribution of basketball income begets more basketball crime. This finding contradicts the findings on crime and income distribution in the general economy.

Part IX concludes the volume with a discussion by Goff and Tollison of possible future research projects in sportometrics.

VI.   Conclusion

Useful economics research can be conducted using sports data, and sports present interesting activities to analyze in and of themselves. We should be clear on one thing, however. We are not concerned with terminology. We are not trying to invent a differentiated product or some new "fill-in-the-blank" economics. As Becker (1971, viii) has pointed out, there is only one kind of economics. We advance sportometrics not as a new kind of economics but as a relevant and useful expansion of economic theory.

Notes

1.   See, for example, Rottenberg (1956), Neale (1964), and Quirk and El-Hodiri (1971). For a survey of this literature, see Cairns, Jennett, and Sloane (1986).
2.   Slovenko and Knight (1967) gives a psychological perspective on how play is related to various subject areas.
3.   See Plott (1982) for a review of this literature.

References

Becker, Gary S. *Economic Theory*. 1971. New York: Alfred Knopf.

Cairns, J., N. Jennett, and P. J. Sloane. 1986. "The Economics of Professional Team Sports: A Survey of Theory and Evidence." *Journal of Economic Studies* 13:1–80.

Neale, W. C. 1964. "The Peculiar Economics of Professional Sports." *Quarterly Journal of Economics* (February): 42–56.

Plott, C. R. 1982. "Industrial Organization and Experimental Economics." *Journal of Economic Literature* 20 (December): 1485–1527.

Quirk, J., and M. El-Hodiri. 1971. "An Economic Model of a Professional Sports League." *Journal of Political Economy* 70 (December): 1302–19.

Rottenberg, S. 1956. "The Baseball Players' Labor Market." *Journal of Political Economy* 64 (June): 242–58.

Slovenko, R., and J. A. Knight, eds. 1967. *Motivations in Play, Games, and Sports.* Springfield, Ill.: Charles C. Thomas Publishing.

II   Sports and Individual Incentives

Richard S. Higgins and Robert D. Tollison

Economics at the Track

I.   Introduction

Aside from an occasional curmudgeon, virtually everyone pays some attention to sports contests. Yet, despite the widespread interest in sports competition, this area of behavior is more or less untouched by modern economic theory. There is, of course, a literature on the economics of sports concerning such matters as the organization of professional sports leagues and the clauses of player contracts, but this is not what we have in mind. Our concern is with the actual play of sports on the field and in the arena. In other words, how can economic theory be used to explain the behavior of players in a game or runners in a race? In this paper, we take a small step toward answering this question for running events in the Olympic Games and for the Kentucky Derby.

Our research strategy is straightforward. The runners in a race face the problem of supplying an efficient level of effort during the race. This problem can be seen as an economic problem: How do runners minimize their running time subject to constraints? By viewing the behavior of runners in this way, a testable economic theory of races can be developed.

The paper proceeds as follows. In Section II, we draw on the theory of contests, as developed by Lazear and Rosen (1981), Holmstrom (1982), and Nalebuff and Stiglitz (1983), to derive the equilibrium distribution of running times in a race. The running-time random variables have expected values that depend on exogenous cost and benefit factors suggested by the maximization model. Based on the distribution of running times, a winning-time distribution is derived whose properties depend on the parameters of the model. In Section III, tests of the economic theory of contests are presented using data on track events at the Olympic Games and on the Kentucky Derby. The tests based on Olympics data presume that runners have homogenous skills. This assumption is relaxed in the test based on Kentucky Derby data, which allow contestants' skills to be held constant. Some concluding remarks appear in Section IV.

II.   The Model
Two Contestants

We first model a race with two runners or contestants. Following Nalebuff and Stiglitz (1983), we posit that each runner supplies effort to produce a running time for a race of a given distance. Thus,

$$t_i = \frac{1}{\theta u_i} + \varepsilon_i, \qquad i = 1, 2 \qquad (1)$$

where t is running time, u is runner effort, θ is a random variable common to both runners, and ε is a random variable specific to each runner. For example, θ may capture weather conditions at the time of the race, and ε may reflect how a particular runner feels at the time of the race.[1] The random variable, θ, has a two-parameter distribution with mean 1 and constant variance and the random variables, ε_i, have zero mean, identical variances (σ^2), and are independent. The terms ε_i and θ also are independent.

There are two prizes: a prize W for winning the race and a prize R if a record is set. In most races, the prize is not limited to the trophy or the purse offered in the race. The prize is the broader commercial gain and personal fame achieved by winning, which may differ across contestants. For example, in the Olympics the value of winning may differ depending on the home country of the contestant. In setting out the contest model, we assume W and R are identical across contestants, but in our empirical test we attempt to control for possible differences.

The runners are assumed to face the same cost-of-effort function, $C(u_i)$. Each runner chooses a level of effort that maximizes expected net gain, where a particular runner's probability of winning depends on his or her effort and that of opponents. As we will show, a ceteris paribus increase in an opponent's effort reduces the probability that the runner will win. Note though that in running races where only speed counts (sprints), the effort of one runner does not affect the time of the others. This may not be true for longer races, such as a marathon, where strategy matters more. In a marathon, a runner may "go out fast" to exhaust opponents, throw "surges" into the middle of a race for the same reason, and so on. In these cases there is an interdependency among contestants' efforts (a runners' oligopoly), which we choose to avoid in this paper by focusing on sprints.

A final introductory point concerns the relevant time horizon of the runners in the model. The analytics do not apply simply and literally to runner decision making during a race. A 100-meter sprint does not afford much time for an economic calculus. Rather the model is designed to predict runner behavior over what might loosely be called the training and racing time horizon. Thus, as we shall see, a runner training for the 1992 Olympics will gauge his or her training effort by such factors as the degree of expected competition, the value of the prize, the level of the record in the event, the state of drug-testing technology, and so forth. This is the sense in which runner decisions are made in our model.

Formally, each runner maximizes

$$WP_i(u_i, u_{j\neq i}, \theta) + R\,\text{Prob}_i(t_i < t^R) - C(u_i) \tag{2}$$

where P_i is the probability that i wins, and $\text{Prob}_i(t_i < t^R)$ is the probability that a record is broken.[2] Denoting the probability density and distribution for the ε_i in (1) as g and G, respectively, we can derive expressions for P_i and Prob_i.

To derive P_i, we note from (1) that i wins when $1/\theta u_i + \varepsilon_i < 1/\theta u_j + \varepsilon_j$, or when $\varepsilon_i < 1/\theta u_j - 1/\theta u_i + \varepsilon_j$. Thus, for a given ε_j, the probability that i wins is $G(1/\theta u_j - 1/\theta u_i + \varepsilon_j)$, and if we integrate over ε_j, we have

$$P_i(u_i, u_{j\neq i}, \theta) = \int_{-\infty}^{\infty} G\left(\frac{1}{\theta u_j} - \frac{1}{\theta u_i} + \varepsilon_j\right) g(\varepsilon_j)\,d\varepsilon_j \tag{3}$$

Furthermore, because $t_i = 1/\theta u_i + \varepsilon_i$, $t_i < t^R$ implies $\varepsilon_i < t^R - 1/\theta u_i$, and we have

$$\text{Prob}_i(t_i < t^R) = G\left(t^R - \frac{1}{\theta u_i}\right) \tag{4}$$

If we replace P_i and Prob_i in (2) by (3) and (4), respectively, the maximand is

$$W\int_{-\infty}^{\infty} G\left(\frac{1}{\theta u_j} - \frac{1}{\theta u_i} + \varepsilon_j\right) g(\varepsilon_j)\,d\varepsilon_j + RG\left(t^R - \frac{1}{\theta u_i}\right) - C(u_i) \tag{5}$$

$$i = 1, 2.$$

The marginal conditions are

$$\frac{W}{\theta}\int g\left(\frac{1}{\theta u_j} - \frac{1}{\theta u_i} + \varepsilon_j\right) g(\varepsilon_j)\,d\varepsilon_j + \frac{Rg}{\theta}\left(t^R - \frac{1}{\theta u_i}\right) - u_i^2 C' = 0 \tag{6}$$

At the symmetric solution, $u_1^* = u_2^*$, the marginal conditions are

$$\frac{W}{\theta}\int g^2(\varepsilon)\,d\varepsilon + \frac{Rg}{\theta}\left(t^R - \frac{1}{\theta u_i^*}\right) - u_i^{*2} C' = 0 \tag{7}$$

Based on (7), the relationship between u^* and the exogenous factors can be derived: $\partial u^*/\partial W > 0$, $\partial u^*/\partial R > 0$, and $\partial u^*/\partial t^R > 0$. Effort rises as the prize value does; effort falls as the record barrier increases (as the record falls, effort falls). The effect of θ on u^* is ambiguous.

As an illustration, consider the special case where $C(u) = cu^2/2$ and ε is uniform on $[-t'/2, t'/2]$. The marginal condition (7) becomes

$$\frac{W}{\theta t'} + \frac{R}{\theta t'} - cu^{*3} = 0, \text{ or } u^* = \left(\frac{W+R}{\theta t'c}\right)^{1/3} \tag{8}$$

Note that in this special case where $g' = 0$, u^* is independent of t^R, and $\partial u^*/\partial \theta < 0$. Because conditions are good when θ is larger, the latter derivative implies that runners reduce effort when running conditions are better. Also, effort falls as the runner-specific element of chance increases in significance (i.e., t' rises) and as c rises.[3]

The running-time random variable in our illustration is

$$t = \theta^{-1}\left(\frac{W+R}{\theta t'c}\right)^{-1/3} + \varepsilon \tag{9}$$

So, $Et|\theta = \theta^{-1}[(W+R)/\theta t'c]^{-1/3}$. We also note that $\partial Et|\theta/\partial \theta$ is ambiguous. Even though effort falls as conditions get better, running time may fall if the increased marginal productivity of constant effort occasioned by an increase in θ outweighs the effect of a reduction in effort. Finally, we see that $Et|\theta$ rises as c and t' rise.

In general, then, mean running time is a function of W, R, and t^R, where $\partial Et|\theta/\partial R < 0$, $\partial Et|\theta/\partial W < 0$, and $\partial Et|\theta/\partial t^R < 0$.

Many Contestants

When there are n runners, runner i wins when $t_i < t_j$ for all $j \neq i$. In this case, $P_i(u_1, \ldots, u_i, u_{i+1}, \ldots, u_n) = \int_{-\infty}^{\infty} \ldots \int_{-\infty}^{\infty} [\Pi_{j \neq i} G(1/\theta u_j - 1/\theta u_i + \varepsilon_j)] \Pi_{j \neq i} g(\varepsilon_j) \, d\varepsilon_i \ldots d\varepsilon_{i-1} \, d\varepsilon_{i+1} \ldots d\varepsilon_n$. The marginal conditions at the symmetric solution are

$$W\left(\frac{n-1}{\theta}\right)\int G^{n-2}(\varepsilon)g^2(\varepsilon) \, d\varepsilon + \frac{Rg}{\theta}\left(t^R - \frac{1}{\theta u_i^*}\right) - u_i^{*2}C' = 0, \tag{10}$$

for all i

From (10) we derive the following:

$$\frac{\partial u^*}{\partial W} > 0, \frac{\partial u^*}{\partial R} > 0, \text{ and } \frac{\partial u^*}{\partial t^R} > 0.$$

The effect of additional contestants on effort is given by

$$\frac{\partial u^*}{\partial n} = \frac{W}{\theta D}[\int G^{n-2}g^2 + (n-1)\int G^{n-2}g^2 \ln G] \tag{11}$$

where D is negative. Thus, $\partial u^*/\partial n < 0$ or > 0 as $|(n-1)\int G^{n-2}g^2 \ln G|$ $>$ or $< \int G^{n-2}g^2$. But because G lies between 0 and 1, $\ln G$ lies between $-\infty$ and zero, so $\partial u^*/\partial n \le 0$. The greater the number of contestants, the less individual running effort will be.

The running-time random variable is

$$t = \frac{1}{\theta u^*(W, R, t^R, n)} + \varepsilon \tag{12}$$

Based on the above comparative statics, $\partial t/\partial W < 0$, $\partial t/\partial R > 0$, $\partial t/\partial t^R \le 0$, and $\partial t/\partial n \ge 0$.

In our special case of a uniform distribution for ε and $C = cu^2/2$, (10) is

$$\frac{W}{\theta t'} + \frac{R}{\theta t'} - cu^{*3} = 0, \text{ or } u^* = \left(\frac{W+R}{c\theta t'}\right)^{1/3} \tag{13}$$

Note that in this case u^* is independent of the number of contestants and t^R.

The Winning-Time Distribution

Our hypothesis is that winning time in a footrace can be explained as a first-order statistic based on the running-time distribution. Specifically, the distribution function for winning time, t^W, is $1 - \{1 - G[t^W - 1/\theta u^*(W, R, t^R, n)]\}^n$. Thus, the winning-time density is $n[1 - G(t^W - 1/\theta u^*)]^{n-1} g(t^W - 1/\theta u^*) \equiv h_n(t^W)$.

To illustrate how the winning-time probability density function varies with n, we resort to our special case where G is the uniform distribution. Figure 1 depicts the winning-time density functions for $n = 1, 2,$ and 3. The greater the number of contestants, the more the density is skewed toward lower running times. Moreover, as n increases, mean winning time declines.

In general, the winning-time random variable is

$$t^W = f(W, R, t^R, n) + \zeta \tag{14}$$

where ζ has zero mean and a variance that declines with n.

As Stigler (1961) notes in the context of search theory, when the underlying distribution (here the running-time distribution) is normal, the expected minimum-order statistic is just the mean of the underlying distribution minus a function of n, times the standard deviation of the underlying distribution, where the function of n rises at a declining rate. In our context, the expected winning-time would be

$$Et^W = \frac{1}{\theta u^*} - f(n)\sigma \tag{15}$$

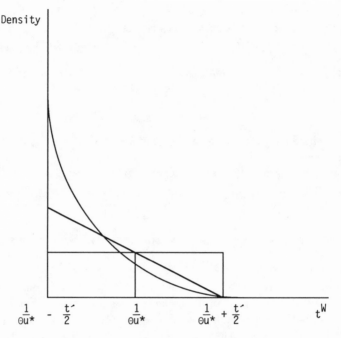

Figure 1. Winning-time density functions

III.   Empirical Analysis
Olympics Sprints

First, we estimate average running time in a race. Expected running time is hypothesized to depend on various exogenous factors that capture the relevant costs and benefits and the degree of competition in our model. Second, expected winning time is estimated. In this case, we test whether expected winning time depends on the mean and standard deviation of running time and on the number of contestants, as predicted by the minimum-order statistic hypothesis.

Average Running-Time Regression. The data used to estimate average running time are running times in the final heats of the 100M, 200M, 400M, and 800M events in the Olympic Games from 1896 to 1980 (Wallechinsky 1984),[4] 426 observations. We pooled the observations across events, normalizing running times by the 100M distance. Thus, our dependent variable, t, is the time in nearest tenths of a second required to run 100M, whether the actual event is the 100M or the 800M. A priori, we expect the rate to rise with overall distance, so dummy variables to allow for differences across events in mean running time per 100M are included as regressors—D100, D200, and D400.

Other explanatory variables are suggested by our model to capture changes over time in the gains from winning, technology, and the number of contestants. Still other regressors are necessary to avoid statistical artifact. Specifically, we note that in several cases the number of running times in an event is less than the number of competitors running in the heat. Most often, this occurs because a runner fell (Mary Decker) or otherwise did not finish. In these cases, the average running time is affected in a manner unrelated to our theory about the relationship between expected running time and the number of competitors. Thus, we include the regressor, *NUMT,* which is the number of recorded times in an event.

Several regressors were included to capture changes over time in technology. Specifically, starting blocks were used for the first time in 1948. Because starting blocks are used only in the 100M, 200M, and 400M, we interacted the *BLOCK* dummy variable (1 from 1948 to 1980; 0 otherwise) with the 100M, 200M, and 400M dummy variables. Also, the running surface has changed over time. In 1968, the cinder track was replaced by artificial surfaces such as the tartan track. To account for this change the dummy variable *SURFACE* was included (1 from 1968 to 1980; 0 otherwise). A third dummy variable, *CURVE,* was defined to mark the date, 1960, when the 200M was run around a curve instead of straightaway. This regressor interacts D200 and *CURVE.* Finally, to capture secular changes in factors such as health and training techniques and shoe technology, we included a trend variable, *T,* which ticks off years from the first Olympics. In this case, we also allowed the effects of these exogenous trend factors to be different for the various events. So, initially, we included D100 *T,* D200 *T,* and D400 *T.*

On the demand side we measured the importance of winning to the contestants in several ways. We included the total number of gold, silver, and bronze medals won by a runner's home country in the year an event was run. *MEDALS* was included to capture the importance of the Olympics in the runner's home country, which presumably is correlated with the gains the individual runner could achieve by winning. We also included a dummy variable, *US,* that indicates whether a contestant is from the United States. *US* is included as a crude indication of the relative value of winning to contestants overall; specifically, *US* is positively correlated with the size of the prize. Finally, we included the variable, *NATIONS,* the number of nations participating in a particular Olympics, which proxies the importance of the Olympics worldwide.

A third set of regressors was included to measure the effect of the number of competitors on average running time. *HEAT* is the number of runners in the final heat. *TOTNUM* is the total number of entrants in a particular event, most of whom are eliminated before the final heat. Strictly speaking, our model analyzes the impact on running time of the actual number of competitors in the race. Nonetheless, the *n* in the model is best interpreted as the degree of competition, at least for purposes of estimating average running time. So we also include *TOTNUM* along with *HEAT*.[5]

Finally, we included the world record time (per 100M) and Olympic record time (per 100M) in effect at the time the event was run to test the implication that runners will supply less effort the harder the record is to break. These variables are *WR* and *OR*, respectively.

To summarize, the regression model we initially estimated is

$$
\begin{aligned}
t_{ijk} = a_0 &+ a_1\, D100_j + a_2\, D200_j + a_3\, D400_j + a_5\, D100_j\, T_k \\
&+ a_6\, D200_j\, T_k + a_7\, D400_j\, T_k + a_8\, T_k + a_9\, NUMT_{jk} \\
&+ a_{10}\, HEAT_{jk} + a_{11}\, NATIONS_k + a_{12}\, TOTNUM_{jk} \\
&+ a_{13}\, MEDALS_{ijk} + a_{14}\, WR_{jk} + a_{15}\, OR_{jk} + a_{16}\, D100_j\, BLOCK_k \\
&+ a_{17}\, D200_j\, BLOCK_k + a_{18}\, D400_j\, BLOCK_k \\
&+ a_{19}\, D200_j\, CURVE_k + a_{20}\, SURFACE_k + a_{21}\, US_{ijk} + \mu_{ijk}
\end{aligned}
\tag{16}
$$

where

t_{ijk}	= running time of contestant *i* in event *j* in Olympics *k* in seconds per 100M (accuracy to nearest tenth of a second);
$D100_j$	= 1 if 100M event; 0 otherwise;
$D200_j$	= 1 if 200M event; 0 otherwise;
$D400_j$	= 1 if 400M event; 0 otherwise;
T_k	= time trend;
$NUMT_{jk}$	= number of recorded times in a particular event in the *k*th Olympics;
$HEAT_{jk}$	= number of entries in final heat of particular event in the *k*th Olympics;
$NATIONS_k$	= number of nations represented in the *k*th Olympics;
$TOTNUM_{jk}$	= total number of entrants in a particular event in the *k*th Olympics;
$MEDALS_{ijk}$	= total number of medals won by home country of runner *i* in event *j* in the *k*th Olympics;
WR_{jk}	= existing world record in the *j*th event in the *k*th Olympics;

OR_{jk} = existing Olympic record in the jth event in the kth Olympics;

$BLOCK_k$ = 1 in Olympics when starting blocks used (1948–80); 0 otherwise;

$CURVE_k$ = 1 in years since 200M was run on curve (1960–80); 0 otherwise;

$SURFACE_k$ = 1 in the years since running surface was a polyurethane composition (1968–80); 0 otherwise;

US_{ijk} = 1 if runner i in the jth event in the kth Olympics represents the United States; and

μ_{ijk} = a random error term.

Our model suggests the following coefficient signs: $a_1 \leq 0$; $a_2 \leq 0$; $a_3 \leq 0$; and $|a_1| \geq |a_2| \geq |a_3|$; a_5, a_6, and a_7 are ambiguous; $a_8 < 0$; a_9 is ambiguous; $a_{10} > 0$; $a_{11} < 0$; $a_{12} > 0$; $a_{13} < 0$; $a_{14} \leq 0$; $a_{15} \leq 0$; $a_{16} < 0$; $a_{17} < 0$; $a_{18} < 0$; $a_{19} > 0$; $a_{20} < 0$; and $a_{21} < 0$.

The regression model was initially estimated using OLS. Based on these results, we combined variables $D100\ T$ and $D200\ T$ when the null hypothesis that $a_5 = a_6$ could not be rejected. We also adjusted for heteroskedasticity. Because we have pooled running times from several events, correcting for possible differences in the variance of running times for different events seems appropriate. Moreover, because our specification of the winning-time regression in the next section depends on the normality of the error distribution, purging the residuals of heteroskedasticity facilitates the test of normality.

To adjust for heteroskedasticity, we first calculated the standard deviation of the residuals from regression (16), with $D100\ T$ and $D200\ T$ replaced by $[(D100 + D200)\ T]$, for each race. Then, based on the model $\sigma_{jk}^2 = \sigma^2\ (NUMT)^{d_1}\ (TOTNUM)^{d_2}\ (D100')^{d_3}\ (D200')^{d_4}\ (D400')^{d_5}$, where $DX00' = e$ when $DX00 = 1$, and $DX00' = 1$ when $DX00 = 0$, we estimated the d_i. We eliminated the variables with insignificant d_i coefficients and reestimated the σ_{jk}^2 relation to find weights to adjust (16) for heteroskedasticity. Ultimately, the weights were

$$W_{jk} = (NUMT_{jk})^{-0.682}\ D_j^{\,0.328}$$

where $D_j = e$ if $D100$ or $D200$ equals 1, and $D_j = 1$ otherwise.

The weighted regression results are

$$Et = 14.32 - 3.57\ D100 - 3.46\ D200 - 1.94\ D400$$
$$(7.52)(-7.50) \qquad (-7.28) \qquad (-6.36)$$

$$+ 0.04\ (D100 + D200)T - 0.004\ D400T - 0.09\ NUMT$$
$$(5.75) \qquad\qquad (-0.36) \qquad\qquad (-6.68)$$

$$+ 0.08 \; HEAT - 0.01 \; NATIONS + 0.005 \; TOTNUM$$
$$\quad (6.56) \qquad (-3.27) \qquad\qquad (3.54)$$

$$- 0.0009 \; MEDALS + 0.06 \; WR - 0.03 \; OR - 0.07 \; T$$
$$(-4.10) \qquad\qquad (0.52) \quad (-2.24) \quad (-5.43)$$

$$- 0.13 \; D100BLOCK - 0.28 \; D200BLOCK$$
$$(-1.94) \qquad\qquad (-4.34)$$

$$+ 0.08 \; D400BLOCK - 0.08 \; D200CURVE$$
$$(0.80) \qquad\qquad (1.17)$$

$$+ 0.03 \; SURFACE - 0.06 \; US$$
$$(0.86) \qquad\qquad (-2.23)$$

$$\text{(17)}$$

$$R^2 = 0.98$$

F-statistic $= 1178.14$

A number of interesting findings appear in (17). First, the variables, *HEAT* and *TOTNUM*, which most clearly measure n, the number of contestants in our theoretical model, have the effect of raising expected running time. This result is consistent with the model's prediction that runners supply less effort the greater the number of competitors.

Second, we included *NATIONS*, *US*, and *MEDALS* as measures of the gains from winning. These were predicted to have negative effects on expected running time, which they do, and significantly.

Third, the effect of the existing record times is found to be negative and significant as predicted for the Olympic record, but the estimated effect is zero for world record time. The harder the Olympic record is to break, the less effort runners will expend to break it. Carl Lewis' pass on Bob Beamon's long-jump record at the 1984 Olympics is a vivid example of this point.

Fourth, the technology variables show some surprises. Apparently, starting blocks have significantly lowered average running time for only the 100M and 200M, and more for the 200M than the 100M. Changes in the running surface have not significantly altered running times, and although the sign on the *D200 CURVE* variable is positive as predicted, it is not significant. Also, the predicted effect of *T* on running time, whether interpreted as secular supply- or demand-side changes, is supported by the coefficient estimates. The 800M running time has declined statistically significantly as indicated by the coefficient on *T*, and as evidenced by the insignificant coefficient for *D400 T*, running time in the 400M has declined in the same way. In the case of the 100M and the 200M, expected running time has changed in the same way secularly, but the positive sign on (*D*100

+ *D200*) *T* indicates these times have decreased less on average than the times for the longer distances. Based on casual knowledge about the relative gains from winning the 100M and 200M over winning the 400M and 800M—for example, in recent times 100M and 200 winners often have gone on to play professional football—we suspect that *T* must be primarily picking up supply-side effects. If this is so, then we can infer that training and health advances have been more productive for the relatively longer distances. In bold terms, stamina can be learned more easily than speed.

Finally, we note as expected that there are diminishing marginal returns to longer distances. The 400M is run, on average, 1.94 seconds per 100M faster than the 800M, and the 100M and 200M are run, on average, approximately 3 seconds per 100M faster than the 800M.

To obtain a predictor of expected running time as a regressor in the winning-time regression in the next section, we first eliminated the insignificant regressors from (17): *D400 T, WR, D200 CURVE, D400 BLOCK,* and *SURFACE*. We then applied OLS to the resulting regression model, calculated race-specific standard deviations, reconstructed weights, and estimated the coefficients again, applying the weights to the regressors. The equation for predicting expected running time is

$$Et = \quad 15.32 \quad - \quad 3.81 \ D100 \ - \ 3.71 \ D200 \ - \ 2.08 \ D400$$
$$(239.02)(-67.11) \qquad (-61.93) \qquad\quad (61.49)$$

$$+ \ 0.05 \ (D100 + D200) \ T \ - \ 0.09 \ NUMT$$
$$(8.01) \qquad\qquad\qquad\qquad (-7.30)$$

$$+ \ 0.08 \ HEAT \ - 0.007 \ NATIONS \ + 0.003 \ TOTNUM$$
$$(7.45) \qquad\quad (-2.89) \qquad\qquad\quad (2.69)$$

$$- \ 0.001 \ MEDALS \ - 0.03 \ OR \ - 0.08 \ T \qquad\qquad (18)$$
$$(-4.23) \qquad\qquad\quad (-6.97) \quad (-12.98)$$

$$- \ 0.18 \ D100 \ BLOCK \ - 0.27 \ D200 \ BLOCK \ - 0.05 \ US$$
$$(-2.71) \qquad\qquad\qquad (-4.34) \qquad\qquad\quad (-2.09)$$

$$R^2 = 0.98$$

F-statistic = 1529.37

$$\sigma_{jk}^2 = 0.008 \ (NUMT_{jk})^{1.358} \ D_j^{-0.654} \text{ where } D_j = e \text{ when } D100 +$$

$$D200 = 1; 1 \text{ otherwise.}$$

The Winning-Time Regression. If the underlying distribution of running times is normal, winning time (which is just the minimum of a sample of times drawn from the running-time distribution) has an expected value equal to $Et - f(n)\sigma$, where Et and σ are the mean and standard deviation of the underlying running-time distribution and $f(n)$ is an increasing function (with $f'' < 0$) of the number of runners in the heat.

We first tested for the normality of the residuals. We applied the Kolmogorov-Smirnov test to the residuals from the weighted regression (18). The null hypothesis (normality) cannot be rejected. The probability that we are accepting the null by mistake is .01; D-max is 0.0515.

Based on our confirmation of a normal running-time distribution, we hypothesized the following winning-time regression model:

$$t^W = a_0 + a_1 Et - \ln (HEAT^d)\sigma + \zeta$$
$$= a_0 + a_1 Et - d(\ln HEAT)\sigma + \zeta \qquad (19)$$
$$= a_0 + a_1 Et + a_2(\ln HEAT)\sigma + \zeta$$

The function $\ln (HEAT^d)$ has the properties predicted by the first-order statistic hypothesis: when $HEAT = 1$, $\ln HEAT^d = 0$, and as $HEAT$ rises, $\ln HEAT^d$ rises at a declining rate. We predict that $a_0 = 0$, $a_1 = 1$, and $a_2 < 0$.

To estimate (19), we defined t^W as the winning time per 100M to the nearest tenth of a second for the 100M, 200M, 400M and 800M final heats in the Olympics from 1896 to 1980. Our measure of Et for each race is the predicted value from (18), based on the value of the regressors in each race. For the independent variables, $MEDALS$ and US, which are runner-specific and not race-specific, we used the average over runners in the race. As an estimate of σ, we used the square root of the predicted value of the variance regression reported in (18).

The regression results are

$$Et^W = \ -0.13 + 1.005M - 0.368(\ln HEAT)\sigma$$
$$\qquad (-0.76) \ (65.90) \quad (-2.33)$$
$$F\text{-statistic} = 2284.4 \qquad n = 73 \qquad (20)$$
$$R^2 = 0.985$$

The estimates in (20) strongly support the hypothesis that winning time satisfies the minimum-order statistic property. The intercept is not significantly different from 0; the coefficient on average running time is not significantly different from 1, and the marginal contribution of σ is negative with $\partial Et^W/\partial HEAT = -\sigma(.368)/HEAT < 0$, and $\partial^2 Et^W/\partial HEAT^2 = \sigma(.368)/(HEAT)^2 > 0$.

The Kentucky Derby

Heterogenous Runners. In the Olympics running-time and winning-time regressions, we assumed that the runners were homogenous.

That is, they have identical cost-of-effort functions. If, instead, runners have different abilities and the selection of runners for the final heat systematically chooses the better runners, the prediction that expected running time is negatively related to the number of contestants does not distinguish the contest model from a random effort, or performance, model. Specifically, if runner performance is a random variable with a mean which varies across runners depending on the skill of each, then the more runners in a race, the lower would be average performance unless runners were selected randomly for the final heat. Moreover, we presume that qualification for the final heat through good performance in preliminary heats systematically selects the better runners for the final heat. Thus, a test of the contest model based on the estimated sign of the running-time–number-of-contestants coefficient would not be appropriate unless runners' skills or predicted performance were held constant.

We were unable to obtain adequate data on runners' skills to provide a strong test of the contest model. Fortunately, information about contestants' skills is available for the Kentucky Derby. We thus can provide a strong test of the economic theory of contests by estimating an expected running-time regression for the Kentucky Derby, holding skill constant.

Although we know of no direct evidence that horses obey the law of demand, we nonetheless expect running times in a professional horse race to conform to the economic theory of contests. Given running ability, owners choose training effort and jockey skills and efforts presumably based on an economic calculus, which we suppose is well described by the contest model.

Expected Running Time with Skill Held Constant. The regression model posits a linear relationship between expected running time in the Kentucky Derby and several regressors suggested by the economic theory of contests. The explanatory variables include the number of horses in the race, the size of the purse, measures of the individual entrant's skill and of the distribution of entrants' skills in the race, jockey experience, technological factors such as the presence or absence of starting gates, and track and weather conditions. The purpose of the regression model, of course, is to test the null hypothesis that the coefficient on the number of contestants is less than or equal to zero. The contest model predicts a positive coefficient.

The Kentucky Derby data, although containing more complete information about contestant skills than the Olympics data, provide less information about running times. Only the winning time is available from each Kentucky Derby. However, the data indicate how many lengths (or fraction of lengths) behind the winner each horse finished. Thus, instead of estimating average running time, we estimate the expected number of lengths behind the winner as a function of the independent variables suggested by the contest model, holding winning time constant. Holding winning time constant enables us to interpret the coefficient on number of contestants as the ceteris paribus effect of the number of contestants on average running time.

To account for heterogenous skills, we use data on the odds that a particular horse will win, reported just prior to post time. The odds are presumably rational predictors of relative performance. They appear to be deficient for our purposes for two reasons.

First, the odds provide information about differences in predicted performance, not just skill differences. This turns out to be a blessing in disguise as relative skill may be ambiguous. That is, one horse may be better than another under normal conditions and worse when running in the mud. Odds at post time automatically adjust for such contingencies and reflect the relative skills that count, among other things. Broadly speaking, the deficiency in the test based on Olympics data is that average runner performance might be systematically related to the number of runners for reasons independent of the contest model's proposition that runners reduce effort in response to an increase in the number of competitors, other things equal. Including odds as regressors holds constant those factors that predict performance and are not accounted for by the other explanatory variables in our regression, for example, contestant skill conditioned on the "state of the world" at post time.

Second, the odds provide predictions only about relative performance. However, including winning time among the regressors converts—partly, at least—the expected relative performance predictors to expected absolute performance predictors. Of course, with winning time as an explanatory variable, the unconditional predictive capacity of the regression model is limited. Overall, the shortcomings of using odds data are insignificant relative to the opportunity they afford in controlling for skill differences.

To further control for skill differences, we collected data on jockeys' prior riding experience in the Kentucky Derby. The jockey experience variable measures absolute skill better, perhaps, than odds and winning time.

We obtained data on the Kentucky Derby (the premier U.S. thoroughbred racing event) from 1920 through 1985 (*The Kentucky Derby* 1986). The length of the race and the weight of jockeys and saddles are constant over all races and horses in these sixty-six years. Two equations are estimated from the data. First, we estimate the length behind the winner for each horse in races over the 1920–85 period. This pooled time-series–cross-section has 954 observations for the dependent variable. Second, we estimate a time series for average lengths behind the winner for the sixty-six years' races.

Equation (21) states the model used to estimate the number of lengths back a horse finished.

$$LENGTHSBACK_{ij} = f(STARTERS_j, ODDS_{ij}, WINTIME_j,$$

$$\$WINNER_j, \$SECOND_j, \qquad (21)$$

$$JOCKEXP_{ij}, DGATE, DTRACK_j, u_{ij})$$

where

$LENGTHS_{ij}$ = number of lengths back from the winner of horse i in race j,

$STARTERS_j$ = the number of starters in race j,

$ODDS_{ij}$ = the odds at post time for horse i in race j,

$WINTIME_j$ = the winning time in race j,

$\$WINNER_j$ = prize money in real terms for the winning horse in race j,

$\$SECOND_j$ = prize money in real terms for the second place horse in race j,

$JOCKEXP_{ij}$ = number of previous Kentucky Derby rides for jockey i in race j,

$DGATE$ = 1 if a horse competed in the pre-starting gate era (pre-1930); 0 for horses after 1930,

$DTRACK_j$ = 1 if the track condition was listed as fast in race j; 0 otherwise, and

u_{ij} = a random error term.

The dependent variable, *LENGTHSBACK*, measures the distance a horse finished behind the winner. It equals 0 for the winner. A nose equals 0 lengths, a head is 0.1 lengths, and a neck is 0.25 lengths.

The number of horses starting a race, *STARTERS*, varies across races. This is the central variable of interest in our test. Controlling for heterogenous skills, do we still find average running time (proxied here by lengths back) positively related to the number of contestants?

ODDS measures the abilities of each horse relative to the abilities of other horses in a race. Specifically, *ODDS* for a particular horse is the ratio of its probability of losing to its probability of winning, ignoring the cost of administering the wagers. The odds are the result of the prerace wagers of individuals. Two special cases exist in the odds data. If two or more horses in a race are under joint control (same owner, trainer, or stable), the horses are grouped together in the wagering. Wagers are cast for the group instead of the individual horses, and the odds for the group are reported for each individual horse. The average horse-specific odds for such groups are approximately equal to the number of horses in the group times the group odds, so we adjusted the group odds in this manner. A similar situation arises when the race contains more than twelve horses. In this case, handicappers select the best twelve horses. The remaining horses are grouped in the betting as in the joint-control case. This is called a field bet, and we again obtain horse-specific odds by multiplying the odds for the group by the number of horses in the group. Higher odds mean a horse has relatively less ability and is a "longer shot" to win the race. The expected sign on *ODDS* is positive.

WINTIME varies across races, and controls for the speed of a race. This allows the effects of the other variables on distance behind the winner to be measured independently of the speed of the race. No sign is predicted a priori.

The remainder of the model controls for a variety of exogenous forces. *$WINNER* and *$SECOND* are the amounts of money going to the winner and to the second place horse in real dollars. Higher payoffs imply more intense competition. The expected sign on both variables is negative. *JOCKEXP* is the number of times the jockey has previously ridden in the Derby. This controls for the human capital of jockeys. More experienced jockeys will choose more efficient paths, stay away from boxes, and avoid collisions. The expected sign is negative. *DGATE* and *DTRACK* are dummy variables to control for technological conditions. Horses running before 1930 started with an elastic tape stretched across the starting line. Starts were often delayed due to horses breaking the tape. Starting in 1930, mechanical starting gates were used. *DGATE* captures this technological change. The expected sign is positive; more even starts should allow the better horses to pull away from the pack earlier. *DTRACK* measures the condition of the running surface on the track. A negative sign is expected. Good track conditions mean less of a chance of horses losing footing, hence a faster race.

Equation (21) is estimated by ordinary least squares. The results are

$$LENGTHSBACK = 30.808 + 0.272 \; STARTERS + 0.107 \; ODDS$$
$$ (0.92) \quad (2.89) (11.70)$$

$$- \; 0.149 \; WINTIME - 0.001 \; \$WINNER$$
$$(-0.57) (-0.63)$$

$$- \; 0.015 \; \$SECOND - 0.285 \; JOCKEXP \qquad (22)$$
$$(-2.82) (-2.89)$$

$$- \; 0.116 \; DGATE - 1.450 \; DTRACK$$
$$(-0.11) (-1.35)$$

$$R^2 = 0.189$$

$$F\text{-statistic} = 27.58 \qquad n = 946$$

Overall, the equation is significant at the 1 percent level. The key variable of interest, *STARTERS*, has a positive sign and is significant at the 1 percent level. Average running time, as proxied by *LENGTHSBACK*, rises with more starters, ceteris paribus. *ODDS* has the expected positive and significant sign. Better horses with lower odds finish closer to the winner than less able horses with longer odds. Winning time is negative but not significant. *$WINNER* is negative but not significant. *$SECOND* and *JOCKEXP* are negative and significant at the 1 percent level. The introduction of starting gates, *DGATE*, had no perceptible effect on the finish of horses. *DTRACK* is negative and significant at the 15 percent level. Fast track conditions lead to closer races.

Equation (23) gives the model used to estimate average lengths behind the winner across races:

$$AVERAGE\ LENGTHSBACK_j = (STARTERS_j,\ MODDS_j,\ SDODDS_j,$$

$$WINTIME_j,\ \$WINNERS_j,$$

$$\$SECOND_j,\ MJOCKEXP_j, \tag{23}$$

$$DGATE,\ DTRACK_j,\ u_j)$$

where the four new variables are defined as follows:

$AVERAGE\ LENGTHSBACK_j$ = the mean length behind the winner for horses in race j,

$MODDS_j$ = the mean odds of the horses in race j,

$SDODDS_j$ = the standard deviation of odds of horses in race j, and

$MJOCKEXP_j$ = the mean years of Derby experience of jockeys in race j, where jockey experience is defined as in (21).

The definitions of the remaining variables are unchanged.

The new dependent variable, *AVERAGE LENGTHSBACK*, allows for the effects of the explanatory variables to be estimated on the mean finish of a horse. Together with *WINTIME*, *MODDS* and *SDODDS* control for the distribution of abilities across races. Ceteris paribus, higher mean odds mean that the average horse is less likely to win the race; that is, average skill is lower. The expected sign of the coefficient of *MODDS* is positive. The expected coefficient of *SDODDS* is zero. Higher *SDODDS* means more variation in abilities, but it is unclear what effect greater variation would have on average lengths back. *MJOCKEXP* controls for the abilities of jockeys in the race. More overall experience should lead to faster times as proxied by average lengths back. *MJOCKEXP* is expected to have a negative sign. The other variables in equation (23) are expected to have the same signs as in equation (21).

Equation (23) is estimated by ordinary least squares. The results are

$$AVERAGE\ LENGTHSBACK\ =\ 47.333\ +0.289\ STARTERS$$
$$(1.02)\quad(1.75)$$

$$+\ 0.103\ MODDS\ -\ 0.063\ SDODDS$$
$$(1.07)\qquad\qquad(-0.82)$$

$$-\ 0.256\ WINTIME\ -\ 0.002\ \$WINNER$$
$$(-0.71)\qquad\qquad(-0.96)\qquad(24)$$

$$-\ 0.005\ \$SECOND$$
$$(-0.66)$$

$$-\ 1.300\ MJOCKEXP$$
$$(-2.25)$$

$$+\ 0.649\ DGATE\ -\ 0.649\ DTRACK$$
$$(0.44)\qquad\qquad(-1.53)$$

$$R^2 = 0.349$$

$$F\text{-statistic} = 3.33\qquad n = 66$$

Overall, the equation explains 35 percent of the variation in average lengths behind and is significant at the 5 percent level. *STARTERS* again has a positive sign and is significant at the 10 percent level. Neither of the odds distribution control variables, *MODDS* and *SDODDS*, has a significant effect. Winning time has a negative sign as in (22) but is again insignificant. Prize money to the winner, *$WINNER*, is negative but insignificant. Second place prize money, *$SECOND*, has a negative sign and is not significant. Jockey experience has a negative sign and is significant at the 5 percent level. *DGATE* has a weak positive sign. Track condition, *DTRACK*, has a negative sign that is slightly below the 10 percent significance level.

The central point, however, is that, in both experiments on the Kentucky Derby data, we are able to find a positive effect of the number of contestants on a proxy for average running time, while controlling for differences in ability. These results bolster our confidence in the prediction that effort to achieve a fixed prize is reduced with a larger number of competitors. The findings are not conclusive, however. The Kentucky Derby is run around an oval track so that positioning along the rail is valuable, and congestion increases with the number of contestants.

IV.   Conclusion

In this paper, we apply contest theory to the example of racing contests. From Nalebuff and Stiglitz (1983), we know that competition serves to re-

duce the incentive problems created by unobservable asymmetric information and to reveal information, which would otherwise be unobservable,
about the environment in which economic agents supply effort. Thus, regardless of whether spectators value the contest as such, a running race
automatically levels the playing field and elicits efficient levels of effort
from the runners, as if the goal were the fastest running time subject to
constraints (conditioned on time and place). Approaching the problem in
this way, we derive an economic theory of running in a footrace. This theory makes certain predictions about the impact of the number of competitors, the value of winning, technology, and so forth on the average running time in a race; and we find these predictions supported in a test using
data from the sprint events (100M to 800M) in the modern Olympic
Games.

Unfortunately, the Olympics running data do not allow for the control of
differential abilities of runners. This blurs the test of the basic implication
of our application of contest theory to running that more runners in a race
lead to a reduction in the supply of effort among runners and hence to a
higher average running time. In effect, we are unable to distinguish a homogenous runners model from a random performance model with differ-
entially skilled runners. To address this issue, we offer empirical evidence
from the history of a horse racing event, the Kentucky Derby. Here we are
able to control for differential running ability with the use of prerace odds
and jockey experience, and we find that our basic result, that more starters
leads to slower races, tests strongly in this data set.

Notes

We are grateful to Dwight Lee, Gerry Butters, and Cliff Huang for helpful comments. We also acknowledge helpful research assistance from Susan Campbell
and Brian Goff. The usual caveat applies.
1.   The relative marginal productivity of effort is constant across runners in
        equation (1). This condition does not necessarily hold. In the 1968 Mex-
        ico City Olympics, for example, it was argued that the Kenyans had an
        advantage over other runners because of the high altitude. Over time, of
        course, runners from other countries can seek altitude training to mute
        such an advantage.
2.   In the event that a contestant whose running time is better than the existing
        record time does not win the race, breaking the record counts for signifi-
        cantly less. In our specification, however, which simplifies the analytics,
        a runner does not have to win to enjoy the benefits of breaking a record.
3.   In team sports, the chance element is less significant than in individual
        sports as other team members or substitutes can compensate for the "bad
        day" of a single player. On the other hand, shirking may be greater in

team sports because of input interdependency, although coaches are unlikely to miss or tolerate shirking by individual players.

4.   The long-distance running events were excluded because they are more likely to entail interdependence among contestants' efforts beyond that captured in our contest model. In short, our model captures only "offense" on the part of contestants. Long-distance running is characterized by strategic behavior; in sprints, running fast is all that counts. The relevant physiological distinction is between aerobic and anaerobic running. Of course, the 800M is not a pure sprint, but we have included it in our data because it is not a long-distance race either.

5.   In the winning-time model, where the minimum-order statistic property is critical, it is more appropriate to restrict number of competitors to *HEAT*.

References

Holmstrom, B. 1982. "Moral Hazard in Teams." *Bell Journal of Economics* 13 (Autumn): 324–40.

The Kentucky Derby, 1875–1985. 1986. Louisville: Churchill Downs, Inc.

Lazear, E. P., and S. Rosen. 1981. "Rank-Order Tournaments as Optimum Labor Contracts." *Journal of Political Economy* 89 (October): 841–64.

Nalebuff, B. J., and J. E. Stiglitz. 1983. "Prizes and Incentives: Towards a General Theory of Compensation and Competition." *Bell Journal of Economics* 14 (Spring): 21–43.

Stigler, G. J. 1961. "The Economics of Information." *Journal of Political Economy* 69 (June): 213–25.

Wallechinsky, D. 1984. *The Complete Book of the Olympics*. New York: Penguin Books.

Kenneth Lehn

Property Rights, Risk Sharing, and Player Disability in Major League Baseball

In *The Economic Organization,* Frank Knight describes five tasks performed in all economic systems. In logical order, the first of these tasks is determination of what is to be produced. Knight describes the second function: "The second step, logically speaking, after the ranking and grading of the uses to which productive power may be put, is that of actually putting them to use in accordance with the scale of values thus established. From a social point of view, this process may be viewed under two aspects: (a) the assignment or *allocation* of the available productive forces and materials among the various lines of industry, and (b) the effective *coordination* of the various means of production in each industry into such groupings as will produce the greatest result." Economists frequently have assumed that the "effective coordination" of inputs is primarily an engineering problem and have directed their attention to questions dealing with allocative efficiency. For example, Knight goes on to state that the effective coordination of inputs "properly belongs to technological rather than to economic science, and is treated in economics only with reference to the interrelations between the organization of society as a whole and the internal organization of the industries" (Knight 1951, 10).

Recent literature in the area of property rights and agency relationships has assumed that the effective coordination of inputs depends on the available contracting technology as well as on the available engineering technology.[1] In this literature, organizations are viewed as networks of contracts involving the voluntary interaction of individuals in pursuit of their self-interest. Embodied in these contracts is an incentive structure which is determined in part by legal arrangements defining property rights and in part by transaction costs, including the costs of monitoring performance. As alternative specifications of property rights result in different incentive structures within the organization, production functions are viewed as more than simply technological relationships. Jensen and Meckling have stated that, "Since such sets of contracts specify the disposition of rewards and costs arising out of the organization's activities, they are important in determining the behavior of the participants and thereby the behavior of the organization as a whole. In particular, in the case of the firm, the nature of the rights and the contracts affects output. This in turn means that the production function of the firm depends on the specification of rights and the laws or rules of the game governing contracting" (Jensen and Meckling 1979, 470).

The property rights–agency literature provides a theoretical perspective from which to examine some effects that recent changes in the assignment of the right to player services have had on contractual incentives in major league baseball. Traditionally, club owners had possessed a well-defined and transferable property right to players' services by virtue of the reserve clause. A labor arbitrator's ruling in 1975 led to a collective bargaining agreement (hereafter referred to as the Basic Agreement) that partially transferred the rights to players' services from the club owners to the players themselves. In addition to affecting the distribution of rents, this transfer has also resulted in a reallocation of risk bearing from players to club owners via a proliferation of guaranteed multiyear player contracts. To the extent that alternative risk-sharing arrangements alter incentives, the behavior of players and club owners will be affected by the allocation of risk bearing and, thus, by the specification of the property rights to player services.

In this paper we empirically investigate some effects of the Basic Agreement on the allocation of risk bearing in the market for players' services. In Section I, we briefly describe how the property rights to players' services were redefined in the Basic Agreement. Section II examines the effect that the Basic Agreement had on the allocation of risk bearing between players and club owners. In Section III empirical results are presented on the effects that the reallocation of risk bearing has had on the disability rate among players. In Section IV, the results of this study are summarized.

I.   The Property Rights of Baseball's Labor Market

The first professional baseball league, the National Association of Professional Baseball Players, was formed in 1871. From 1871 through 1901, professional baseball experienced the entry and exit of several leagues. In an attempt to control both the movement of players across clubs and the level of players' salaries, in 1884 the two existing leagues (the National League and the American Association) signed the National Agreement, which contained a provision commonly known as the "reserve clause." The reserve clause provided club owners with an exclusive option to renew the contracts of eleven players (later changed to all players) on their rosters, thereby precluding negotiation between these players and other clubs for the players' services.

In *Federal Baseball Club of Baltimore v. National League of Professional Baseball Clubs,*[2] the Supreme Court unanimously upheld both the legality of the reserve clause and professional baseball's exemption from federal antitrust laws on the grounds that baseball was not interstate commerce and thus was not subject to federal antitrust laws. For more than fifty years after this Supreme Court ruling, organized baseball's antitrust exemption and the absence of competition from other professional baseball leagues combined to give major league club owners a well-defined and transferable right to the services of major league players.

The contractual changes which provide the impetus for this paper arose from legal developments which occurred in the 1970s. In 1975, pitchers Andy Messersmith and Dave McNally challenged the reserve clause, and in December, 1975, labor arbitrator Peter Seitz ruled that both players were eligible to sell their services to any major league club. Upheld in a U.S. district court, this decision resulted in a collective bargaining agreement in July, 1976 (retroactive to January, 1976) between the players' association and baseball management that substantially altered the structure of contracting rights in the market for players' services. Under the Basic Agreement, players with at least six years of major league experience who had not signed a contract with their current club for the following baseball season were eligible to participate in a "reentry draft." The reentry draft, held in November each year, established the clubs' negotiating rights to eligible players. This draft was described in the Basic Agreement:

> At the Selection Meeting, Clubs shall select in inverse order of their standing in the championship season just concluded. . . . Each of the 24 (26 beginning in 1977) participating Major League Clubs may make one selection in each round. As the proceedings advance, round by round, each Player may be selected by a maximum of 12 Clubs (13 beginning in 1977), not counting the Player's former club which need not select such a Player. The selections will continue until each eligible Player has been selected by 12 Clubs (13 beginning in 1977) or until each Club has indicated that it desires to make no further selections. At the conclusion of the selections, the former Club of each Player will be asked to indicate whether it wishes to have negotiation rights with respect to that Player, and if it does desire to have such rights, it will then be added to the list of Clubs eligible to negotiate and contract with that Player.[3]

Under the Basic Agreement, a club which lost a player through the reentry draft was compensated by the club which signed the player. The signing club provided the player's former club with one of its selection rights in the Amateur Player Draft the following June. While this compensation system partially attenuated a player's right to contract with clubs which selected him in the reentry draft, it is generally acknowledged that the relatively low value of amateur draft choices in professional baseball had not affected the mobility of most players who participated in the reentry draft.[4]

II.   Property Rights, the Distribution of Rents, and Risk Sharing in the Market for Player Services

Since an ostensible purpose of the reserve clause had been to promote an equitable distribution of playing talent across clubs, most economic analyses of the market for player services have studied the reserve clause for its effect upon two phenomena: the distribution of rents between the players and club owners and the allocation of players across clubs.[5] Because the reserve clause did not preclude clubs from transacting player contracts among themselves, there are theoretical grounds to believe that the allocation of players across clubs is independent of the assignment of the property right to player services. In a classic paper on the market for player services, Rottenberg stated: "It seems, indeed, to be true that a market in which freedom is limited by a reserve rule such as that which now governs the baseball labor market distributes players among teams about as a free market would. . . . The difference is only that in a market subject to the reserve rule part of the price for the player's services is paid to the team that sells his contract and part of his value is kept by the team that holds his contract; in the free market the player gets his full value."[6]

With the existence of binding roster constraints, the reserve clause had no effect on the total stock of major league players. Consequently, the conventional efficiency loss resulting from underutilization of the seller's resource in a monopsonistic market cannot be associated with the reserve clause. As a result, the reserve clause primarily has been viewed as affecting the distribution of rents between club owners and players.[7]

Available empirical evidence supports the hypothesis that the relaxation of the reserve clause has involved a redistribution of rents from club owners to players. Table 1 lists the average nominal salary for major league players on an annual basis for the years 1971–80. We have deflated these figures by the Consumer Price Index and also list the average real salary in 1975 dollars for each year. These figures show a dramatic increase in average real salary from 1976 to 1977. As the Basic Agreement was signed in mid-1976, the 1977 season was the first full season played under the Basic Agreement. Thus, in the first full year of the Basic Agreement, the average real salary of major league players increased by more than 38 percent. After a 21.95 percent increase in 1978, the average real salary of major league players leveled off for the next two years.[8]

Table I

Average Nominal Player Salary, Average Real Player Salary (in 1975 Dollars), and Percentage of Change in Average Real Player Salary, 1971–80

Year	Average Nominal Salary	Average Real Salary	Change in Average Real Salary (%)
1971	31,543	41,918	. . .
1972	34,092	43,860	4.63
1973	36,566	44,285	0.97
1974	40,839	44,570	0.64
1975	44,676	44,676	0.24
1976	51,501	48,692	8.99
1977	76,066	67,560	38.75
1978	99,876	82,392	21.95
1979	113,558[a]	84,204	2.20
1980	130,592[b]	85,299	1.18

Source: Average nominal salary data are from *Sports Illustrated* 36 (January 5, 1981).

[a] This was the first year that the Players Association discounted deferred payments. They used a 9 percent rate to discount deferred payments without interest.

[b] This figure is based on the Players Association's estimate that salaries increased by about 15 percent in 1980. The Player Relations Committee's estimate of the average 1980 salary is $146,500.

In addition to the average salary data, there are also frequent media reports of the wealth effect associated with the Basic Agreement. A popular magazine reported two cases in which players received dramatic increases in their compensation: "The bonanza is all so new, so overwhelming, that recent free-agent prospectors like Larry Hisle and Lyman Bostock, former Minnesota Twins, give the impression that they have struck fool's gold. Hisle, whose salary leaped from $47,200 to $525,833 when he joined the Milwaukee Brewers this season, will not talk about his good fortune. . . . Bostock talks about his big raise—from $20,000 to $450,000, compliments of the California Angels. . . ." (Kennedy and Williamson 1978). This anecdotal evidence provides additional support for the view that the Basic Agreement has involved a large redistribution of rents.

Effect of the Basic Agreement on the Allocation of Risk Bearing between Players and Club Owners

In addition to redistributing rents from club owners to players, the Basic Agreement has had a substantial effect on the way in which players and club owners share the risk associated with the value of the players' performance. Data are not available on individual player contracts prior to 1976, but several baseball executives have indicated in private conversation that prior to the Basic Agreement virtually all of the 600 major league players

Table 2
Number of Players by the Number of Guaranteed Years on Their Contract for 650 Players in 1980

Guaranteed Years on Contract (N)	Players (N)
0	352 (54.15)
1	26 (4.00)
2	45 (6.92)
3	57 (8.77)
4	41 (6.31)
5	92 (14.15)
6	29 (4.46)
7	4 (.62)
8	0 (.00)
9	0 (.00)
10	4 (.62)

Note: Figures shown in parentheses are percentages.
Source: Contract data were obtained from the Major League Baseball Player Relations Committee on all players who performed in the major leagues in 1980.

had a one-year contract.[9] Furthermore, these contracts typically were not guaranteed by the club. Depending on his seniority, if a player was released by his club or sent to the minor leagues during a baseball season, he received a prorated share of his salary for the time that he spent in the major leagues. During the Basic Agreement there was a sizable increase in the number of guaranteed multiyear player contracts. Table 2 lists the number of players by the number of guaranteed years on their contract for 650 players who were on the active opening-day roster of a major league club in 1980. Thirty-five percent of the players in 1980 had at least three guaranteed years on their contract.

This contractual change under the Basic Agreement can be viewed as a reallocation of risk bearing from players to club owners. The risk associated with the value of a player's performance involves the risk of disability and the risk that expectations of the player's performance will not be met. In part, player contracts stipulate the way in which this risk is to be shared between the player and the club owner. The post-1976 increase in the number of guaranteed multiyear player contracts indicates that players are bearing less employment risk under the Basic Agreement than they were under the reserve clause. This observation leads to the following question: Why is the allocation of risk bearing between players and club owners dependent on the rules governing contracting rights in the market for player services?

To address this question it is useful to view the reserve clause as an implicit long-term contract between players and club owners that provided the owners with an option to renew the contract annually. Since the standard explicit contract was for one year, the risk associated with the discounted value of a player's performance was shared by both the player and the owner under the reserve clause. To illustrate this, for simplicity assume a two-state world in which i is a discrete index that defines the state of a player's disability. Let $i = 0$ if the player is not disabled, 1 if the player is disabled. Further assume that the value of the rent associated with a player's skills is dependent on whether the player is disabled: $R_t(i) =$ rent associated with the player's skills in year t, and $R_t(0) > R_t(1)$, all t. Assume that players perform for T years. The discounted value of rents that are lost due to the occurrence of the risky event, that is, the total size of the wager, is

$$W = \sum_{t-1}^{T} \frac{R_t(0) - R_t(1)}{(1 + r)^t}$$

Let $\alpha =$ players' share of the rents under the reserve clause, $0 < \alpha < 1$; and $1 - \alpha =$ club's share of the rents under the reserve clause. The total wager can be written as: $W = W_p + W_c$, where

$$W_p = \alpha \sum_{t-1}^{T} \frac{R_t(0) - R_t(1)}{(1 + r)^t} = \text{player's wager}$$

and

$$W_c = (1 - \alpha) \sum_{t-1}^{T} \frac{R_t(0) - R_t(1)}{(1 + r)^t} = \text{club's wager.}$$

Thus, under the reserve clause, players and club owners bore risk in proportion to their respective shares of the rent associated with the players' performance.

For a given assignment of property rights, the terms of a contract (including, of course, the way in which risk is shared) are negotiated to the mutual advantage of the contracting parties. If both players and club owners preferred alternative contractual arrangements to the explicit one-year contract observed under the reserve clause, presumably these preferred arrangements would have evolved. Note that the pre-1976 contracts did not preclude players from purchasing the clubs' option to renew their contracts annually. Assuming that both players and club owners are risk averse, a player could have signed a guaranteed multiyear contract with his club, by accepting a guaranteed wage that was less than his expected future wage.

That the standard explicit contract under the reserve clause was a one-year contract implies that the club owners valued the option to renew the players' contract annually more than the players valued the security of guaranteed multiyear contracts.

Now consider the effect that a transfer of the right to player services (from club owners to players) has on the choice of contractual arrangements. As a benchmark against which the observed contractual changes can be contrasted, consider the case in which the transferred right affects only the distribution of rents. If all other contractual stipulations are independent of the assignment of the right to player services, then clubs would retain the option to renew the players' contracts annually, that is, the standard contract would continue to be an annual contract. Since the player owns the right to his services, he receives the full value of the rent associated with his skills (that is, $\alpha = 1$ in the example above). Accordingly, under this contractual arrangement the player bears the entire risk associated with the value of his performance.

We have indicated, however, that there has been an increase in the number of guaranteed multiyear player contracts under the Basic Agreement. At first glance, this contractual change may appear to be an attempt by clubs to replicate the reserve clause by signing players to multiyear contracts, thereby precluding the players from joining other clubs. But a multiyear contract is consistent with any risk-sharing arrangement. Clubs could replicate the reserve clause with an explicit long-term contract that takes the form of a series of one-year contracts, renewable each year at the club's option. Under this contractual arrangement, in each year that a club renews his contract, the player receives a predetermined wage which is an unbiased estimate of his marginal revenue product, plus a premium that reflects the shadow value of the club's option.[10] Thus, while the increased number of long-term contracts under the Basic Agreement can be explained, at least in part, by a desire of clubs to replicate the reserve clause, this explanation cannot account for the fact that, in practice, clubs typically guaranteed every year of a player's multiyear contract.

Coase's proposition (Coase 1960) provides an analytical framework within which to examine the observed increase in the number of guaranteed multiyear contracts under the Basic Agreement. Coase stated that with zero transaction costs and neutral wealth effects, the allocation of resources is independent of the initial assignment of property rights. In the case of baseball contracts, we have observed that the allocation of risk bearing is dependent on the initial assignment of the right to players' services. Since the transaction costs associated with the allocation of risk bearing between players and club owners are presumably low, this observed relationship suggests the following: the value which players place on insuring their stream of income, relative to the value which clubs place on the option to renew the players' contracts annually, is dependent on the assignment of the right to the players' services.

One explanation for the relationship between the allocation of risk bearing and the assignment of the rights to players' services is that the wealth transfer associated with the Basic Agreement has increased both the willingness and the ability of players to insure their stream of income. An increase in the players' willingness to sign guaranteed multiyear contracts is consistent with the postulate of nondecreasing relative risk aversion, a postulate that is conventionally assumed to characterize behavior toward risk when an individual's wealth and wages increase in the same proportion.[11] From the example above, if α goes from a value of less than one during the reserve clause to a value of one during the Basic Agreement, both the players' wealth and their wages increase by a factor of $(1/\alpha)$. The hypothesis of constant or increasing relative risk aversion predicts that players are willing to pay a higher premium to insure their stream of income under the Basic Agreement than they were willing to pay to insure their stream of income under the reserve clause. Given the size of the wealth transfer associated with the Basic Agreement, this wealth-induced effect is likely to be nontrivial. In addition to affecting the players' willingness to sign guaranteed multiyear contracts, the increase in their wealth position has increased their capacity to "purchase" these contracts. With a positive wealth elasticity of demand for security, then, players will choose to consume part of their additional wealth in the form of increased security.

One implication resulting from the reallocation of risk bearing in the market for players' services concerns the incentive effects of alternative risk-sharing arrangements.[12] If the probability of a risky event is in part endogenous to the behavior of at least one party to a contract, then the way in which the parties share the risk may affect the probability that the event occurs. The cost borne by an individual from the occurrence of a risky event is inversely related to the extent to which the individual has insured against the event, resulting in an inverse relationship between the extent to which an individual has insured against an event and the incentive that the individual has to prevent the event from occurring.

Since the probability of both player disability and deviations in player performance is, in part, endogenous to the behavior of players and clubs, the use of guaranteed multiyear player contracts has implications for the likelihood that these events occur. As the risk associated with these events is shifted from players to club owners, there is a reduced incentive for players to prevent the risky events. This effect unambiguously predicts that the probability of player disability and unmet expectations in player performance is directly related to the extent to which players have insured their future income through guaranteed multiyear contracts.

In addition to the behavior of players, the behavior of clubs is also likely to affect the probability of player disability and/or unmet expectations in player performance. As the risk associated with these events is shifted from players to club owners, the owners have an increased incentive to prevent the occurrence of these events. For two reasons, however, we do not expect guaranteed multiyear contracts to affect the owners' behavior significantly with respect to prevention of these events. First, since clubs received most of the rents associated with the players' employment under the reserve clause, the incremental increase in the clubs' wager is likely to be small. Guaranteed player contracts in part simply transform the club's wager from one that had consisted of potentially forgone losses under the reserve clause into one that consists of potentially explicit losses. If the value of the club's wager had not changed during the Basic Agreement, then this distinction would not alter the club's behavior with respect to its prevention of the risky events. The only part of a guaranteed contract that will elicit a behavioral response from the club owners is the proportion of the risk, which the players bore under the reserve clause, that is now borne by the owners. Even in the limiting case where the club guarantees the entire stream of the player's future income, its wager increases only by $\alpha/1 - \alpha$ percent, and not by the entire value of the guaranteed contract.

A second reason for suspecting that guaranteed multiyear contracts have induced a relatively small behavioral response from club owners is that, in part, the owners can diversify this risk across players. With frictionless markets, players would also be able to diversify this risk through buying and selling shares in their uncertain future income. Since there are limited diversification opportunities for players, however, clubs have a comparative advantage in bearing the risk associated with future player performance. As a result, an incremental change in risk bearing is likely to elicit a greater behavioral response from players than from club owners.

III.   Empirical Evidence:
The Effect of Guaranteed Multiyear Contracts on
Player Disability

In the previous section, we attempted to show that the Basic Agreement resulted in both a transfer of wealth from club owners to players and a reallocation of risk bearing from players to club owners. In this section the effect that guaranteed multiyear player contracts have had on player disability is examined.[13]

Concomitant with the Basic Agreement has been a significant increase in the disability rate among players in major league baseball. To document this increase, data have been collected for each year from 1974 to 1980 on all players who spent time on a major league club's disabled list.[14] Conveniently, the rules concerning placement of players on a club's disabled list have not changed over this period. These rules are described in *The Baseball Blue Book:*

> Upon written application to its League President and the Commissioner, a club may request that a player, unable to render service because of a specific injury or ailment, be placed on the disabled list. The Commissioner may approve such requests when certified by the League President, but only after the Commissioner has received written evidence from a doctor detailing the extent of the disability. . . . Players on the Regular Disabled List shall count on the overall roster but not on the active list. . . . Clubs must designate at the time they request permission to place [a] player on a disabled list whether he is to be placed on the Emergency Disabled List for not less than sixty (60) days, on the Regular Disabled List for not less than twenty-one (21) days or on the Supplemental Disabled List for not less than fifteen (15) days.[15]

Clubs are not permitted to have more than three players on the regular disabled list at the same time nor more than one player (excluding pitchers) on the supplemental disabled list at the same time. Clubs are permitted, however, to have an unlimited number of players on the emergency disabled list simultaneously.

The total number of players who spent time on a major league club's disabled list is shown in the second column of Table 3 for each of the seven years for which we have compiled these data. The average number of players who spent time on the disabled list has increased from 89 players per season in the 1974–76 period to 131 players per season in the 1977–80 period. Part of the 47 percent increase in the average number of disabled players is the result of an expansion of the major leagues in 1977. This expansion increased the stock of active major league players by 8.33 percent from 600 players in each of the 1974–76 seasons to 650 players in each of the subsequent seasons. To adjust the disability data for the 1977 expansion we have divided the flow of disabled players in each season by the stock of active players in each of these seasons. These figures are reported in the third column of Table 3. As a percentage of the total stock of active players, the per season flow of disabled players in the major leagues has increased from approximately 15 percent in the 1974–76 period to 20 percent in the 1977–80 period. This represents a 33 percent increase in

Table 3
Disability Statistics for All Players in Major Leagues during Each Season, 1974–80

Year	Total Number of Players Who Spent Time on Disabled List	Players Who Spent Time on Disabled List (%)	Total Number of Days Spent by All Players on Disabled List	Average Number of Days Spent by All Players on Disabled List	Average Number of Days Spent by Disabled Players on Disabled List
1974	83	13.8	4,177	6.962	50.325
1975	103	17.2	5,210	8.683	50.583
1976	81	13.5	4,700	7.833	58.025
1977	128	19.7	6,155	9.469	48.086
1978	114	17.5	5,393	8.297	47.307
1979	141	21.7	7,738	11.905	54.879
1980	142	21.9	7,311	11.248	51.486
1974–76	267	14.8	14,087	7.826	52.760
1977–80	525	20.2	26,597	10.230	50.661

Note: The disability data for the years 1974–79 were obtained from *The Baseball Yearbook* for each corresponding year. Disability data for 1980 were obtained from the Player Relations Committee.

the percentage of active players who spent time on a disabled list in the 1977–80 period over the same percentage during the 1974–76 period.

The total number of days spent by all players on a major league club's disabled list is shown in the fourth column of Table 3 for each of the seven seasons. To calculate the average number of days spent on a disabled list by all players, this total has been divided by the total stock of active players in each season. These averages are reported in the fifth column of Table 3. The average number of days spent on a disabled list by all players increased by approximately 31 percent during the 1977–80 period over the same average during the 1974–76 period.[16]

Several explanations for baseball's increased disability rate have been offered by baseball executives, team physicians, sportswriters, and baseball fans. Some conventional explanations which have been offered are:

1. *Artificial turf.* Allegedly, artificial turf results in more injuries.
2. *Advent of the "designated hitter" rule in the American League.* This rule apparently allows pitchers to pitch more innings per game than they would in the absence of the rule. It has been hypothesized that this places greater strain on pitchers' arms and thereby increases the likelihood of injuries among American League pitchers.
3. *Growing sophistication of sports medicine.* It has been hypothesized that injuries which previously went undetected are now diagnosed.
4. *The 1977 expansion of the American League.* This expansion sup-

posedly has increased the proportion of younger players in the league.[17]
Proponents of this theory contend that young players, particularly young pitchers, are more susceptible to injuries than are older players.

While there has been much speculation concerning the increase in player disability, there is little empirical support for the offered explanations. This is illustrated in the following excerpt from an article dealing with baseball's disability rate:

> The difficulty of deriving an intelligent trend from the increased number of injuries is underlined by the two distinct ways baseball's two leagues differ. The N. L. has the majority of baseball's artificial turf fields. So one could expect a greater injury rate. Yet, at one point in the 1980 season, 22 nonpitchers were disabled in the N. L., compared to 39 in the A. L. (whose two extra franchises can't account for the difference). And the A. L. with its DH would seem more threatening to the welfare of pitchers. But 15 of its hurlers went on the disabled list, compared to 18 Nationals during the early part of the season. (Singer 1980, 35)

The explanation which is offered here for the increase in baseball's disability rate is that the proliferation of guaranteed multiyear player contracts under the Basic Agreement has reduced the price of disability to players, thereby inducing an increase in the players' "consumption" of disability. This hypothesis assumes, of course, that the probability of a player becoming disabled is in part endogenous to the player's behavior. While undoubtedly there is a large random element associated with disability, it is also clear that players' behavior can affect the probability that they become disabled. First, it is likely that proper physical conditioning reduces the probability of a disabling injury. Two club physicians, discussing the increased disability rate, have explicitly commented on the relationship between conditioning and disability: ". . . it behooves us, as doctors, to try to work out a bonafide off-season program for players. It requires sacrifice on their part. They must dedicate themselves. . . . A guy who works out has less chance of injury. Players don't use muscles the way they should. If you don't loosen up regularly, you stretch those muscles in the spring and they get pulled" (Singer 1980, 35). Assuming that conditioning is not costless for players, that monitoring the players' condition is not costless for clubs, and that guaranteed multiyear contracts reduce the cost borne by players from "improper" conditioning, it follows that a guaranteed multiyear contract reduces a player's incentive to prevent disability through physical conditioning.

For a given level of conditioning, the behavior of players can affect the probability that they spend time on the disabled list in another way. The cost of both revealing an injury and recovering from an injury is lower for players with guaranteed multiyear contracts than it is for players who have short-term contracts that reward the players for their playing performance. Since it is costly for clubs to diagnose player disability and to monitor the players' recovery, alternative contractual arrangements are likely to affect the willingness of players to perform when they are injured. Even if clubs could costlessly detect player disability, however, the increased wealth position of players is likely to affect the players' marginal rate of substitution between playing when they are injured and leisure. Thus, both the price and wealth effects of guaranteed multiyear contracts reduce the probability that players will perform when they are injured.

We wish to test the hypothesis that the increase in baseball's disability rate has resulted, in part, from changes in contractual incentives. Specifically, the following two hypotheses are tested:

H1: At a point in time, players with guaranteed long-term contracts are more likely to be disabled than are players with short-term contracts.

H2: Players experience more disability after signing guaranteed long-term contracts than they do prior to signing such contracts.

Empirical Evidence

To test the first hypothesis, disability data are analyzed for all players in the sample who played the entire 1980 season at the major league level. In this analysis, we do not include players who at any time during the 1980 season (a) were sent by their club to the minor leagues,[18] (b) were released by their club,[19] (c) were suspended by their club (or by their league),[20] or (d) voluntarily retired.[21]

Summary statistics on player disability are listed in Table 4 by the number of guaranteed years remaining on the contracts of all players in the sample who spent the entire 1980 season in the major leagues. There is a direct relationship between the number of guaranteed years remaining on the players' contracts and the average number of days which players spent on a major league club's disabled list in 1980. On average, each additional guaranteed year remaining on the player's contract is associated with a 25 percent increase in the average number of days spent on the disabled list. Players with three or more guaranteed years remaining on their contract spent, on average, 79 percent more time on the disabled list than players with one or two guaranteed years remaining on their contract.[22]

In order to control for some of the other factors which frequently are cited as determinants of baseball's disability rate, we also estimate a logit model in which the dependent variable is *LNDL,* the log of the odds that a

Table 4
Average Number of Days Spent on Disabled List in 1980 and Other Summary Statistics for 526 Players Who Spent Entire 1980 Season in Major Leagues

Number of Guaranteed Years Remaining on Contract in 1980	N	Average Number of Days Spent by All Players on Disabled List in 1980	SD	Minimum	Maximum	Coefficient of Variation
0–1	328	9.424	25.973	.000	201.000	275.605
2	60	14.683	31.853	.000	158.000	216.938
3	43	18.116	37.815	.000	192.000	208.744
4	42	15.024	34.826	.000	132.000	231.803
5+	53	21.189	42.313	.000	179.000	199.693
0–2	388	10.237	26.987	.000	201.000	263.622
3+	138	18.355	38.568	.000	192.000	210.123

Source: See table 3 and notes 18–24.

player spent time on the disabled list in 1980. Among the independent variables in the model is *GUARYEARS*, the number of guaranteed years remaining on the player's contract. Our hypothesis predicts a positive estimated coefficient for this variable. The other independent variables are: (*a*) *AGE*, the player's age in 1980; (*b*) *ARTITURF*, the percentage of games which the player's club played on artificial turf in 1980;[23] (*c*) *PITCHER*, which takes on the value of 1 if the player is a pitcher and 0 otherwise; (*d*) *AL*, which takes on the value of 1 if the player performed in the American League for the entire season in 1980 and 0 otherwise; (*e*) *ALPITCH*, which takes on the value of 1 if the player was a pitcher in the American League in 1980 and 0 otherwise.

Results from estimation of this model are reported in Table 5. The variable *GUARYEARS* has an anticipated positive coefficient, and it is statistically significant. The only other independent variable that has a statistically significant coefficient in this equation is the dummy variable that standardizes for whether the player is a pitcher in the American League. Counter to the theory that the designated-hitter rule is in part responsible for the increase in player disability, American League pitchers were less likely to be injured in 1980 than other players.

Tables 4 and 5 contain cross-sectional evidence which supports the hypothesis that changes in contractual incentives are, in part, responsible for the recent increase in baseball's disability rate. Some longitudinal analysis is also possible: the contract data can be used to test directly the hypothesis

Table 5
Logit Estimate of Odds that Player Spent Time on Disabled List in 1980
for 503 Players in 1980

Variable	Logit Model (Dependent Variable = LNDL)
INTERCEPT	−1.710
	(3.31)
GUARYEARS	.125
	(3.46)
AGE	.005
	(.03)
ARTITURF	−.057
	(.01)
PITCHER	.363
	(1.36)
AL	.269
	(.72)
ALPITCH	−.838
	(3.45)
N	503
D-statistic	.014
Model χ^2 statistic	7.29 (6 df)

Note: χ^2 statistics are shown in parentheses.
Source: See table 3 and notes 18–24.

that players spend more time on the disabled list after signing guaranteed multiyear contracts than they do before signing these contracts. The sample for this test is the set of 249 players who either were reentrants when they signed their contract or who would have been eligible for the next reentry draft at the time that they signed a multiyear contract with their current club. This group of players is selected since they had a well-established disability record before signing their contract.

For each eligible player, the total number of days spent on the disabled list is calculated in the three seasons before and in all seasons after signing his contract. Players are then classified by the number of years in which their contract is guaranteed against disability. For each category, the average number of days spent on the disabled list per season by this group of players in the three seasons before, and in all seasons after, they signed their respective contracts is calculated. These averages are listed by the number of guaranteed years on the players' contracts in Table 6.

It is seen that there is a significant increase in the number of days spent

Table 6
Average Age, Precontract and Postcontract Average Number of Days Spent on Disabled List, and Postcontract Change in Disability by Number of Guaranteed Years on Contract for 249 Eligible Players in Sample

Guaranteed Years on Contract (N)	N	Average Age When Signed Contract	Average Number of Days Spent on Disabled List per Season in Three Seasons Prior to Signing Contract	Average Number of Days Spent on Disabled List per Season in All Seasons after Signing Contract	Change in Average Number of Days Spent on Disabled List (%)
0	53	31.019	7.987	5.977	−25.17
1	18	34.722	5.333	.913	−82.88
2	23	34.652	5.841	5.833	−.13
3	36	32.278	5.009	12.206	143.67
4	29	31.379	3.483	8.972	157.60
5+	90	30.056	5.019	13.849	175.92
0–2	94	32.617	6.939	5.171	−25.48
3+	155	30.819	4.729	12.551	165.40

Source: See table 3 and notes 18–24.

on the disabled list after players sign a guaranteed contract of more than two years in length. The per season average number of days spent on the disabled list decreases from 6.939 to 5.171 for ninety-four players who signed contracts which are guaranteed from zero to two years. For the 155 players who signed contracts which were guaranteed for three or more years, the corresponding average increases from 4.729 days to 12.551 days. This represents a 165 percent increase in postcontract disability for players who signed guaranteed contracts which were more than two years in length.[24]

Of the 155 players who signed contracts which were guaranteed for three or more years, thirty-eight (approximately 25 percent) had contracts which contained bonuses related to the frequency with which they were to perform, the number of awards that they were to win, and/or the judgment of the general manager of the club for which the players were to perform. In Table 7 the average number of days spent on the disabled list by this group of players in both the precontract period and the postcontract period is listed. These averages are also listed for the 117 players who had guaranteed multiyear contracts which did not contain incentive bonuses. Among the former group of players, the average number of days spent on the disabled list increased by 27.25 percent, from 4.763 days in the precontract

Table 7
**Average Number of Days Spent on Disabled List in Precontract
and Postcontract Periods for Players with Guaranteed Contracts of
at Least Three Years in Length by Whether the Contracts Contained
Incentive Bonuses**

	N	Average Number of Days Spent on Disabled List per Season in Three Seasons Prior to Signing Contract	Average Number of Days Spent on Disabled List per Season after Signing Contract	Change in Average Number of Days Spent on Disabled List (%)
Without incentive bonuses	117	4.717	14.445	206.23
With incentive bonuses	38	4.763	6.061	27.25

Source: See table 3 and notes 18–24.

period to 6.061 days in the postcontract period. Among the latter group of players, the corresponding increase was 206.23 percent, from 4.717 days in the precontract period to 14.445 days in the postcontract period. Thus, it appears that the disincentive effects of guaranteed multiyear player contracts can be mitigated considerably by the inclusion of incentive bonuses in the players' contracts.

IV.   Conclusion

Adopting the perspective that contracts serve as a conduit through which performance is affected by rules governing contracting rights, this study has examined empirically some effects that a change in the assignment of ownership rights to players' services has had on players' contracts in major league baseball. An unambiguous relationship has been found among the assignment of the right to players' services, the allocation of risk bearing between players and club owners, and player disability. These results suggest that, in addition to affecting the distribution of rents between players and club owners, the assignment of the right to players' services also affects the nature of what is produced in major league baseball.

One interpretation of these results is that the 1975 arbitration decision changed the property rights in the market for players' services so dramatically that it is unlikely that there has been an instantaneous adjustment to a new equilibrium contractual form. During the past five years information has been obtained regarding the incentive effects of different contractual forms.[25] If the results on player disability were unanticipated by the club owners, then in the future it is expected that the risk associated with the value of a player's performance will be reallocated, at least in part, to the players, in the form of fewer guaranteed multiyear contracts and more incentive contracts.

Notes

Generous financial support for this research was provided by the Center for the Study of American Business and the H. B. Earhart Foundation. I would like to thank Lee Benham, Alexandra Benham, Edward Greenberg, William Landes, William Marshall, David Schap, and Barry Weingast for helpful comments.

1. See, for example, Alchian and Demsetz (1972), Jensen and Meckling (1976, 1979), and Cheung (1969).

2. *Federal Baseball Club of Baltimore v. National League of Professional Baseball Clubs,* 259 U.S. 200 (1922).

3. Basic Agreement between the American League of Professional Baseball Clubs and the National League of Professional Baseball Clubs and Major League Baseball Players Association, effective January 1, 1976 (retroactively), art. XVII, C(1b) and (1c), 35–36.

4. Three reasons account for the relatively low value of amateur draft choices in professional baseball vis-à-vis the value of amateur draft choices in other professional sports. First, most players selected in the amateur player draft are not ready to perform at the major league level when selected and require, on average, three to five years of seasoning in the minor leagues. In footall and basketball, draft picks are usually expected to play at the major league level immediately. Second, unlike college football and college basketball, college and high school baseball does not have a wide national following. Thus, there is little name recognition value in baseball draft picks. Third, there likely is greater variance attached to forecasting player talent in baseball than other major sports. The higher degree of specialization in pro football and the dominance of size and quickness in pro basketball make it relatively easy to rank prospects in these sports compared to pro baseball.

5. See, for example, Rottenberg (1956), Hodiri and Quirk (1971), Hunt and Lewis (1976), Holahan (1978), Spitzer and Hoffman (1980), and Daly and Moore (1981).

6. Rottenberg (1956, 255). Rottenberg's article preceded publication of the "Coase theorem" (see Coase 1960). His argument, however, is consistent with Coase's proposition, which states that in a world of zero transaction costs and neutral wealth effects, the allocation of resources is both efficient and invariant with respect to the initial assignment of ownership rights. The efficiency result is tautologically true with the assumption of zero transaction costs, and the assumption of neutral wealth effects as-

sures the invariance result. Since there are differences in the revenue potential of the markets in which major league clubs perform, a player's marginal revenue product may be dependent on the club for which he plays. The Rottenberg-Coase insight is that, independent of whether clubs or players possess the property right to player services, equilibrating market forces result in an allocation of players across clubs such that each player performs in the market in which his marginal revenue product is highest. Spitzer and Hoffman (1980) have empirically examined the first-year effect of the Basic Agreement on the allocation of players across clubs. They could not reject the null hypothesis that the same percentage of players changed clubs during the first year of the Basic Agreement as had changed clubs in the nine previous years. Introduction of positive transaction costs and/or nonneutral wealth effects may result, however, in a relationship between the assignment of the right to players' services and the allocation of players across clubs. Generally, cash sales of front-line players in baseball, from one club to another club, are prohibited. This prohibition can be viewed as increasing the costs associated with the transaction of players' contracts, since clubs must engage in barter exchange (that is, trades of players' contracts are the way in which clubs transact in players). Daly and Moore (1981) argue that this transaction cost results in a systematic effect between the assignment of the right to players' services and the allocation of players across clubs.

7.   Holahan (1978) examines an argument which states that teams which were marginally profitable with the reserve clause would become insolvent with the abolition of the reserve clause. One implication of this argument is that if some teams dissolve, then clearly the Coase theorem is violated. Holahan argues, however, that with sufficient inter-team transfers of revenue no team's existence is dependent on the retention of the reserve clause. Furthermore, Holahan states that these transfers would be consistent with joint maximization of teams' profits since league balance presumably is directly related to league profits. Holahan also examines whether or not the reserve clause is necessary for the continued existence of the minor leagues, where young players are trained. Applying Becker's theory (1964) of human capital Holahan argues that the assignment of rights to player services affects the way in which training costs are shared between players and club owners, but it should have little effect on the overall level of investment in player development.

8.   While these numbers are strongly suggestive, there are several problems associated with using these data to estimate the wealth transfer induced by the Basic Agreement. First, only in 1979 did the source for these data begin discounting deferred compensation in calculating the players' average salary. Because the number of contracts with deferred compensation began to increase in 1977, an upward bias is introduced in the 1977 and 1978 average salaries that are reported in Table 1. Second, these figures do not control for possible changes in the demand for baseball that would have affected the value of the players' marginal product during this pe-

riod. Third, the average salary figures in Table 1 are calculated for all players in the major leagues. In 1980, more than 60 percent of players had less than six years of major league service. Thus, they were unable to sell the right to their services in a competitive market. Assuming that more than 60 percent of players in all included years had less than six years of experience, the average salary figures underestimate the wealth effect involved when individual players receive the property right to their services.

9. Raymond Grebey, director of the Major League Baseball Player Relations Committee; John Clairborne, former senior executive vice-president and chief operating officer of the St. Louis Cardinals; Robert Fontaine, director of player personnel for the San Francisco Giants; Joseph McDonald, general manager of the St. Louis Cardinals; and Martin Appel, former associate director of information for the commissioner's office, have all stated this in private conversation.

10. Joe Sullivan, former general manager of the St. Louis Cardinals football team, has indicated in private conversation that a series of one-year contracts is the typical form that long-term contracts take in professional football.

11. Pratt (1964) and Arrow (1965) independently developed the concepts of absolute risk aversion and relative risk aversion.

12. A large body of literature exists on these incentive effects. Among the most important articles are Arrow (1963), Pauly (1968), Zeckhauser (1970), and Marshall (1976).

13. We are also in the process of examining the effect of guaranteed multi-year contracts on players' performance. Since one player's performance depends in part on the performance of both his teammates and his opponents, this is a more formidable task than examining the effect of guaranteed multiyear contracts on player disability. It is difficult to detect the effect that the Basic Agreement has had on the absolute level of pitching and batting, since a pitcher's performance statistics depend in part on the quality of batters, and vice versa. Thus, if the absolute quality of both pitching and batting has declined during the Basic Agreement, unless the relative quality of the two has changed, there will be no change in overall batting and pitching statistics.

14. There are two difficulties involved with using time spent on the disabled list as a proxy for player disability. First, not all disabled players are placed on a club's disabled list. Since players must spend a minimum of fifteen days on the disabled list and clubs are limited in the number of players that they are allowed to have on the supplemental and regular disabled lists simultaneously, players with minor injuries frequently will not be placed on a disabled list. The second difficulty with this proxy is that, on occasion, clubs allegedly place healthy players on the disabled list in order to free a spot on their active roster for another player. Thus, it is unlikely that all players on the disabled list are actually disabled.

15. *The Baseball Blue Book* (1981), § MR2 (e),>2, 511.

16.   The post-1977 increase in this average has resulted from an increase in the frequency of player disability rather than from an increase in the average number of days spent by disabled players on a disabled list. The latter average has been calculated for each year from 1974 through 1980 and it is listed in the sixth column of Table 3. This average has actually declined in the 1977–80 period by approximately 4 percent when compared to the same average over the 1974–76 period.

17.   For a discussion of these explanations, see Singer (1980).

18.   The sample for this section consists of all 576 players who were on the opening-day roster of a major league club in 1980 and who had at least one full season of major league experience prior to 1980. The following players are excluded from the sample because they were sent to the minor leagues during 1980: Joe Kerrigan, Stan Papi, Miguel Dilone, Don Werner, Mike Paxton, Andres Mora, Julio Gonzales, Jerry Terrell, Willie Norwood, Kevin Kobel, Dave Hamilton, Glenn Burke, Donnie Moore, Roy Thomas, Mike Parrott, Gary Wheelock, Dave Rajisch, Nelson Norman, and Willie Upshaw. In 1980 a rule was instituted whereby clubs could send disabled players to one of the club's minor league teams for a period of rehabilitation not to exceed twenty days. Officially, these players remain on the major league club's disabled list and this time is counted as major league service for the players. Thus, players who were sent to the minor leagues under this clause are included in the sample.

19.   The following twenty-one players are excluded from the sample because they were released by a major league club during 1980: Larvell Blanks, Ted Sizemore, Ralph Garr, Steve Ontiveros, Ken Henderson, Dave Tomlin, Jack Billingham, Steve Busby, Steve Braun, Mike Marshall, Dale Murray, Jose Cardenal, Lerrin LaGrow, Darold Knowles, Bernie Carbo, Fred Kendall, Von Joshua, Roger Metzger, Bob Stinson, Tom Buskey, and Balor Moore.

20.   The following eight players are excluded from the sample because they were suspended or placed on the disqualified list in 1980: Joe Nolan, Bob Horner, Al Cowens, Rick Auerbach, Bill Almon, Bert Blyleven, Mike Ivie, and Ferguson Jenkins.

21.   Two players, John Hiller and Willie McCovey, are excluded from the sample because they voluntarily retired during the 1980 season. Only four of the fifty players who are excluded from the sample for this test spent time on the disabled list in 1980 (for a total of 106 days). Thus, we have not biased the sample by excluding players who were sent to the minor leagues or released because of disabling injuries.

22.   The evidence presented in Table 4 is relevant for the hypothesis that the increase in baseball's disability rate is accounted for by a growing sophistication in sports medicine. The evidence in Table 4 does not refute this hypothesis. However, this hypothesis does not predict that at a point in time there should be a significant difference in the average number of days spent on the disabled list by players with guaranteed long-term con-

tracts and the average number of days spent on the disabled list by players with short-term contracts.

23. Twenty-three players in the sample of 526 played for more than one club in 1980 and were deleted from the sample for this estimate because of computational difficulties with respect to this variable.

24. One hypothesis is that, with one-year contracts, clubs are more willing to release disabled players than they are to release players who have guaranteed, multiyear contracts. Thus, the argument goes, players who previously would be released now show up on the disabled lists because of their multiyear contracts. To test this hypothesis, we calculated the average number of days spent on the disabled list in the first season after signing their contract for the 249 players in Table 6. Since all of these players are established players, it is not likely that they would be released during the first year of their contracts, regardless of their disability status (that is, it is likely that they would show up in the disability statistics even if they had a one-year contract). Among the 94 players who had less than three guaranteed years on their contract the average number of days on the disabled list decreased from 6.939 days before signing the contract to 4.596 days in the first season after signing the contract. Among the 155 players whose contracts were guaranteed for at least three years, the corresponding average increased from 4.729 days before signing the contract to 10.323 days in the first season after signing the contract, an increase of approximately 116 percent. These results refute the argument that the relationship between guaranteed multiyear contracts and player disability can be explained by sample bias.

25. The following passage, which is an attachment to the Basic Agreement, supports the view that there has not been an instantaneous adjustment to a new equilibrium contractual form during the Basic Agreement: "The Parties recognize that the provisions of the Agreement concerning player control establish a new dimension in their collectively bargained relationship and, therefore, to a degree must be regarded as experimental."

References

Alchian, Armen A., and Harold Demsetz. 1972. "Production, Information Costs, and Economic Organization." *American Economic Review* 62:777.

Arrow, Kenneth J. 1963. "Uncertainty and the Welfare Economics of Medical Care." *American Economic Review* 53:941.

————. 1965. *Aspects of the Theory of Risk-Bearing.* Amsterdam: North Holland.

Becker, Gary S. 1964. *Human Capital: A Theoretical and Empirical Analysis with Special Reference to Education.* New York: National Bureau of Economic Research.

Cheung, Steven. 1969. "Transaction Costs, Risk Aversion, and the Choice of Contractual Arrangements." *Journal of Law and Economics* 12:23.

Coase, Ronald H. 1960. "The Problem of Social Cost." *Journal of Law and Economics* 3:1.

Daly, George, and William J. Moore. 1981. "Externalities, Property Rights, and the Allocation of Resources in Major League Baseball." *Economic Inquiry* 19:77.

El-Hodiri, Mohamed, and James Quirk. 1971. "An Economic Model of a Professional Sports League." *Journal of Political Economy* 79:1302.

Holahan, William L. 1978. "The Long-Run Effects of Abolishing the Baseball Player Reserve System." *Journal of Legal Studies* 7:129.

Hunt, Joseph W., Jr., and Kenneth A. Lewis. 1976. "Dominance, Recontracting, and the Reserve Clause: Major League Baseball." *American Economic Review* 66:936.

Jensen, Michael C., and William Meckling. 1976. "The Theory of the Firm: Managerial Behavior, Agency Costs, and Ownership Structure." *Journal of Financial Economics* 3:305.

————. 1979. "Rights and Production Functions: An Application to Labor Managed Firms and Codetermination." *Journal of Business* 52:469.

Kennedy, Ray, and Nancy Williamson. 1978. "Money in Sports: Part 2." *Sports Illustrated* 36 (July 24).

Knight, Frank H. 1951. *The Economic Organization.* New York: Harper and Row.

Marshall, John M. 1976. "Moral Hazard." *American Economic Review* 66:880.

Pauly, Mark V. 1968. "The Economics of Moral Hazard: A Comment." *American Economic Review* 53:531.

Pratt, John. 1964. "Risk Aversion in the Small and in the Large." *Econometrica* 32:122.

Rottenberg, Simon. 1956. "The Baseball Players' Labor Market." *Journal of Political Economy* 64:242.

Singer, Tom. 1980. "Why Is the Major League Injury Rate Rising?" *Baseball Digest* 39:33.

Spitzer, Matthew, and Elizabeth Hoffman. 1980. "A Reply to Consumption Theory, Production Theory, and Ideology in the Coase Theorem." *Southern California Law Review* 53:1187.

Zeckhauser, Richard J. 1970. "Medical Insurance: A Case Study of the Tradeoff between Risk-Spreading and Appropriate Incentives." *Journal of Economic Theory* 2:10.

Robert E. McCormick and Robert D. Tollison

Crime on the Court

I warne you wel, it is no childes pley.
—Geoffrey Chaucer, *Canterbury Tales*

I.   Introduction

The economic approach to crime (Becker 1968; Tullock 1971; Barro 1973; Ehrlich 1973, 1975; Becker and Landes 1974; Becker and Stigler 1974) develops the concept of a market for criminal activities. The supply of crime is a function of the costs and benefits of illegal activities and individual risk preference. The demand for crime derives from the free-lunch theorem—not all crime is worth preventing. In this paper we employ these demand and supply functions to discuss the impact of the number of law enforcers on the arrest rate.

Our interest centers on the impact that a small change in the number of enforcers has on the number of arrests. Does a greater number of policemen lead to more or fewer arrests, other things equal?[1] To address this question we develop a theory that models the behavior of enforcers and criminals simultaneously. We motivate the discussion of the theory with an example from the world of sports. Our question in this context is, What is the impact of the addition of a third official in college basketball on the number of fouls called per game? Sports provide an economic laboratory with a history of accurate reporting of events. This is unlike most criminal data, which are generally held to be subject to various types of reporting error. We thus apply our theory in Section III by using the complete history (1954–83) of the Atlantic Coast Conference (ACC) basketball tournament. Employing data on fouls per game and controlling for a variety of ceteris paribus conditions (players' ability and experience, rule changes, attendance, and so forth), we find a statistically important *negative* association between the number of officials and the number of fouls called per game. Since this result can be due to several effects at work in our model, we present evidence in Section IV that the negative relation is due to better officiating and cleaner play. Concluding remarks are offered in Section V.

II.   A Theory of Law Enforcement

In any given time period the probability that a criminal will commit a crime is a function of the expected costs and benefits of crime. The expected cost of crime is the probability of arrest and conviction times the fine associated with conviction; the expected benefit of crime is the probability of not being detected times the rewards of illegal behavior.

Formally,

$$P_C = P(D, F, B), \tag{1}$$

where $D = 1 - (1 - P_{A/C})^N$. P_C is the probability of criminal activity; D is the probability of detection and conviction given that a crime has been committed; $P_{A/C}$ is the probability that any one policeman will make an arrest given that a crime has been committed; F is the fine; N is the number of police; and B is the benefit of criminal activity. We assume that P_C decreases with an increase in D, an increase in F, and a reduction in B.[2]

The police can make an arrest whether or not a crime has been committed, and vice versa. Hence, we write

$$P_{A/C} = A(N) \tag{2}$$

and

$$P_{A/G} = G(N), \tag{3}$$

where $P_{A/C}$ and N are defined as above and $P_{A/G}$ is the probability of a false arrest. The signs of A_N and G_N, are both ambiguous.

In the general case of N policemen, the probability of an arrest is

$$P_A = 1 - P_C(1 - P_{A/C})^N - (1 - P_C)(1 - P_{A/G})^N. \tag{4}$$

Inserting the behavior of the actors into (4) yields

$$P^A = 1 - P(D, F, B)[1 - A(N)]^N - [1 - P(D, F, B)][1 - G(N)]^N, \tag{5}$$

with $D = 1 - [1 - A(N)]^N$, which is a reduced-form demand and supply theory of criminal activity.

We illustrate one comparative static result of the model, which addresses the central theme of the paper. Namely, the derivative of (5) with respect to N predicts the change in the number of arrests for an increase in the number of police, ceteris paribus. This derivative is:

$$\frac{\partial P_A}{\partial N} = P_D D_N [(1 - G)^N - (1 - A)^N] + NPA_N (1 - A)^{N-1} \tag{6}$$

$$+ N(1 - P)G_N (1 - G)^{N-1} - P[(1 - A)^N \ln (1 - A)]$$

$$- (1 - P)[(1 - G)^N \ln (1 - G)],$$

where $D_N = NA_N = NA_N (1 - A)^{N-1} - [\ln (1 - A)](1 - A)^N$.

We cannot predict the sign of (6). Increasing N increases the number of police officers who might detect a crime or make a false arrest (the last two terms are positive), but it changes the probability that each will do so (the second and third terms are ambiguous). A fortiori, criminal behavior adjusts to changes in the probability of arrest, the first term in (6). Even if we could sign the impact of N on police behavior—for example, that more police means better detection and more arrests—the response of criminals would be to commit fewer crimes, and the total effect remains ambiguous.[3] Even if more police reduces the probability that any one police officer will catch a criminal, the larger number of police might lead to an increased probability of detection as N increases. Consequently, it is not possible to say a priori whether more police is associated with more or fewer arrests.[4] Since the sign of $\partial P_A / \partial N$ cannot be determined logically, we seek an empirical estimate of its sign in the next section.

III.   An Application to College Basketball

Our theory does not predict a sign for (6), that is, for what happens to the arrest rate when the number of police officers increases. To the extent that rules violations in basketball are analogous to criminal behavior, a data source is available that allows us to estimate the sign of (6) and to draw inferences about the impact of N on A and G. We recognize that the typical sanction meted to a basketball player who violates the rules is not the same thing as incarceration. However, many of the sanctions imposed for rules violations are parallel to putting someone in jail. For example, a player with five fouls goes out of the game. Two technical fouls on a coach lead to his ejection from the game. Strictly speaking, monetary fines are not imposed for rules violations (although they are in an opportunity cost sense). Rather, possession of the ball or a free throw is given to the other team. There is an empirical symmetry between basketball rules violations and crime, which means that an estimate of equation (6) in a basketball economy may be useful in predicting its sign in general.

In 1978, an experiment began in college basketball. The number of officials in the Atlantic Coast Conference (ACC) was increased from two to three per game. This change allows us to estimate the impact of more enforcers on the arrest rate, which is the number of personal fouls committed by each team in a game. Our data base consists of the history of the ACC tournament.[5] Beginning with the 1979 tournament, there were three officials assigned to each game. Prior to 1979, there were two. For most of the games we can identify the officials by name. In addition to the change in the number of officials, there have been other rule changes. In 1983, a 30-second shot clock and a three-point shot from 19 feet were in effect. Starting in 1973, the first six fouls committed by either team in a half resulted in the other team gaining possession of the ball. Prior to 1973, a single free throw was taken by the fouled player. Beginning in 1963, an offensive foul cost a possession; prior to 1963, a fouled defensive player was awarded a free throw.

To estimate the sign of $\partial P_A / \partial N$, we also need to control for changes in F and B, the costs and benefits of fouling. We estimated the number of fouls called on the winning and losing team in each game as a function of the other team's field goal and free throw accuracy in the game, $FGPCT$ and $FREEPCT$; the total score of the game, $SCORE$; the year of the tournament, $TIME$; the difference in the height of the winning and losing team, $HITEDIFF$; the difference in the experience of the winning and losing team measured by the number of lettermen, $PLAYEXP$; the difference in coaching experience measured by the number of years as coach at the respective schools, EXP; attendance at the game, $ATTEND$; and the experience of the referees as measured by the average number of ACC tournament games officiated by the crew, $OFFEXP$. $SHOOT$ and $CHARGE$ control for the two rule changes discussed above. $SHOOT$ is one for years when all fouls were awarded a free throw and zero for years when the first six fouls were penalized by loss of possession. $CHARGE$ is zero for years when an offensive foul cost the offending team possession and one for years when it cost a free throw. $OFFICIAL$ controls for the number of referees calling the game; it takes the value 2 or 3. We anticipate that $SCORE$ controls for the 1983 rule changes. An appendix that gives our data and information about their derivation is available from the authors. The data were obtained from Barrier (1981) and various editions of the *Atlantic Coast Conference Basketball Yearbook*.

The results of estimating this model by ordinary least squares are reported in Table 1. In both the winner's and the loser's equation, $OFFICIAL$ has a negative and statistically significant coefficient.[6] The magnitude of the coefficient suggests that adding the third official reduced the number of fouls called per game by about 17. Over the whole period, 1954–83, there were on average 52.2 fouls called per game. Hence, the effect of adding the third official was substantial—a 50 percent increase in the number of enforcers was associated with a 34 percent reduction in the number of arrests.

The other results in Table 1 are consistent with rational behavior on the part of the participants. The time trend has been to increase the number of fouls called by about two per game per year. $SCORE$, as a proxy for speed and action on the court, is positively associated with more fouls per game; more action begets more fouls although the direction of effect could be the opposite. Each set of ten points scored is associated with about one more

Table I
Regression Results—Basketball Fouls

	Parameter Estimate	Standard Error	t-Ratio	Prob > |t|
	Number of Fouls Committed by Winner (F-ratio = 14.90; R^2 = .5471)			
INTERCEPT	−4,709.49	602.680559	−7.8142	.0001
TIME	2.426270	.308124	7.8743	.0001
SCORE	.104337	.022676	4.6012	.0001
FREEPCT	−12.721683	4.687295	−2.7141	.0074
FGPCT	−14.601949	8.443828	−1.7293	.0858
SHOOT	11.107982	2.999642	3.7031	.0003
OFFICIAL	−21.059024	2.631219	−8.0035	.0001
HITEDIFF	.724399	.408193	1.7746	.0780
EXP	.238277	.085598	2.7837	.0061
PLAYEXP	−.398640	.247292	−1.6120	.1091
OFFEXP	−.428517	.152126	−2.8169	.0055
ATTEND	−.000145	.000397	−.3652	.7155
CHARGE	14.461917	3.670531	3.9400	.0001
	Number of Fouls Committed by Loser (F-ratio = 10.67; R^2 = .4639)			
INTERCEPT	−3,458.62	531.447697	−6.5079	.0001
TIME	1.778320	.271717	6.5447	.0001
SCORE	.124287	.023660	5.2531	.0001
FREEPCT	−3.950536	5.439805	−.7262	.4688
FGPCT	−22.704364	9.475005	−2.3962	.0178
SHOOT	9.922577	2.620516	3.7865	.0002
OFFICIAL	−13.784749	2.332086	−5.9109	.0001
HITEDIFF	−.138335	.358248	−.3861	.6999
EXP	.124235	.075083	1.6546	.1001
PLAYEXP	−.145511	.214533	−.6783	.4987
OFFEXP	−.280478	.134300	−2.0884	.0385
ATTEND	.000232	.000353	.6577	.5118
CHARGE	9.881283	3.360302	2.9406	.0038

foul. The better either team shoots, as proxied by *FREEPCT* and *FGPCT*, the less it is fouled. On average a 1 percentage point increase in free throw accuracy by one team is associated with about eight fewer fouls per game by the opponent. The greater the difference between the heights of the two teams, the more fouls per game. The more disparate is the experience of the two coaches in a given game, the more fouls are called. The opposite is true for players' experience. Referees' experience has a negative and significant coefficient. Attendance is a proxy for the importance of the outcome of the game.[7] The two rule changes, *SHOOT* and *CHARGE*, both have strong positive signs of about the same magnitude. This is interpreted to mean that players and coaches would rather give their opponents a free throw than possession of the ball.[8]

IV.   Two versus Three Officials

The negative relationship between arrests and the number of enforcers in the case of basketball can be due to two things. More referees are associated with either fewer false arrests, fewer criminal acts, or both. If the probability of a false arrest decreases with N, it is likely that the probability of a good arrest increases. Although it is not logically required that these two effects be of opposite sign, intuition suggests they are as an empirical matter. In addition, if the probability of arrest increases with the number of police, we expect that the probability of detection also increases. Consequently, we contend that the response of criminals to an increase in N will be to commit fewer crimes. Therefore, if the number of false arrests decreases with N, the negative sign on (6) must be due to two things—fewer false arrests and fewer crimes committed. On the other hand, if the evidence indicates that the number of false arrests increases with N, the negative relationship must be due to fewer good arrests, a negative marginal product for the third official, or more referee shirking.

Upsets

Quantifying the number of false arrests is not an easy task. Therefore, we first attempt to sign G_N indirectly by examining the time series of upsets in ACC tournament competition. We argue that the fewer mistakes made by officials, the more likely the better team will win the game. Specifically, official error (Type I or Type II) increases the variance of the outcome of the game and decreases the probability that the better team will win. Assume that the number of officials is mean preserving with respect to the scoring of each team but that official error increases the variance of each team's scoring. It follows that the mass of probability that the expected loser will win must increase. We define an upset as a tournament game in which a lower-seeded team defeats a higher-seeded team. Tournament seeds are based on regular season records against conference opponents. If the quality of officiating increases with N, going from two to three officials reduces the number of upsets, and vice versa.

Consider the following model. The probability of an upset is a function of the costs and benefits of winning, the technical abilities of the teams, and luck. For example, young teams (in our data teams with few lettermen) may acquire relatively more basketball capital over a season than old teams. This implies that a young team will lose relatively more of its early conference games and enter the tournament with a low seed. By the end of the season the difference between the abilities of the old and the young team will have decreased. This will increase the probability of an upset, ceteris paribus. A similar human capital argument can be advanced for coaches. *PLAYEXP* and *EXP* control for the difference in player and coaching experience. To control for changes in the costs and benefits of winning, we also entered *TIME, SCORE, SHOOT,* and *CHARGE.* Finally, we included a variable, *NCAA,* which controls for changes in the rules for advancing to postseason play. Prior to 1975, only the winner of the ACC tournament advanced to the National Collegiate Athletic Association tournament. From 1975 to 1979, the tournament winner and one other team could advance. Since 1980, 4.25 teams have advanced on average. These rule changes reduce the incentive of the top-seeded teams to win the tournament; they are already assured a place in the NCAA tournament based on their regular season performance.

We report ordinary least squares and logistic regressions of the upset model in Table 2, including *OFFICIAL.* The change from two to three officials is associated with a reduced probability of upsets, and the result is statistically significant at the 10 percent level.[9] We interpret this result to mean that the quality of officiating increased with the advent of three officials. That is, three officials reduced the variance in the outcome of tournament games, which implies that the quality of officiating increased with three referees. In turn this suggests that the negative sign of $\partial P_A / \partial N$ is due to fewer false arrests and reduced fouling.[10]

Crime and Output

Transfers, including transfers due to crime, are associated with redistributive competition. Individuals compete to capture transfers and to resist having their wealth taken away. In other words, real resources are consumed in the transfer process. What is the implication of this argument for crime and output? As Tullock (1967, 231) says, "A successful bank robbery will inspire potential thieves to greater efforts, lead to the installation of improved protective equipment in other banks, and perhaps result in the hiring of additional policemen." This means that economies with high crime rates will be associated with low real production, ceteris paribus.

In basketball terms, Tullock's point can be put this way. Fouling but not being caught in the act will induce players to foul and to practice avoiding fouls or techniques to draw the attention of officials when they are fouled, and may lead to the addition of more referees. Such behavior reduces scor-

Table 2
Regression Coefficients—Upset Model
OLS Estimates (F-Ratio $= 3.35$; $R^2 = .1310$)

	Parameter Estimate	Standard Error	t-Ratio	Prob $> |t|$
INTERCEPT	−23.566823	27.882899	−.8452	.3991
TIME	.012449	.014161	.8790	.3806
SCORE	−.000456	.001149	−.3975	.6915
EXP	−.011492	.004219	−2.7236	.0071
PLAYEXP	−.037984	.011627	−3.2670	.0013
SHOOT	.032936	.141496	.2328	.8162
CHARGE	.195689	.157978	1.2387	.2171
OFFICIAL	−.355691	.192095	−1.8516	.0657
NCAA	.083083	.076524	1.0857	.2791

Logistic Regression Estimates (Model $\chi^2 = 24.50$, $df = 8$)

	Parameter Estimate	Standard Error	χ^2 Statistic	Prob $> \chi^2$
INTERCEPT	−130.31612147	166.51167003	.61	.4338
TIME	.06808087	.08443313	.65	.4201
SCORE	−.00235112	.00658561	.13	.7211
EXP	−.06130248	.02484204	6.09	.0136
PLAYEXP	−.21896673	.07135558	9.42	.0022
SHOOT	.42417153	.86915017	.24	.6255
CHARGE	1.04057746	.94075572	1.22	.2687
OFFICIAL	−2.81048966	1.67979328	2.80	.0943
NCAA	.76486641	.67016956	1.30	.2537

ing because spending time in this way decreases a player's ability to perform other basketball feats such as scoring. For this reason we argue that expected errors in officiating induce players to learn and perform skills that *reduce* scoring. We can use this argument to estimate the signs of G_N and A_N. If the addition of the third official is associated with more scoring on the basketball court, we have another piece of evidence that three officials led to a lower crime rate in terms of the number of fouls actually committed during a game. If three officials are associated with less scoring output, we would infer that the basketball crime rate actually rose in the three-official era. A positive association between officials and output would imply that the crime rate declined.

In a purely technical sense, output on a basketball court is the score of each team. This does not mean that the economic output of a basketball game is the score. Winning the game may be paramount to the fans. As a wise coach once observed, an ugly win is better than a pretty loss. Nonetheless, we believe that economic output and technical output are monotone transformations of each other.[11]

We can estimate the impact of more officials on scoring output in a basketball economy. Consider the following model of the winner's and the loser's score. *TIME* controls for trend. *SHOOT* and *CHARGE* control for rule changes. *HITEDIFF*, *PLAYEXP*, and *EXP* control for differences in players' and coaches' ability and experience across the two teams in a given game. *FREEPCT* and *FGPCT* control for game-specific performance of players. *FOULS* represents a form of victim compensation for detected crime. The more a team is fouled, the more victim compensation it receives in the form of possession of the ball or free throws and the higher its score on average. *OFFICIAL* is used to determine whether there is more or less real output with more police.

Table 3 reports ordinary least squares estimates of the model. The results are not sensitive to model specification.[12] The coefficient on *OFFICIAL* is positive in both equations, but it is only statistically significant in the winner's equation. There is therefore some reason to believe that three officials are associated with increased scoring output on the court. Further evidence on this point can be gained from the results on officials' experience. The coefficient on this variable is positive and significant in both equations. More experienced officials are associated with higher scores, presumably because they call a better game. More referee learning means better refereeing, better refereeing means fewer fouls committed, and fewer fouls committed means more real output. This is additional evidence that more basketball officials reduces the number of fouls committed and the number of bad calls.

V.   Conclusion

We present a model of criminal and police behavior where the behavior of each is endogenous. One important result of the model is that the arrest rate may be a misleading statistic when attempting to evaluate the quality and quantity of law enforcement. The mass of the sports evidence suggests that increasing the size of the police force reduces the arrest rate and increases the quality of law enforcement. No policy implications follow from this result, however. Increasing the size of the police force is not free, and we are not prepared to argue that such changes would be cost effective in practice. We can note, however, that the supply of crime in our data is rela-

Table 3
Regression Coefficients: Output Model

	Parameter Estimate	Standard Error	t-Ratio	Prob > |t|
		Winner's Score (F-ratio = 11.63; R^2 = .4853)		
INTERCEPT	3,010.916	1,023.48	2.9418	.0038
TIME	−1.540839	.524111	−2.9399	.0038
OPPONENT'S FOULS	.713351	.130790	5.4542	.0001
CHARGE	.610939	5.984444	.1021	.9188
SHOOT	−10.106034	4.648230	−2.1742	.0313
OFFICIAL	7.286445	4.485530	1.6244	.1064
HITEDIFF	1.027700	.619922	1.6578	.0995
EXP	.037159	.132085	.2813	.7789
PLAYEXP	.205872	.371958	.5535	.5808
ATTEND	−.000745	.000607	−1.2263	.2221
OFFEXP	.539729	.231331	2.3331	.0210
FREEPCT	22.587973	9.298198	2.4293	.0163
FGPCT	126.528813	13.920502	9.0894	.0001
		Loser's Score (F-ratio = 4.64; R^2 = .2734)		
INTERCEPT	2,569.971	1,095.331	2.3463	.0203
TIME	−1.293030	.561771	−2.3017	.0227
OPPONENT'S FOULS	.524618	.120858	4.3408	.0001
CHARGE	−1.912368	6.038176	−.3167	.7519
SHOOT	−14.397993	4.787349	−3.0075	.0031
OFFICIAL	2.023766	4.921747	.4112	.6815
HITEDIFF	−.397539	.648689	−.6128	.5409
EXP	−.137062	.138543	−.9893	.3241
PLAYEXP	−.222621	.392002	−.5679	.5710
ATTEND	−.000392	.000625	−.6270	.5316
OFFEXP	.405802	.242835	1.6711	.0968
FREEPCT	22.806112	7.402350	3.0809	.0025
FGPCT	45.123960	13.307594	3.3908	.0009

tively elastic. We find that a 50 percent increase in the number of officials is associated with a 34 percent reduction in arrests. Our other evidence suggests that the crime rate went down even more than this. We find that referee competency went up with the move to three officials and that the number of fouls called went down. So the crime rate must have decreased by more than 34 percent. This implies an elastic response by criminals to changes in the probability of being arrested.

Notes

We are indebted to the Clemson University Athletic Department, especially Bob Bradley, Bill Foster, and Bobby Robinson for their assistance on this project. Without implicating them, we are also grateful to Gary Becker, Rex Cottle, Marty Geisel, Michael Maloney, James Savarese, Edward Steitz, Earl Thompson, Gordon Tullock, and Lee Wakeman for helpful comments and interventions on our behalf.

1. Swimmer (1974) addresses this problem in the context of seven different crimes. However, as he notes, there are several problems with his data. In particular, there are nonnormal errors in the reporting of crime statistics across cities and income groups by the offended person, and there is also nonnormality in the errors of police reports about crime statistics. We attempt to avoid such problems by applying our model to a data set that does not suffer from these problems.

2. The individual's preference toward risk is crucial in mapping D, F, and B into P_C. For our purposes, however, the degree of risk aversion is not important. Whatever it is, we assume it is constant. Moreover, we interpret the fine associated with detected crime to mean any sanction, including incarceration.

3. Indeed, the first and second terms in (6) are probably of opposite sign. If A_N is positive, D_N is also positive, and the first term in (6) is negative $(A > G)$. If increasing the size of the police force increases the individual police officer's probability of arrest (and if $A > G$), criminals respond by committing fewer crimes. The reverse is possible although not logically required.

4. By similar argument it is also impossible to predict the impact of police competency on the number of arrests. Highly trained and experienced police forces may be associated with low arrest statistics. Moreover, in a profit-maximizing setting no owner would willingly bear the extra cost of adding an enforcer, such as shoplifting detectives in a department store, unless the crime rate would decrease. But as we have just noted, this does not imply more arrests. Decreases in the commission of crime do not necessarily reduce the arrest rate because more false arrests could be forthcoming as the number of police officers increases. The problem is compounded in nonproprietary settings because crime minimization may not be the objective function.

5. The ACC holds its basketball tournament each March at the end of regular season play. Generally, there have been eight member schools, although from 1972 to 1979 there were only seven schools. The University of North Carolina team did not participate in the 1961 tournament because it was guilty of a rule violation (playing an ineligible player). The

teams are seeded according to regular season records, and the tournament is a single-elimination event. This means that eight teams yield a seven-game tournament and seven teams a six-game tournament. The first tournament was played in 1954, and we have data on the 1983 tournament. We are missing data for 1955 and 1962, and hence we have a total of 201 games in our data set.

6.   We estimated the winner's and the loser's foul equation by the method of seemingly unrelated regressions. The results are comparable to those reported in Table 1. Deleting the experience variables or *ATTEND* does not alter the results. We tested for equality of the *OFFICIAL* coefficients across the winner's and loser's equation in each of these specifications. In every case the impact of the third official is larger (more negative) on the winner than the loser. In the specification in Table 1 the F-statistic is 4.28, which is significant at the 5 percent level. In the other two specifications, deleting the experience variables and deleting the experience variables plus *ATTEND*, the test suggests equality.

7.   Attendance is a poor proxy for the importance of the game for at least two reasons. We do not know ticket prices, and we cannot measure the extent of the television audience or revenues. Face value of tournament tickets is not very relevant since the schools employ two-part pricing schemes to allocate tournament tickets. We were unable to obtain a time series of these pricing schemes by schools.

8.   We tried several other control variables. These include whether there was an overtime, the halftime score, the difference in the final score, the difference in the halftime score, and the total number of field goals attempted per game. None of these variables are statistically important, nor did their inclusion affect the other results.

9.   The other results in the upset model are consistent with economic behavior. For example, the NCAA rule changes decreased the incentive of top-seeded teams to win the tournament. Alternative specifications, for example, deleting changes in the rules of play or including the experience of officials, do not affect the results. It may be true that differences in player and coach experience and ability do not perfectly control for the expected closeness of the game. For example, it would be nice to have betting odds or some other measure of pregame point spreads, but we were unable to locate such data for our time series.

10.   This result squares with the reasons given for the move to three referees by basketball intellectuals. For example, Professor Edward Steitz of Springfield College, secretary-editor of *NCAA Basketball Rules*, made such a case for three officials in a phone conversation with us. For an introduction to the art of officiating, including a technical discussion of two vs. three officials, see Bunn (1968, 177–247). Alternative explanations for the move to the third official include attempts to improve the enforcement of rules other than fouling and the potential for wealth redistribution. The wealth redistribution argument will not stand empirical

scrutiny on several grounds. The regular season and tournament winning percentages across schools during the two- and three-official era appear to be normally distributed. In addition, only two schools voted against the change to three officials. Finally, given that sports is an income-inelastic good in the quality dimension, we expect sports entrepreneurs to add officials and other monitoring technology over time as a means of reducing official error and nonproductive behavior by players. We note that during the drafting of the final version of this paper, the United States Football League announced that it will employ instant replays to reduce officials' errors in the 1984 season.

11. One casual piece of evidence to support this contention is the prevalence of shot clocks in professional basketball. We also observe the emergence of a shot clock in college basketball as the scoring in games declined due to the increasing number of teams that resorted to stall-like play on offense. Viewed in this way, slowdown basketball, such as the four corners, is simply an extreme investment of basketball talent in a wasteful way.

12. We also estimated the output model and the foul model simultaneously where each team's score and fouls are endogenous using the method of three-stage least squares. The estimates were not substantially different from the ordinary least squares estimates reported in Tables 1 and 3.

References

Barrier, Smith. 1981. *The ACC Basketball Tournament Classic.* Burlington, N.C.: Metro Sports.

Barro, Robert J. 1973. "The Control of Politicians: An Economic Model." *Public Choice* 14 (Spring): 19–42.

Becker, Gary S. 1968. "Crime and Punishment: An Economic Approach." *Journal of Political Economy* 76 (March–April): 169–217.

Becker, Gary S., and William M. Landes, eds. 1974. *Essays on the Economics of Crime and Punishment.* New York: Columbia University Press for the National Bureau of Economic Research.

Becker, Gary S., and George J. Stigler. 1974. "Law Enforcement, Malfeasance, and the Compensation of Enforcers." *Journal of Legal Studies* 3 (January): 1–18.

Bunn, John W. 1968. *The Art of Officiating Sports.* Englewood Cliffs, N.J.: Prentice-Hall.

Ehrlich, Isaac. 1973. "Participation in Illegitimate Activities: A Theoretical and Empirical Investigation." *Journal of Political Economy* 81 (May–June): 521–65.

———. 1975. "The Deterrent Effect of Capital Punishment: A Question of Life and Death." *American Economic Review* 65 (June): 397–417.

Office of the Commissioner and the Service Bureau. 1954–83 (various editions). *Atlantic Coast Conference Basketball Yearbook.* Greensboro, N.C.: Atlantic Coast Conference.

Swimmer, Eugene. 1974. "Measurement of the Effectiveness of Urban Law Enforcement—A Simultaneous Approach." *Southern Economic Journal* 40 (April): 618–30.

Tullock, Gordon. 1967. "The Welfare Costs of Tariffs, Monopolies, and Theft." *Western Economic Journal* 5 (June): 224–32.

———. 1971. *The Logic of the Law.* New York: Basic Books.

III   Sports and Managerial Incentives

Robert C. Clement and Robert E. McCormick

Coaching Team Production

What is meant by performance? Input energy, initiative, work attitude, perspiration, rate of exhaustion? Or output? . . . sometimes by inspecting a team member's input activity we can better judge his output effect. . . . It is not always the case that watching input activity is the only or best means of detecting, measuring, or monitoring output effects of each team member, but in some cases it is a useful way.

         —Armen Alchian and Harold Demsetz

I. Introduction

A major tenet of the Alchian-Demsetz (1972) representation of the firm is that managers are hired by workers to prevent shirking and malfeasance in their own ranks. Absent overseers, individual workers bear only a fraction of the cost of shirking, and hence, everyone undersupplies labor relative to its opportunity cost. In this world, the managerial function is to monitor inputs and meter rewards, thereby reducing the incentive to shirk and raising each worker's marginal productivity. The more dependence there is in the marginal products of laborers, the more important the role of management. This view of supervision is simultaneously intuitively pleasing and difficult to quantify. This paper investigates the role of management in a setting where, indisputably, there is team production: intercollegiate basketball.[1]

Data on 3,012 college basketball players across ten years and 65 teams are used to replicate one aspect of coaching—the allocation of playing time. Next, we attempt to link coaching decisions to winning. The goal is to determine if coaches who manage well, by our standards, are successful.

Section II motivates the paper. In Section III the empirical methodology is detailed; the monitoring function is estimated and related to coaching success. Section IV contains a summary and conclusion.

II. Coaching Decisions

The essence of team production is interdependence and the inherent immeasurability of marginal productivity across workers. However, this does not meant that *proxies* for marginal productivity cannot be developed. Managers monitor worker inputs and deduce marginal products accordingly. Of course, some inputs are more cheaply quantified than others. Attitude is hard to measure, but heart rate is easy. Sweat is observed cheaply, but workers can feign exhaustion.

In the famous Chinese boatpullers fable, the coxswain uses his whip to ensure that coolies pull efficiently, to persuade each worker to give the appropriate effort.[2] McManus (1975, 341) relates a story told by Cheung: " . . . boats are pulled upstream by a team of coolies prodded by an overseer with a whip . . . an American lady, horrified at the sight of the overseer whipping the men as they strained at their harness, demanded that something be done about the brutality. She was quickly informed . . . 'Those men own the rights to draw boats over this stretch of water and they have hired the overseer and given him his duties.' " Here the monitor uses his vision, intuition, and experience to determine shirking, counseling the loafers with his whip. But employing subjective observation is just one way to monitor. Alternatively, work effort is objectively quantified by skin galvanometers, sphygmomanometers, and the like. Subjective evaluation requires human capital and physical presence while objective measurement necessitates investment in physical capital. Both methods mute the team production problem, and the choice turns on relative marginal products and the cost of machines versus manager's talent. Conceptually, competent subjective evaluation ought to be able to reproduce the outcome of proficient objective quantification, and vice versa.

Consider a team pulling boats under the two different monitoring techniques. The first manager is experienced and competent. He knows when to wield the whip (when the coolies are shirking) and when to shield it. Therefore, he uses subjective, visual evaluation of the workers to assess inputs. By contrast, the other manager is less subjectively adept, making relatively more type I and type II errors with the whip. Instead of relying on intuition, he attaches sphygmomanometers et al. to the workers, counseling with the whip on the basis of meter readings. Naturally, most managers use some combination of subjective and objective monitoring methods, depending on the relative costs.

This is precisely the research design here. Measures of basketball players' work effort come from published statistics on performance. It is not assumed or asserted that managers use these measures, though they might. If Alchian and Demsetz (1972) are correct, it is conceptually possible to mimic the coach's subjective evaluation of inputs, his allocation of playing time, using quantitative measures of player efforts.[3]

The goal is to reproduce managerial decisions regardless of how they are made, and then to determine if there is a link between a team's success and *our* ability to replicate coaching decisions. If coaches' decisions can be cloned using only objective measures of player skill and if coaches who appear to employ this model win more games, then at least one conclusion follows: coaches who assign playing time based on quantifiable playing skills are more successful. Moreover, a link between our ability to mimic managerial decisionmaking on the basis of quantifiable worker inputs and managerial success (winning) constitutes testimony in support of the view that managers are hired by workers to police malfeasance in their own ranks—the Chinese coolie story.

Consider the theoretical alternative. Suppose (i) managerial decisions could be replicated using only quantifiable measures of worker skills. Specifically, imagine that the way coaches allocate playing time in a basketball game can be successfully modeled using individual player characteristics. But (ii) suppose there was *no* relation between our ability to reproduce an individual coach's allocation of playing time and his winning record. What would this mean? For one thing, it would imply that the primary managerial function is not to monitor inputs and meter rewards, but some other unidentified job. Thus, a necessary but not sufficient condition for us to be successful is for managers to be integrally involved in the organization of team production, delimiting malfeasance and motivating workers.

Of course, the coaching function in basketball has many dimensions: recruiting, training, scheduling, organizing practice, devising offensive and defensive strategies, and motivating, above and beyond allocating playing time. Nevertheless, a positive relation between (i) the assignment of playing time and quantifiable player inputs and (ii) winning can be interpreted to mean that a necessary condition for coaching success is the ability to pick the right team members. Managers are indifferent between workers who, on the one hand, *can* supply 100 foot-pounds of effort, but shirk and supply only 90; and those on the other hand who do not shirk but can supply only 90 foot-pounds of effort. Empirically, one can observe only the manager's choice, not the shirking. Hence, if a coach's decisions regarding playing time can be replicated then there exists a single proxy for three managerial chores: finding the efficient production frontier, choosing the right team members, and monitoring shirking.[4] The next two sections are devoted to duplicating coaching decisions with regards to assigning playing time.

III.   Empirical Methodology

The research design is straightforward. First we attempt to reproduce coaches' assignment of playing time. Here the minutes played throughout an entire season by each player on the team are estimated as a function of his individual playing skills. The more competently a coach monitors players' skills, prevents shirking, uses the right combination of players, and trains them, the more likely his team is to win, other things equal. Hence, the next question is whether a coach's winning record is a function of our ability to reproduce his playing time decisions. If the probability that playing time is rewarded based on quantifiable measures of player skills is linked with winning, then successful coaches do at least two things: find the efficient production frontier and employ the requisite inputs.

The data include inputs by 3,012 players from 65 schools over as many as ten years,[5] with the season average or total for each player of points scored, field goal and free-throw shooting percentage, rebounds garnered, personal fouls committed, steals made, turnovers committed, shots blocked, and assists earned. Also included is the playing time each individual was awarded by the coach—the total minutes played throughout the season. Summary statistics for all players are reported in Table 1. The per minute data for some players are distorted by the fact that they played very little. For this reason, summary statistics are also reported for players who played a minimum of 100 minutes. The average player in the sample played 467 minutes and scored 164 points or .3237 points per minute. In the class of players with more than 100 minutes, the average playing time was 605 minutes and points scored was 214 or .3276 per minute.[6]

Several versions of equation (1) were estimated:

$$Min = \alpha I + \varepsilon \tag{1}$$

where Min = minutes played per season,

   I = a vector of measurable player skills (inputs)
   α = a vector of coefficients, and
   ε = an error term,

by weighted least squares for four categories of players (all, more than 100 minutes' playing time, more than 500 minutes, and less than 100 minutes); the results reported in Table 2 speak for our ability to reproduce coaching decisions about playing time.[7] Specifically, players who shoot better from the field or the free-throw line are assigned more playing time. Players who rebound more, score more, garner more steals, block more shots, commit fewer turnovers, make more assists, and foul less, play more. The R^2 is .52; the monitoring model explains just over half of coaches' decisions with regards to the assignment of playing time. Given the folklore about the complexity of coaching and the intricacies of managing a sports team, the ability of this model to explain coaches' behavior is impressive. All told, these results speak highly for the hypothesis that managers monitor inputs and assign playing time on the basis of quantifiable player skills.

One important coaching duty is to train players. For this reason some players should get to play more than their skill levels dictate, especially if they are young and educable. This suggests that quantifiable inputs are less useful in determining playing time for individuals who play just a bit, ones being trained, and are best for players who play a lot, those already trained.

Table 1
Summary Statistics

Variable	N	Mean	Standard Deviation	Minimum Value	Maximum Value
			All players		
Games played	2768	22.675	8.888	1.0	37.0
Minutes played	2982	466.973	368.604	1.0	1354.0
Field goal percentage	2963	451.091	130.791	0.0	1000.0
Free throw percentage	2905	638.712	188.542	0.0	1000.0
Rebounds	2982	72.798	72.201	0.0	500.0
Assists	2982	34.546	41.939	0.0	367.0
Steals	2982	15.755	16.505	0.0	113.0
Turnovers	2808	33.789	28.502	0.0	145.0
Blocked shots	2968	7.037	14.297	0.0	207.0
Fouls	2982	45.249	32.763	0.0	168.0
Points	2979	164.403	163.301	0.0	1090.0
Rebounds/minute	2982	0.165	0.098	0.0	1.0
Points/minute	2979	0.323	0.148	0.0	2.0
Fouls/minute	2982	0.117	0.065	0.0	1.0
Steals/minute	2982	0.034	0.038	0.0	1.205
Blocked shots/minute	2968	0.014	0.028	0.0	.514
Turnover/minute	2808	0.081	0.069	0.0	2.0
Assists/minute	2982	0.069	0.057	0.0	0.600
			Players with more than 100 minutes' playing time		
Games played	2091	26.822	5.014	5.00	37.0
Minutes played	2257	604.846	317.935	101.00	1354.0
Field goal percentage	2266	475.473	73.898	43.00	846.0
Free throw percentage	2266	672.503	127.447	0.00	1000.0
Rebounds	2257	93.971	70.926	0.00	500.0
Assists	2257	44.870	43.388	0.00	367.0
Steals	2257	20.354	16.405	0.00	113.0
Turnovers	2127	43.439	26.169	0.00	145.0
Blocked shots	2247	9.122	15.861	0.00	207.0
Fouls	2257	58.013	27.218	0.00	168.0
Points	2254	213.619	158.934	4.00	1090.0
Rebounds/minute	2257	0.155	0.072	0.00	.435
Points/minute	2254	0.327	0.114	0.0128	.812
Fouls/minute	2257	0.105	0.037	0.00	.294
Steals/minute	2257	0.032	0.018	0.00	.228
Blocked shots/minute	2247	0.014	0.019	0.00	.187
Turnovers/minute	2127	0.074	0.026	0.00	.228
Assists/minute	2257	0.071	0.051	0.00	.538

Table 2
Minutes Played per Season
Weighted by fouls

	All players			
	F-ratio = 326.30 R^2 = .5239			
	n = 2679			
Variable	Estimate	s.e.	t-ratio	Prob > |t|
Intercept	358.848	44.695	8.0288	.0001
Field goal percentage	0.67421	0.0639	10.550	.0001
Free throw percentage	0.28550	0.0388	7.3578	.0001
Rebounds/minute	303.808	77.726	3.9087	.0001
Points/minute	504.948	43.261	11.671	.0001
Fouls/minute	−3923.5	120.56	−32.54	.0001
Steals/minute	480.044	224.85	2.1349	.0329
Blocked shots/minute	1,350.27	212.26	6.3612	.0001
Turnovers/minute	−891.67	180.87	−4.929	.0001
Assists/minute	722.945	110.98	6.5138	.0001

	Players with more than 100 minutes' playing time			
	F-ratio = 254.57 R^2 = .5199			
	n = 2126			
Variable	Estimate	s.e.	t-ratio	Prob > |t|
Intercept	388.910	52.102	7.4643	.0001
Field goal percentage	0.68774	0.0751	9.1524	.0001
Free throw percentage	0.27105	0.0444	6.0984	.0001
Rebounds/minute	368.665	87.000	4.2375	.0001
Points/minute	483.917	47.988	10.083	.0001
Fouls/minute	−4,268.7	147.77	−28.88	.0001
Steals/minute	833.557	287.21	2.9022	.0037
Blocked shots/minute	1,327.12	236.42	5.6134	.0001
Turnovers/minute	−770.52	217.95	−3.535	.0004
Assists/minute	616.968	125.75	4.9063	.0001

Coaches also reward players with playing time for reasons other than direct output; for example, they are kin, they practice hard, or their parents are rich alumni.[8] In general, coaches are not likely to play these players much in total, and most likely they will play only when the outcome of the game is in little doubt.[9] All told, this means that players who get playing time for all these other reasons do not play much.

Due to this effect, the sample of players was bifurcated. Arbitrarily, they were split into those with more and those with less than 100 minutes' playing time per season. The coefficient estimates are reported separately in

Table 2
(Continued)

Players with more than 500 minutes' playing time
F-ratio = 113.82 R^2 = .4546
$n = 1239$

Variable	Estimate	s.e.	t-ratio	Prob > |t|
Intercept	656.789	55.798	11.77	.0001
Field goal percentage	0.52026	0.0780	6.669	.0001
Free throw percentage	0.09595	0.0471	2.035	.0420
Rebounds/minute	253.664	81.829	3.099	.0020
Points/minute	358.484	44.316	8.089	.0001
Fouls/minute	−3,632.9	178.65	−20.3	.0001
Steals/minute	1,234.37	281.26	4.388	.0001
Blocked shots/minute	601.907	215.61	2.791	.0053
Turnovers/minute	−455.38	226.39	−2.01	.0445
Assists/minute	386.289	115.72	3.337	.0009

Players with less than 100 minutes' playing time
F-ratio = 14.31 R^2 = .1926
$n = 578$

Variable	Estimate	s.e.	t-ratio	Prob > |t|
Intercept	67.4877	4.4060	15.317	.0001
Field goal percentage	0.03797	0.0066	5.6920	.0001
Free throw percentage	0.00794	0.0041	1.8939	.0588
Rebounds/minute	−0.4350	9.7861	−0.044	.9646
Points/minute	−34.098	7.9303	−4.299	.0001
Fouls/minute	−84.952	11.747	−7.231	.0001
Steals/minute	8.58841	16.178	0.5308	.5957
Blocked shots/minute	41.9937	26.910	1.5605	.1192
Turnovers/minute	−56.438	15.328	−3.681	.0003
Assists/minute	6.42270	18.011	0.3566	.7215

Table 2, and they are not the same (the tests of equality are uniformly significant at the 5 percent level); moreover, the overall fit of the less-than-100-minutes equation is substantially weaker. The R^2 is .193, contrasted with .524. The two F-ratios are significantly different at the 1 percent level.

Alternative Specifications

There are two potential problems with the specification of the playing time equation. First the model does not constrain the number of minutes available for assignment, although the allocable minutes in a game are finite. This means that the error terms for the monitoring equations must sum to zero in a particular year.[10] Furthermore, coaches whose teams play more

Table 3
Playing Time Equation with Player Inputs Normalized for Relative Skill Weighted by fouls

	All players			
	F-Ratio = 319.76 R^2 = .5188			
	n = 2679			
Variable	Estimate	s.e.	t-ratio	prob > $|t|$
Intercept	283.908	39.583	7.172	.0001
Normalized field goal percentage	273.332	25.070	10.90	.0001
Normalized free throw percentage	171.411	21.403	8.008	.0001
Normalized rebounds/minute	84.9239	11.209	7.575	.0001
Normalized points/minute	167.639	12.274	13.65	.0001
Normalized fouls/minute	−368.08	12.503	−29.4	.0001
Normalized steals/minute	16.4769	6.2581	2.632	.0085
Normalized blocks/minute	6.36101	1.6091	3.953	.0001
Normalized turnovers/minute	−93.152	12.547	−7.42	.0001
Normalized assists/minute	65.5410	6.8753	9.532	.0001

Note: Each player's skills are normalized by the average player skills on his team.

games will, by our specification, appear to reward players more than the average, given each player's skill. To account for this, the playing-time equation using the *proportion* of allocable minutes played as the dependent variable was also estimated. The results are not significantly different from those reported in Table 2. Secondly, the apportionment of playing time takes place as part of a complex simultaneous problem as compared to the static characterization. For example, suppose that a coach's decisions are based not just on a player's absolute skill level, but on his relative ability compared to all other players on his team. Econometrically, the error terms for a single coach are not independent across players. They are across many coaches. To address this, the monitoring equations normalizing each player's skills by the average skills of his teammates were also estimated. The normalized results reported in Table 3 are not substantially different from the absolute results reported in Table 2.

The playing time equations were also estimated in log and semi-log form. The sample sizes are smaller because some players have zero inputs, but overall the basic results are the same. The regressions are highly significant, the coefficients have comparable signs, and the explanatory power of the models is approximately the same.[11] In all events, the results reported in Table 2 are not overly sensitive to model specification.

The next step is to estimate the parameters of equation (1), the assignment of playing time model, for each coach individually, and then to relate them to his winning performance to see if our ability to replicate playing time maps into higher winning percentages.

Winning Percentages of Individual Coaches

The monitoring function was estimated separately for fifty-five coaches by weighted least squares.[12] Summary statistics on these regressions are reported in Table 4. The coaches in the sample, their coaching records, and the individual regression parameters are reported in Table 5.[13] In order to relate a coach's performance record to his coaching ability it is imperative to control for his stock of talent. Each coach's average stock of inputs was calculated and normalized relative to the overall average stocks of inputs. For example, we calculated the average points per minute that a particular coach's players scored, weighting each player's points by the number of minutes he played, and then divided this number by the overall weighted-average points scored per minute from the entire pool of players. Similarly talent ratios were calculated for all seven player skills that are valuable,[14] and then the average of these ratios for each player. The resulting variable, *Talent*1, measures a player's overall talent relative to his peers. Similarly, a player's bad work characteristics were calculated, measured by his personal fouls committed relative to his peers and the relative number of turnovers he caused. The average of these two last player characteristics is called *Talent*2, and it measures a player's undesirable work habits. Then each coach's winning percentage was regressed on his relative stock of inputs, *Talent*1 and *Talent*2, and measures of his coaching ability, as measured by the playing time model. Several proxies are used for the last; R^2, weighted R^2 (R^2 times F-ratio), the degrees of freedom, and the F-ratio, all from his individual playing time equation.[15] Each of these regression statistics is a measure of our ability to reproduce an individual coach's playing time deci-

Table 4
Summary Statistics: Individual Coaches' Assignment of Playing Time Equations

	Mean	Standard Deviation	Minimum	Maximum
F-Ratio	10.654	18.097	0.4800	137.42
Level of Significance	0.038	0.120	0.0001	0.82
Degrees of Freedom	38.527	29.604	1	123
R^2	.672	.144	.3585	.99

Table 5
Coaching Records and Individual Coaching Equations

Coach	$(R^2) \cdot (F\text{-Ratio})$	R^2	F-Ratio	DFE	Winning Percent
Digger Phelps	137.20	.9984	137.4	2	0.6955
Eldon Miller	15.916	.6753	23.57	102	0.6015
Stan Morrison	13.449	.8216	16.37	32	0.5690
Gary Colson	12.999	.9916	13.11	1	0.5000
Hugh Durham	12.241	.9825	12.46	2	0.7059
Guy Lewis	11.611	.5915	19.63	122	0.6913
Terry Holland	10.281	.5693	18.06	123	0.6909
J. D. Barnett	10.185	.6370	15.99	82	0.7191
Nebraska[a]	9.8935	.6712	14.74	65	0.6098
Billy Tubbs	9.8863	.7599	13.01	37	0.7012
Bobby Knight	9.6505	.6619	14.58	67	0.6895
Rollie Massimino	9.3325	.6832	13.66	57	0.6937
John Thompson	9.2408	.6312	14.64	77	0.7985
Bob Weltlich	8.0429	.8502	9.46	15	0.5667
M. K. Turk	7.6517	.6501	11.77	57	0.5185
Dave Bliss	7.3346	.6584	11.14	52	0.5333
John McLeod	7.1424	.8796	8.12	10	0.6207
Lou Henson	6.8443	.5569	12.29	88	0.6361
Dwayne Morrison	6.6774	.7081	9.43	35	0.4306
Steve Yoder	6.5736	.7761	8.47	22	0.3929
Don Devoe	6.0968	.5714	10.67	72	0.6436
Mike Krzyzewski	5.6922	.6642	8.57	39	0.5604
Bill Cofield	5.4713	.6120	8.94	51	0.3796
Lee Hunt	5.3674	.7147	7.51	27	0.4368
Tom O'Neill	5.3402	.7197	7.42	26	0.2209
Jerry Tarkanian	5.2694	.7984	6.60	15	0.8507
VMI[a]	5.1845	.7151	7.25	26	0.3095
John Orr	5.0790	.6325	8.03	42	0.4759
Jim Harrick	4.9610	.5920	8.38	52	0.6386
Sonny Allen	4.5813	.6319	7.25	38	0.4091
Frank McGuire	4.3684	.9538	4.58	2	0.5926
Jim Haller	4.1518	.5399	7.69	59	0.4121
Gene Bartow	3.9600	.5706	6.94	47	0.6770
Len Stevens	3.9548	.7785	5.08	13	0.4107
Jim Killingsworth	3.7080	.6669	5.56	25	0.5556
Marshall[a]	3.6846	.5379	6.85	53	0.6127
Jim Boeheim	3.6164	.7550	4.79	14	0.7021
U. of Pittsburgh[a]	3.4436	.9183	3.75	3	0.4643
Gerry Gimelstob	3.4178	.6341	5.39	28	0.5133
Gary Williams	3.3981	.7154	4.75	17	0.7143
Bill Foster	3.0605	.4858	6.30	60	0.5607
Tom Davis	2.9141	.7005	4.16	16	0.7258
MTSU[a]	2.8405	.4940	5.75	53	0.5282
Rich Falk	2.7720	.5923	4.68	29	0.4070
Joe Williams	2.6239	.7169	3.66	13	0.5574

Table 5
(Continued)

Coach	$(R^2) \cdot$ (F-Ratio)	R^2	F-Ratio	DFE	Winning Percent
Cliff Ellis	2.0959	.5175	4.05	34	0.6033
Bruce Parkhill	2.0770	.6552	3.17	15	0.2407
Dick Harter	2.0093	.4239	4.74	58	0.5626
Bill Foster-USC[b]	1.9607	.4051	4.84	64	0.5909
Rick Majerus	1.9138	.6934	2.76	11	0.6066
Baptist College[a]	1.2844	.6116	2.10	12	0.4727
Gene Keady	1.0212	.5461	1.87	14	0.7159
George Raveling	0.9364	.4237	2.21	27	0.5632
John Bach	0.5772	.3585	1.61	26	0.3718
Lefty Driesell	0.3890	.8104	0.48	1	0.6417

[a] Our data sources did not identify the coaches at these schools for the relevant period. We assumed that the coach was unchanged over the period of the data.

[b] This Bill Foster coached at the University of South Carolina during the period of our data.

Table 6
Coaches' Winning Performance as a Function of Playing Time Assignment

Independent Variable	Coefficient/($|t$-ratio$|$)			
Intercept	0.1383 (0.64)	0.1363 (0.63)	−0.0018 (0.01)	0.1363 (0.63)
F-ratio $\times$ R^2	0.0014 (1.95)	0.0014 (2.02)		
R^2			.1759 (1.61)	
F-ratio				0.0014 (2.02)
Talent1	0.8679 (6.56)	0.8416 (6.24)	0.8225 (5.99)	0.8416 (6.24)
Talent2	−0.5503 (2.91)	−0.5374 (2.84)	−0.4964 (2.55)	−0.5374 (2.84)
Degrees of Freedom in Playing Time Equation		0.0004 (0.79)	0.0009 (1.57)	0.0003 (0.76)
R^2	.527	.536	.522	.536
F-ratio	18.91	14.42	13.67	14.42
Number of observations	55	55	55	55

sions. It is our assessment of a coach's ability to put the right players on the court.

The regression results are reported in Table 6. Using any metric, there is a positive relation between our measure of coaching performance and winning percentage. The elasticity of winning with respect to quantifiable playing time assignment using weighted R^2 (the first specification in Table 6) is 0.0196 at the mean; a 10 percent increase in the use of quantifiable player input to allocate playing time is associated with a 0.196 percent increase in winning percentage.

The evidence presented here can also be interpreted to mean that team selection is a viable task in almost any team production setting. Arguably, collegiate basketball is the ultimate team production process, and yet over half of coaches' decisions with respect to awarding playing time are described by a single equation, using only the publicly generated data on player inputs. If we were privy to other quantifiable input data which coaches surely are (such as number and extent of injuries, arrival time at practice, and the like), we expect that our ability to predict playing time would improve. For example, we do not know player position (guard, forward, or center), or height, age, or weight. This reduces the ability to predict playing time, but there is no reason to expect that our existing predictions are biased by the omissions.

As noted earlier, for each individual coach, the error terms are not independent; the coach must resolve an optimization problem subject to the constraint that only five players participate at any one time. Moreover, different positions on the floor require different skills (guards versus centers). Earlier inquiries suggest that this is not a serious problem; nevertheless, Table 7 lists the highest 20 residuals and the lowest 20 in the sample of players who played more than 100 minutes. Our suspicion is that injured players dominate in the negative residuals category, and friends, family, and rich kids are the bulk of the positive errors. For example, Vince Hamilton of Clemson was injured for a large portion of the 1982 season, and as a consequence, his per minute statistics predict he should have played more than he did. The authors will supply the errors for all observations on request. There is no obvious pattern in the tails of the errors, that is, all guards, implying that the omitted variables problems are not serious.

In addition, the average stock of talent available to each coach was calculated, using the average of a player's good and bad work skills, *Talent*1 and *Talent*2. These are proxies for the coach's overall ability to evaluate talent, recruit players, and train them, as distinct from his on-the-court assignment of playing time. Based on the average of good player skills, *Talent*1, in order, Guy Lewis, Jerry Tarkanian, Billy Tubbs, John Thompson, Jim Boeheim, Jim Harrick, Joe Williams, Sonny Allen, Gene Bartow, and

Table 7
Highest and Lowest Residuals from the Minutes Played Equation

Player	School	Year	Minutes Played	Predicted Minutes	Residual	t-ratio
			Negative Residuals			
John Briggs	SMU	83	150	956.24	−806.24	−3.457
Gary Carter	Tennessee	81	228	998.59	−770.59	−3.306*
Mark Newlen	U. Va.	75	131	867.97	−736.97	−3.167
Paul Crowley	S. Miss.	84	133	841.55	−708.55	−3.051
D. Shaffer	Clemson	83	165	861.00	−696.00	−2.992
Boyzi Perry	Baptist	82	305	994.37	−689.37	−2.957
Simcik	UAB	82	219	895.74	−676.74	−2.970
Ed Littleton	Tennessee	81	112	775.92	−663.92	−2.848*
K. Lambiotte	U. Va.	82	122	765.94	−643.94	−2.761
R. Whitman	Indiana	79	145	786.54	−641.54	−2.753
Petrovic	Northwestern	84	137	775.73	−638.73	−2.741
G. Stepheson	MTSU	84	126	763.34	−637.34	−2.730
V. Hamilton	Clemson	82	114	748.39	−634.39	−2.719**
(unknown)	S. Ala.	83	229	849.77	−620.77	−2.666
Arnold	FSU	84	170	790.63	−620.63	−2.666
G. Jefferson	U. Va.	78	190	809.77	−619.77	−2.660
G. Montgomery	Illinois	84	462	1,071.76	−609.76	−2.615
Kevin Woods	Tennessee	81	180	777.47	−597.47	−2.563
K. Cadle	Penn St.	75	104	699.04	−595.04	−2.563
G. Shropshire	VCU	82	140	731.92	−591.92	−2.540
			Positive Residuals			
K. Hammonds	MTSU	84	1,076	624.10	451.90	1.937
L. Heard	Georgia	82	1,117	662.43	454.57	1.952
B. Bender	Duke	79	1,089	632.88	456.12	1.955
D. McClain	Villanova	84	1,191	731.04	459.96	1.970
D. Brown	Houston	79	503	41.27	461.73	1.982
G. McClain	Villanova	84	1,210	747.04	462.96	1.984
K. Mitchell	Wisconsin	78	204	−263.00	467.00	2.012
V. Garlick	Penn State	82	119	−349.86	468.86	2.025
E. Smith	Georgetown	81	1,166	696.38	469.62	2.012
B. Douglas	Illinois	84	1,174	687.58	486.42	2.086
Huffman	VMI	84	1,109	621.74	487.26	2.089
D. Meagher	Duke	83	942	446.27	495.73	2.122
F. Brown	Georgetown	81	955	458.69	496.31	2.130
T. Amaker	Duke	83	1,235	737.25	497.75	2.134
Laurence Held	Pacific	82	932	431.81	500.19	2.144
R. Whitman	Indiana	78	1,258	752.47	505.53	2.167
Cucinella	TCU	82	1,002	491.92	510.08	2.189
V. Taylor	Duke	79	1,119	606.99	512.01	2.193
J. Bryan	Duke	81	146	−369.95	515.95	2.231
Mann	Ga. Tech	79	999	462.49	536.51	2.302

*Declared academically ineligible in midseason.

**Injured during the season.

Other players may be have been injured or quit; data sources are incomplete in this regard.

Cliff Ellis are ranked at the top. In reverse order, Dwayne Morrison, Bob Weltlich, Tom O'Neill, Lee Hunt, Rich Falk, and Jim Haller rank at the bottom. That is, they had the worst players to work with, the players who scored the least, shot the worst, and so forth. Using undesirable player skills, Talent2, Tom O'Neill, Dick Harter, Gary Colson, Bill Cofield, and John Bach had the worst players, those that made many turnovers and fouled a lot. Using this latter metric, Gene Keady, Jim Killingsworth, Billy Tubbs, and Lefty Driesell had the best players.[16]

The coach's average pool of talent, Talent1, was regressed on the metric of his ability to assign playing time efficiently (the weighted R^2 from the playing time equation). There is no relation. At least in this sample, good on-court coaching is not linked with quality recruiting, and vice versa. This implies that good coaching encompasses two completely different talents. This suggests that using only a coach's winning record to assay his on-court management ability may be inappropriate. From a managerial perspective, it is consistent with the casual observation that personnel and other management decisions are frequently separated.

IV.   Conclusions

The actual function of managers is difficult to measure. What has been accomplished here is the quantification of one dimension of managing team production: the choice of workers. Managerial choice is quantified by attempting to replicate coaching decisions on the assignment of playing time in basketball games using the actual performances by the players. Our ability to reproduce management decisions varies considerably across coaches; and more importantly, the coaches for whom we best replicate decisions have the highest winning percentages, other things the same. Several implications follow from this result. First, coaches who base their playing-time decisions on player performance are more likely to win. This means that coaches who observe player performance best, most quickly assimilate that information, and make the appropriate substitutions are most likely to win. This suggests that some coaches are better monitors than others, perhaps not a surprising result; but it also implies that recruiting, pregame planning, cajoling of referees, scheduling, and the rest are not the only management chores. Coaches must also monitor players and mete out rewards.

Clearly, the role of managers in the firm is complicated. They must organize production, write a multitude of complex contracts, and make product line, financial, and investment decisions. What has been demonstrated here is that there is a great deal of evidence that the first of these functions is an

important and time-consuming activity of managers, and the tradition in
the property rights literature is not denied; managers are the employees of
workers.

Notes

We are grateful to the Clemson University Athletic Department, especially Bob
Bradley, for help on this project. We also thank Armen Alchian, Tom Borcherding,
Harold Demsetz, Matt Lindsay, Mike Maloney, and two referees for their com-
ments. The standard caveat applies.

1. There is a small literature on the application of economics to sports and
   vice versa. For example, see El-Hodiri and Quirk (1971), Scully (1974),
   Hunt and Lewis (1976), Holahan (1978), Zak, Huang, and Siegfried
   (1979), Daly and Moore (1981), Lehn (1982), Porter and Scully (1982),
   McCormick and Tollison (1984; 1986), Higgins and Tollison (1986),
   Fleisher et al. (1988), and Goff, Shughart, and Tollison (1986).

2. Cheung (1983, 8) repeats his story, and Nardinelli (1982) discusses a
   similar phenomenon in British textile mills.

3. This is a sufficient but not necessary condition. Our inability to reproduce
   coaching decisions does not mean that someone else, perhaps luckier or
   more qualified, could not.

4. This follows regardless of the methodology used to replicate coaching
   decisions. Some player skills are inherently unquantifiable to outside ob-
   servers; they are only seen through the eyes of the individual coach.
   These include defensive alignment, movement away from the ball, rebounding position in a team rebounding sense, hustle, and the like. If
   these skills are collinear with quantifiable characteristics such as rebounding and scoring, we will have no problem reproducing coaching decisions; otherwise we will have trouble. The evidence is presented in
   section IV.

5. The data were obtained from the individual schools. Requests were
   mailed to all NCAA Division I schools that participate in basketball, asking for ten years' data, generating some seventy-five replies. Of these, ten
   did not report the required data, and many supplied less than ten years'
   data. The remaining sample includes sixty-five schools, varying in number of years.

6. Per minutes statistics are employed as the measures of inputs because
   each of the characteristics is a positive function of minutes played. The
   more a player plays, the better chance he has to score, rebound, and foul.
   Hence, rebounds per minute and so forth are the appropriate assessment
   of a player's physical abilities.

7. Given the nature of the data, we anticipated the problem of heteroskedasticity, linked with points scored or fouls committed. Consequently,
   the log of the squared OLS residuals from equation (1) were regressed on
   the log of points, fouls, and several other variables that could have been

linked to the variance of the error term. Only fouls is significantly associated with the estimated variance of the error term. Consequently,
weighted least squares is appropriate. For brevity's sake the OLS estimates are not reported. We will supply them on request. The only significant difference is that the coefficient on rebounds per minute has a
negative coefficient.

8.   We note that other managers have similar discretion, commonly referred
       to as agency costs.

9.   Two sons of coaches, Danny Tarkanian and Chuck Driesell, had positive
       residuals in playing time more than two standard errors above the predic-
       tions of our equation.

10.   This problem is partially muted by the use of many years' data for some
       coaches.

11.   It can be argued that including points scored in the minutes equation
       along with shooting percentages amounts to overidentifying the equation.
       This problem is handled in several ways. First, by argument, points
       scored is distinct from shooting percentage and is not logically a linear
       transformation of shooting percentage and/or minutes played. Players
       with the ability to get open, players with a lot of confidence, players who
       command the respect of their teammates get the ball more, and hence
       they have the capacity to shoot more. Second, points per minute are de-
       leted from the regressions, and the basic results are unaltered (the R^2
       declines to .4998). Third, the positive and significant coefficient on
       points per minute stands as testimony to its usefulness.

12.   Of course, winning is but a means to an end for players and coaches;
       salary is the real goal. Moreover, the data come from a nonproprietary
       setting. Hence, the classic problems of the labor-managed firm stand to
       be present. That is, university officials may not have the right incentives
       to ensure that coaches have the right encouragement. It turns out that
       neither of these appears to be a serious problem. Although complete sal-
       ary data are not generally available for college (or professional) basket-
       ball coaches, *USA Today* (December 9, 1986, 10–12C) reports survey
       data for some public school coaches. They list base salary and perquisites
       for 21 of our 55 coaches. We regressed first base salary and then full
       salary on average winning percentage across the 21 coaches in levels,
       logs, and using weighted least squares. In all cases the relation was posi-
       tive and significant at the 1 percent level. On average, the winning elas-
       ticity of salary was about 1.0. We will supply the salary data or the
       estimates on request. To us, this means that even if winning is not the
       only measure of output on the basketball court, it certainly is an appropri-
       ate proxy.

13.   The coaches are ranked in the table on the basis of weighted R^2 (weighted
       by F-ratio). As such the table reflects our ranking of these coaches' abil-
       ity to ascertain player skills and meter playing time accordingly.

14.   These are field-goal shooting percentage, free-throw shooting percent-

ages, rebounds, assists, steals, blocked shots, and points scored (all per minute).

15. We included degrees of freedom to control for variations in sample size across coaches. It also proxies the probability for type II error.

16. Note that there is a *positive* statistical relation between *Talent*1 and *Talent*2 in the data set. The R^2 is very low, .0144, but the *F*-ratio is 39.39, significant at the 1 percent level with 2,707 observations. That is, players that foul the most per minute and make the most turnovers per minute are also the ones that score the most, rebound the most, make the most assists and steals, and shoot the best.

References

Alchian, Armen, and Harold Demsetz. 1972. "Production, Information Costs, and Economic Organization." *American Economic Review* 62 (December): 777–95.

Cheung, Steven. 1983. "The Contractual Nature of the Firm." *Journal of Law and Economics* 26 (April): 1–21.

Daly, George, and William J. Moore. 1981. "Externalities, Property Rights, and the Allocation of Resources in Major League Baseball." *Economic Inquiry* 18 (January): 77–95.

El-Hodiri, M., and James Quirk. 1971. "An Economic Model of a Professional Sports League." *Journal of Political Economy* 79 (November–December): 1302–19.

Fleisher, Arthur A., III, Brian L. Goff, William F. Shughart II, and Robert D. Tollison. 1988. "Crime or Punishment?: Enforcement of the NCAA Football Cartel." *Journal of Economic Behavior and Organization* 10 (December): 433–51 (also in this volume).

Goff, Brian L., William F. Shughart II, and Robert D. Tollison. 1986. "Homo Basketballus." Unpublished manuscript, George Mason University (also in this volume).

Higgins, Richard, and Robert D. Tollison. 1986. "Economics at the Track." Unpublished manuscript, George Mason University (also in this volume).

Holahan, William L. 1978. "The Long-Run Effects of Abolishing the Baseball Player Reserve System." *Journal of Legal Studies* 7 (January): 129–37.

Hunt, Joseph W., and Kenneth A. Lewis. 1976. "Dominance, Recontracting, and the Reserve Clause: Major League Baseball." *American Economic Review* 66 (December): 936–43.

Lehn, Kenneth. 1982. "Property Rights, Risk Sharing, and Player Disability in Major League Baseball." *Journal of Law and Economics* 25 (October): 343–65.

McCormick, Robert E., and Robert D. Tollison. 1984. "Crime on the Court." *Journal of Political Economy* 92 (April): 223–35.

———. 1986. "Crime and Income Distribution in a Basketball Economy." *International Review of Law and Economics* 6 (June): 115–24.

McManus, John. 1975. "The Costs of Alternative Economic Organizations." *Canadian Journal of Economics* 41 (August): 334–50.

Nardinelli, Clark. 1982. "Corporal Punishment and Children's Wages in Nineteenth Century Britain." *Explorations in Economic History* 19 (July): 283–95.

Porter, Philip K., and Gerald W. Scully. 1982. "Measuring Managerial and Allocative Efficiency: The Case of Baseball." *Southern Economic Journal* 48 (January): 642–50.

Scully, Gerald W. 1974. "Pay and Performance in Major League Baseball." *American Economic Review* 64 (December): 915–30.

Zak, Thomas A., Cliff J. Huang, and John J. Siegfried. 1979. "Production Efficiency: The Case of Professional Basketball." *Journal of Business* 52 (July): 379–92.

Philip K. Porter and Gerald W. Scully

Measuring Managerial Efficiency:
The Case of Baseball

I.   Introduction

In economic analysis the role of the entrepreneur is paramount to the production process. The entrepreneur is engaged in a Darwinian game of efficiently transforming scarce resource inputs into outputs. In the modern business organization this role is delegated to managers. Despite the conceptual importance of the role of management in the production function, very little is known about the actual effect on output of variations in managerial skill. In part this is due to the lack of proprietary data. In part it is due to difficulties in measuring the outputs and inputs of complex production processes in a meaningful way. A number of investigators have employed the concept of the frontier production function, as developed by Forsund and Hjalmarsson (1974) and Timmer (1971) and more recently by Schmidt and Lovell (1979), to measure the effect on technical and price efficiency of various property rights structures or institutional constraints. To our knowledge estimates of managerial efficiency have not been obtained with firm specific data, except for some regulated industries.

In this study we estimate managerial efficiency by manager and by firm, managerial marginal revenue product, the rate of change in managerial efficiency over years of experience and relative factor price efficiency. We use major league baseball teams over the period 1961–80 as our data source. What is particularly appealing about the choice of major league baseball teams as the industry for analysis is that outputs (win percent) and inputs (player skills) are unambiguously measured, and the production function is simply specified, as shown by Scully (1974b). Our results indicate that managerial skill in baseball contributes very substantially to the production process.

The paper will evolve as follows. First, the concept of the frontier production function is briefly outlined. Then, estimates of managerial efficiency by manager and by team are provided and discussed, a managerial efficiency learning curve is estimated, an estimate of managerial marginal revenue product provided, and the managerial efficiency profile of expansion teams discussed. Finally, we examine the relative factor price efficiency of baseball teams.

II.   Measuring Managerial Efficiency: Technical Considerations

Major league baseball teams produce a constant number of games per season, the quality of which is measured by percent win records. The teams' percent wins, W, is related to vector inputs of player skills, which measure team hitting performance, H, and team pitching performance, P (Scully, 1974b, 917–19).[1]

$$W = AH\alpha P^{1-\alpha}, \qquad 0 < \alpha < 1. \tag{1}$$

The managers of major league baseball teams are the economic agents responsible for transforming inputs into percent wins. In addition to training and motivating players and maintaining team morale, managers make a wide array of technical and strategic decisions that directly affect the outcome of the games. These decisions include such matters as the composition of the team roster, the order of the starting lineup, the choice of the starting and relief pitchers, substitutions in the hitting lineup, and a variety of other strategic decisions during the game. How well these choices are made indicates the skill of the manager.

There is considerable variation among baseball teams in the quality of player skills fielded during a season.[2] Hence the efficiency of a manager must be measured free of the level of team playing strength. Managerial performance must be measured in terms of the difference between actual performance achieved and performance which could have been achieved under "best" practice techniques. To remove the effect of variations in playing talent among teams, the production function in (1) is divided by the output level.

$$1 = Ah\alpha p^{1-\alpha} \tag{2}$$

where $h = H/W$ and $p = P/W$ are the unit hitting and pitching inputs, respectively. Of course, equation (2) may be converted into a rectangular hyperbola of the form:

$$p = ah^b \tag{3}$$

where $a = A^{1/(\alpha-1)}$ and $b = \alpha/(\alpha - 1)$ is the elasticity of substitution between pitching and hitting inputs.[3]

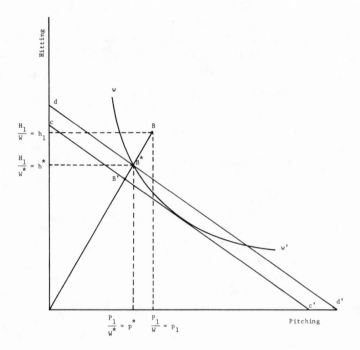

Figure 1. Measures of efficiency

If all major league baseball managers were equally efficient in transforming their unit inputs of player skills into unit outputs of wins, they would lie along the unit isoquant, w–w' in Figure 1 where w–w' reflects equation (3) and team hitting and pitching inputs are measured relative to team win percent. However, given the level and complexity of skill required to manage a major league baseball team, it is likely that there will be considerable variation in managerial efficiency. To measure the degree to which managers fail to realize the maximum possible output for their given player inputs, we apply the concept of the frontier unit isoquant, which has been utilized in different contexts by Timmer (1971) and Forsund and Hjalmarsson (1974).

Managers that fail to attain the maximum output possible for their inputs of playing talent lie to the northeast of the frontier unit isoquant along rays through the origin. That is, such managers require greater quantities of inputs per unit of output than is indicated by the frontier production function in equation (2). In the figure, B represents the actual performance of the manager (utilizing P_1 and H_1 input units to produce W) and B^* is the best possible performance of the manager for its chosen input combination. W^* exactly satisfies equation (2). Managerial performance relative to potential performance is measured by the distance OB^*/OB. More formally, relative managerial efficiency is measured as:

$$E = OB^*/OB = (h_1^2 + p_1^2)^{1/2}/[(h^*)^2 + (p^*)^2]2]^{1/2} = W/W^*, \quad (4)$$

where $0 \leq E \leq 1$.

III.   Empirical Estimates of Managerial Efficiency in Baseball

Following Scully (1974b), team hitting is measured by the team slugging average (total bases divided by times at bat) and team pitching by the team strike out to walk ratio.[4] Team performance is measured by team wins.[5] The input and output measures are normalized by their respective (league) sample means. More precisely, the empirical equivalents to the theoretical variables are as follows.

$$w_i = 2W_i/(W + L).$$

Thus, relative team wins, w, for team i, is team wins (W) divided by expected wins, $(W + L)/2$.

$$h_i = SA_i \bigg/ \left[(1/n) \left(\sum_{i=1}^{n} SA_i \right) \right].$$

Relative team slugging average, h_i, is team slugging average (SA) divided by league slugging average.

$$p_i = (SO/BB)_i \bigg/ \left[(1/n) \sum_{i=1}^{n} (SO/BB)_i \right].$$

Relative team pitching, p_i, is the team strike out to walk ratio, SO/BB, divided by the league strike out to walk ratio.

Empirical estimates of the frontier unit isoquants for each of the major leagues and for each of the years 1961 to 1980 were obtained using a linear programming technique. In particular, the linear programming technique required that all observations of inputs per unit of output lie on or above the isoquant and minimized the sum of the squared deviations from the observations to the isoquant along rays through the origin. The parameter estimates of the isoquants do not merit attention, although the reader should note that they were reasonably well behaved and plausible. What merits interest is the measure of managerial efficiency presented in summary form in Table 1. Major league baseball managers are ranked by mean lifetime

Table I
Performance Measures of Major League Baseball Managers with Five or More Years of Experience, 1961–80

Manager	Team(s)	Years of Experience	Years in Sample	Mean Efficiency	Standard Deviation
Weaver, E.	Bal.	13	13	.987	.023
Anderson, S.	Cin., Det.	11	11	.961	.049
Alston, W.	Bkn, L.A.	23	16	.945	.089
Virdon, B.	N.Y., Hou.	7	7	.936	.062
Schoendienst, R.	St. L.	12	12	.933	.060
Murtaugh, D.	Pit.	14	10	.931	.057
Lopez, A.	Chi.	6	6	.918	.089
Walker, H.	Pit., Hou.	9	8	.916	.087
Dark, A.	S.F., Cle., Oak.	9	9	.913	.091
Martin, B.	Min., Det., Tex., N.Y., Oak.	11	11	.912	.068
Williams, D.	Bos., Oak., Cal., Mon.	13	13	.909	.068
Bauer, H.	K.C., Bal.	7	7	.909	.081
Ozark, D.	Phi.	7	7	.907	.045
Rigney, B.	L.A./Cal., Min., S.F.	17	12	.905	.078
Tanner, C.	Chi., Oak., Pit.	10	10	.902	.082
Franks, H.	S.F., Chi.	7	7	.900	.045
Berra, Y.	N.Y., N.Y.	5	5	.898	.078
Houk, R.	N.Y., Det.	16	16	.886	.107
Hodges, G.	Was., N.Y.	9	9	.886	.074
Mele, S.	Min.	7	7	.877	.109
Mauch, G.	Phi., Mon., Min.	21	20	.874	.104
Lemon, J.	Was., K.C., Chi., N.Y.	7	7	.870	.060
Bristol, D.	Cin., Sea., Atl., S.F.	11	11	.869	.078
Durocher, L.	Bkn/L.A., N.Y., Chi.	24	7	.856	.071
Harris, L.	Bal., Hou., Atl.	6	6	.837	.075
Zimmer, D.	S.D., Bos.	7	7	.831	.081
Westrum, W.	N.Y., S.F.	5	5	.822	.107
Johnson, D.	Bos., Sea.	7	7	.793	.099
Other Active			<5	.881	.093
Other Inactive			<5	.824	.094

(1961–1980) efficiency. Also presented are their respective standard deviations of efficiency, their years of experience and the teams which they managed. Earl Weaver emerges as the premier manager, in terms of efficiency, of the sample of managers over the period. Not only is Weaver's average performance extraordinarily high (.987), his performance is very consistent ($\sigma = .023$). The second most efficient manager in baseball is Sparky Anderson (.961 ± .049). The mercurial Billy Martin ranks only tenth. We leave it to the reader to peruse the list further, and to the sports aficionados among them to disagree.

Examination of Table 1 reveals a rough correlation between a manager's efficiency and his longevity. Examination of the annual efficiency measures of the managers (not presented here to conserve space) indicates a systematic improvement in efficiency for managers who remain with one team for any duration. The pattern is reminiscent of a learning curve. A managerial efficiency learning curve was estimated with the following result.

$$E_{it} = .8923 + .00828t - .00033t^2 - .05150ORIG,$$
$$(61.27) \quad (2.16) \quad\quad (1.70) \quad\quad (4.52)$$

where E is the efficiency measure of ith manager in year t, t is the year of experience, $ORIG$ is a dummy variable equal to zero if the manager is with his original team, and t-values are presented in parentheses below the coefficients. With efficiency at about 89 percent of potential, managerial performance increments at 0.8 percent per year at a diminishing rate, reaching a maximum of 94.4 percent after 12.5 years. Managers who change teams during their careers incur a five percentage point decrease in efficiency.[6]

While some teams retain managers for very long periods (e.g., Weaver at Baltimore, Anderson at Cincinnati, Alston at Los Angeles, Schoendienst at St. Louis, Murtaugh at Pittsburgh), many teams change managers with some frequency, either to improve team performance or assuage the fans. It is useful, therefore, to estimate mean managerial efficiency by team. The average and standard deviation of managerial performance, along with the mean percent win record is presented by team, ranked in order of efficiency, in Table 2. Cincinnati, Los Angeles, and Pittsburgh dominate the National League; and Baltimore, New York, and Kansas City dominate the American League. Not surprisingly, these teams are among the top winning teams. But, the correlation between managerial efficiency and win record is by no means perfect, even at this high level of aggregation. Note San Francisco in the National League and Boston, Detroit, and Minnesota in the American League, among others. However, the expansion teams (e.g., Montreal, Houston, New York, San Diego, Kansas City, Milwaukee, Seattle, and Toronto) in general and on average finish in the lower division and are managed relatively inefficiently. By focusing attention on the expansion teams a rough estimate of the time necessary to efficiently transform player inputs into output (wins) can be obtained (see Table 3). In general, managerial efficiency increases over time for these teams. The improvement in efficiency is particularly consistent and strong during the first three seasons. Thereafter, efficiency rises, although somewhat erratically, through the tenth year of existence when the managers of these expansion teams are as efficient as the league average (about $E = .88$). In terms of

Table 2
Managerial Performance Measures by Team 1961–80

Team	Mean Efficiency	Standard Deviation	Mean Per-cent Win	Team	Mean Efficiency	Standard Deviation	Mean Per-cent Win
National League				American League			
Cincinnati	.968	.049	.581	Baltimore	.965	.046	.580
Los Angeles	.942	.081	.557	New York	.930	.073	.554
Pittsburgh	.924	.069	.544	Kansas City	.921	.083	.526
St. Louis	.919	.067	.519	California	.875	.087	.474
San Francisco	.899	.059	.525	Boston	.869	.090	.520
Atlanta	.857	.081	.488	Oakland	.868	.109	.480
Philadelphia	.856	.115	.497	Detroit	.863	.090	.522
Montreal	.846	.096	.460	Chicago	.853	.094	.492
Houston	.836	.108	.470	Minnesota	.849	.077	.521
Chicago	.825	.077	.471	Cleveland	.837	.072	.470
New York	.804	.121	.418	Milwaukee	.834	.079	.459
San Diego	.800	.107	.410	Texas	.834	.070	.444
				Seattle	.714	.032	.381
				Toronto	.703	.053	.361

Table 3
Mean Managerial Performance by Year for Expansion Teams, 1961–80

Year	Montreal	Houston	New York	San Diego	Kansas City	Milwaukee	Seattle	Toronto	Average All Expansion Teams
1	.637	.645	.496	.669	.749	.709	.686	.615	.650
2	.855	.764	.719	.689	.813*	.767*	.717	.718	.755
3	.885	.832*	.666	.774	.998	.902	.767	.723	.759
4	.868	.683	.659*	.722*	.855	.848	.688	.759*	.760
5	.840	.817*	.916	.661	1.000*	.915*			.858
6	.902	.700	.753	.761*	.860	.837			.802
7	.800	.854*	.827*	.787	.888*	.826			.830
8	.685*	.754	1.000	.909	.955	.769*			.845
9	.844*	.864	.959	.859	.936	.717			.863
10	.897	.967	.980	1.000*	1.000	.944*			.965
11	.973	.851	.817*	.815	1.000	.950			.901
12	.972	.844*	.944	.955*	1.000*	.824			.923
13		.927*	.798						.862
14		.666*	.843						.754
15		.988	.761*						.874
16		.896	.756*						.826
17		.858	.792						.825
18		1.000	.808						.904
19		.983	.783						.883

*First year under new manager.

managerial efficiency, then, it takes about a decade for an expansion team to transform player inputs into output as well as the average team.

IV.   The Marginal Revenue Product of Managerial Efficiency

In a previous paper Scully (1974b) estimated the marginal revenue product of baseball player skills. What is the effect of a one percentage point increase in managerial efficiency on team revenues? It was estimated that in 1969 a one point increase in the team win rate increased team revenues by $10,330. At the average baseball win rate of .500, a 1 percent increase in managerial efficiency yields a .005 point increase in the team win rate. In 1969 prices, a one percent increase in managerial efficiency increases team revenues by $51,650. Earl Weaver is 13.1 percent better than the average manager. Hence, his marginal product is .065 points to the team win rate. In 1969 prices, Earl Weaver's marginal revenue product is $675,000 (at current ticket prices, his marginal revenue product is somewhat in excess of one million dollars). By comparison, Scully (1974b, 922) estimated Sandy Koufax's marginal revenue product at $725,000. Thus, a manager of the quality of an Earl Weaver or a Sparky Anderson or a Red Schoendienst or a Danny Murtaugh contributes as much to team revenues as does a superstar player of the caliber of a Reggie Jackson. Little is known about the salaries of managers of this caliber, but it is very unlikely that they earn more than a modest fraction of the salaries paid to today's superstar baseball players.

V.   Relative Factor Price Efficiency

The manager attempts to maximize the win percent for a given input of player skills. Any combination of skill input along the frontier production function is technically efficient, but not necessarily price efficient or cost minimizing. It is the front office of major league baseball teams, principally the owner and general manager, who are responsible for selecting an input combination that minimizes cost (see Figure 1). Knowledge of the relative price of the two unit inputs h and p allows one to establish the minimum cost per unit of output (C^*). The isocost line is shown as cc', the minimum isocost line tangent to the frontier unit isoquant. Again, consider the team at point B. Point B' represents the amounts of h and p that the minimum cost per unit (C^*) will purchase, if the input ratio indicated by $B(h_1, p_1)$ is maintained. If maximum potential output for this team is attained (i.e., if its actual win percent is W^*), its per unit cost will be higher, say C, indicated by isocost line dd'. It is easily demonstrated that:

$$\lambda = OB'/OB^* = (C^*/Q)/(C/Q) = C^*/C, \qquad 0 < \lambda \leq 1 \qquad (5)$$

Thus, price efficiency, λ, is the ratio of minimum cost to actual cost for a given input ratio.

How price efficient are major league baseball teams? Since we do not know whether the relative price or relative marginal products of hitting and pitching were constant over the entire period, we focused on the years 1968 and 1969, where corroborating evidence is available (Scully 1974b). The output and input data of all teams for 1968–69 were normalized by their respective annual league means and the isoquant estimated by linear programming techniques previously explained. Then, subject to the constraint of the parameters of the estimated frontier unit isoquant, relative price ratios ranging from .5 to 1.5 were hypothesized and an iterative procedure began which searched for the "best fitting" relative factor price line. Average price efficiency was at a maximum (.933) for a relative price ratio of 1.0, and there was relatively little dispersion among the teams. Confidence in the efficacy of this procedure and the result is enhanced when it is noted that Scully (1974b, 919) found the ratio of the marginal products of hitting to pitching equal to 1.02. We conclude that baseball teams do indeed select cost-minimizing combinations of hitting and pitching talent.

Notes

1. A first approach to this problem included fielding as an input but subsequent analysis revealed this input does not contribute to the accuracy of the measure of output because year-end team fielding averages do not differ significantly between teams. The absolute range of team fielding averages over the twenty years of our sample was only .97 to .98.
2. See Quirk and El-Hodiri (1971) for an elegant development of the theory of relative team playing strengths.
3. Equation (3) is the form of the frontier unit isoquant utilized by Forsund and Hjalmarsson (1974).
4. The measures of hitting and pitching performance chosen here are not in the lexicon of the average baseball fan. Most fans would rate hitting performance in terms of batting averages, home runs, and runs batted in. For pitchers, season won-lost records or earned run averages are more commonly utilized. The problem with many of the measures of player performance is that they do not completely measure performance or that they are not wholly independent of factors beyond the player's control. For example, extra-base hits are not recognized in the batting average, so there is a bias against the long-ball hitter, who may go down swinging at the plate more often and have fewer hits, but whose hits have greater scoring power. A pitcher's won-lost record is not independent of the entire team's performance. And, the earned run average shows surprisingly little variation between great and not-so-great pitchers. For a thorough discussion of this problem see the section on "Measuring Player Ability" in Scully (1974b, 251–53).

5.   The data utilized in this study are from *The Baseball Encyclopedia* or from official major league baseball sources.
6.   Theory would suggest that some portion of management skill is general and, hence, transferable between teams and that some portion of skill is team specific. At least the talents and uses of the new players encountered must be mastered. One also suspects that the best managers tend to stay with their original teams for a longer period.

References

Forsund, F., and L. Hjalmarsson. 1974. "On the Measurement of Productive Efficiency." *Swedish Journal of Economics* 76:131–53.

Quirk, James, and Mohamed El-Hodiri. 1971. "An Economic Model of a Professional Sports League." *Journal of Political Economy* 70 (December): 1302–19.

Schmidt, P., and C. A. K. Lovell. 1979. "Estimating Technical and Allocative Inefficiency Relative to Stochastic Production and Cost Frontiers." *Journal of Econometrics* 9 (February): 343–66.

Scully, Gerald W. 1974. "Discrimination: The Case of Baseball." In *Government and the Sports Business.* Washington, D.C.: The Brookings Institution, 221–73.

———. 1974. "Pay and Performance in Major League Baseball." *American Economic Review* 64 (December): 915–30.

Timmer, C. 1971. "Using a Probabilistic Frontier Production Function to Measure Technical Efficiency." *Journal of Political Economy* 79 (July): 776–94.

Thomas A. Zak, Cliff J. Huang, and John J. Siegfried

Production Efficiency:
The Case of Professional Basketball

Sports, like politics and religion, is a subject to be avoided if peace and quiet are to be maximized. Asking a fan "whose team is best" is akin to speculation about whose god is best. Yet an important difference exists: Even if gods have won-lost records, the statistics are not readily available. Sport, however, results in violent disagreements despite well-documented records. Many disputes center on teams with "great potential" somehow wasted or, conversely, those teams with seemingly inferior talent that consistently "play over their heads" and compile excellent records. Does the best team always win? By estimating a production frontier, this paper considers the possibility that a team with the greatest potential may not prevail as league champion due to inefficient use of its resources. Estimating the production function also allows us to examine the determinants of a team's performance.

Method of Estimating the Production Frontier and Efficiency

Actually, no theoretical distinction can be drawn between a production function and a production frontier. Both define the maximum output attainable for a given combination of inputs. Differences in the economics literature arise because until the late 1950s empirical estimates of production functions were actually estimates of an average production function. Recent econometric research has provided a number of techniques for estimating the frontier production function. Timmer (1971) has applied linear programming techniques in his estimates, while Afriat (1972) and Richmond (1974) rely on a multiplicative error term to arrive at an estimate of the frontier.

For a given vector of inputs x, the maximum output, or the frontier production function, is denoted by $F(x)$. The observed output Y differs from the frontier output by a factor u, that is,

$$Y = F(x) \cdot u. \tag{1}$$

If we restrict u to between 0 and 1, then u can be used as a measure of production efficiency.[1] At the extremes, if a firm always receives the maximum output from a given set of inputs, then observed output equals frontier output, and the firm is 100 percent efficient. The term u has the value 1. If, however, a firm receives no output from its inputs (a case as unlikely as the first), then it rates a zero measure of efficiency, that is, $u = 0$. Obviously the efficiency, u, is a random variable in the sense that it varies from firm to firm or from game to game.

Afriat suggests that a beta distribution may be appropriate for the efficiency term u. In the case of a Cobb-Douglas form for the production frontier $F(x)$, however, he and Richmond assume that $v = -\ln u$ has a gamma distribution with parameter λ. Richmond goes on to show that the mean of the efficiency term, u, is equal to $2^{-\lambda}$. Geometrically, when $\lambda < 1$ and hence $2^{-\lambda}$ (i.e., the mean efficiency) is larger than $1/2$, the distribution of u shows that most observations are fairly efficient; when $\lambda = 1$ a uniform distribution of efficiencies results; and where $\lambda > 1$, the distribution of u indicates that most observations are relatively inefficient. Thus, by estimating the gamma distribution parameter λ, we can reveal the distribution of efficiency across firms or across games of a team and evaluate a team's average efficiency.

Taking the logarithm of the production function, equation (1) yields

$$\ln Y = \ln F(x) + \ln u$$
$$= [\ln F(x) - \lambda] + [\lambda - v]. \tag{2}$$

Since the mean and variance of a gamma distribution are both equal to the parameter λ, the random variable $(\lambda - v)$ has mean zero and constant variance λ. Using the ordinary least squares (OLS) method to estimate equation (2), we can therefore estimate λ (i.e., the variance of the regression), hence the mean efficiency $2^{-\lambda}$ and the production frontier $F(x)$.

A critical aspect of production-function estimation is the requirement that output and all inputs be measurable. Accurate measurement is one of the principal advantages of using professional sports team data. Statistics are extensive, and, unlike industrial data, few disclosure problems are encountered. Furthermore, the unit of observation, a contest, is analogous to a production run in a factory; this enables us to estimate the production function for individual firms (teams) as well as for the industry (league) as a whole.[2]

Empirical estimation of the production frontier for professional basketball teams using the Richmond method enables us to separate team potential (its frontier) from a measure of its technical efficiency (how close it normally comes to the frontier). Combining the two elements associated with each team's production function—efficiency and potential—allows us

to calculate an index of team quality. In the absence of random distur-
bances (luck), the quality index should result in a ranking identical with the
actual records.

In addition, the production-function approach serves as an indicator of
the relationship between inputs and their contribution to output. Computa-
tion of team-specific marginal products can identify those areas in which a
team's best opportunities for improvement lie. Of course this assumes that
one input is as easily expanded as the next, an assumption that may conflict
with reality. The seriousness of this assumption is mitigated somewhat
by the fact that the measured inputs (rebounds, assists, etc.) are jointly
produced by individual ballplayers. Therefore, given a choice between two
ballplayers (willing to work for the same salary), a team can choose the one
making the larger contribution to output.

Empirical Example: Professional Basketball

Using a Cobb-Douglas production function and data for individual games
during the 1976–77 National Basketball Association (NBA) season, we
estimate the equation $Y = F(x) \cdot u$, where the production frontier is

$$F(x) = A\left(\prod_{i=1}^{8} X_i^{\alpha_i}\right) e^{\alpha_9 X_9 + \alpha_{10} X_{10}} \tag{3}$$

and

Y = ratio of the final scores,
X_1 = ratio of field goal percentages (+),
X_2 = ratio of free throw percentages (+),
X_3 = ratio of offensive rebounds (+),
X_4 = ratio of defensive rebounds (+),
X_5 = ratio of assists (+),
X_6 = ratio of personal fouls (−),
X_7 = ratio of steals (+),
X_8 = ratio of turnovers (−),
X_9 = binary variable for location (home = 1) (+), and
X_{10} = difference in number of blocked shots (+)

(expected signs are shown in parentheses).

The specification of the error term u is multiplicative since the ratio
$u = Y/F(x)$ measures the degree of efficiency. For the convenience of estimation it is natural to specify the production frontier $F(x)$ to be a multiplicative (Cobb-Douglas) functional form too. In addition to this attribute,
the Cobb-Douglas form has other desirable properties. First, the marginal
products of each input in the Cobb-Douglas form depend on the levels of

other inputs. This is an intuitively attractive characteristic for professional basketball. For example, the marginal product of shooting skills should depend on the number of times the team acquires the ball (via rebounds, steals, turnovers by the opposing team, and opposing-team scores) and has an opportunity to shoot. Second, the coefficients of the Cobb-Douglas form are easy to interpret—namely, as elasticities. Finally, the Cobb-Douglas form is a widely used specification, with which many people are familiar. It possesses an appealing simplicity. Consequently, we chose the Cobb-Douglas form for the estimated production frontier.

Measuring output as the ratio of final scores captures the relative closeness of each game. Alternatively, one might use absolute score differences to measure output. The two measures will not yield identical results. For example, a game with a final score of 130 to 120 is a "closer" contest than a game ending 90 to 81 when using ratios, although the latter contest has a smaller point difference. Our principal concern, however, is the use of a "relative" measure. Using total points scored is sensitive to an opponent's playing style (a freewheeling, fast-breaking club or a slowdown-pattern one). Besides, if a team averages 120 points per game (the highest in the league) but yields 125 points per game on average, one would not want to say that team has the largest output. In fact, the essence of sports competition is to gauge one's performance relative to others'. The possibility of using a binary variable for winning/losing is rejected because of the Cobb-Douglas form of the production function (estimated using logarithms). The decision to use a ratio output measure instead of differences is arbitrary; however, we believe that normalizing the margin of victory by the number of points scored reflects some of those aspects of defense not included in the direct input measures, as well as controlling for teams with different offensive tactics.

On the input side the case for using ratios is stronger. Once again, logic argues for a comparative measure of inputs. Does it matter if a team gets 50 rebounds if the opposing team has 75? If both teams capture the same number of rebounds, the use of differences would result (in the Cobb-Douglas specification) in zero output. Consequently, we employ ratios on the input side as well, except for those variables which might have an observed value of zero (location and blocked shots in our equations).

Relative shooting percentages, both field goal and free throw, should make an important contribution to team output. Everything else equal, the better a team shoots relative to its opponent, the larger its output. Shooting percentages are used because they reflect how effectively a team shoots the ball more accurately than does the total number of shots. Moreover, the quality of a team's shooting is, for our purposes, as important as the quantity of shots.

Rebounding is also expected to have a relatively large impact on the outcome of a game. Outrebounding the opposition should improve a team's chances of winning. Unlike shooting percentages, where we believe field-goal shooting makes a larger contribution to output than free-throw shooting (more points are scored in a game from the field than from the free-throw line), we cannot infer greater a priori importance for either offensive or defensive rebounds.

Assists are included to capture those aspects of ball handling and teamwork not captured in improved shooting percentages. Of course, we anticipate that assists will make a positive contribution to output.

The ratio of steals and the difference in blocked shots should reflect aspects of defense that do not appear in reduced shooting percentages. While not expected to add a great deal to output, we expect a positive effect.

Inputs that should reduce output are personal fouls (essentially allowing the other team to shoot more free throws) and turnovers (relinquishing the ball without a shot). All else equal, as the number of turnovers increases, output will be adversely affected. In one sense turnovers are the converse of assists; they may measure the lack of cohesiveness of a team during a game. They also proxy aspects of an opponent's defense.

A binary variable, taking the value of one if a team is playing at home and zero if an away game, is also included in the estimated equations to account for the possibility that location affects the outcome of a game. Examination of estimated coefficients for this variable should indicate the magnitude of any advantage the home team enjoys.

In terms of quantifiable measures, the above list exhausts the data source and covers nearly every aspect of the game (shooting, rebounding, ball handling, and defense).

Data were gathered from official NBA box scores for the five Atlantic Division teams (Boston Celtics, Buffalo Braves, New York Knicks, New York Nets, Philadelphia 76ers) during the 1976–77 season. Although the sample is based on these five teams, every other team in the NBA is represented approximately 20 times. Each team plays an 82-game schedule against the other 21 teams in the league. Therefore, teams face each other approximately four times during a season.[3] Some data are lost because the official score sheet was not received, or, in some instances, all of the information was not available for a given game. This accounts for the disparity between the number of observations in the estimates and 82. Since each team faced common foes a similar number of times, the information can be pooled for the Atlantic Division teams to estimate a production function for the entire NBA. For the aggregate NBA estimate the number of observations is further reduced to avoid double counting. For example, a Boston versus Buffalo contest is included only once, instead of as both Boston versus Buffalo and Buffalo versus Boston. This problem is encountered, how-ever, only when two Atlantic Division clubs play one another.

Empirical Results

Regression results are reported in Table 1. The logarithmic form of the es-timated relationship permits us to interpret most of the coefficients as elas-ticities of output with respect to the various inputs. Overall the results confirm our hypotheses. At the 5 percent level all statistically significant coefficients exhibit the predicted signs, and most of the coefficients are sta-tistically significant. As expected, the largest output elasticities are asso-ciated with shooting percentages, especially field-goal percentage. This means that the larger a team's field-goal-shooting percentage is relative to its opponent's field-goal percentage, the larger its final point total will be relative to the opposition's. However, a 1 percent increase in the ratio of shooting percentages results in a less than 1 percent increase in the ratio of points scored.[4] In the case of the aggregate NBA regression, a 1 percent increase in field-goal-shooting percentage leads to a 0.61 percent increase in the ratio of final scores.

The elasticity of score ratios with respect to free-throw-shooting percent-age is less than that for field goals. This is to be expected for several rea-sons: first, free throws made contribute only one point to score rather than the two points awarded for field goals, and, second, missed free throws provide less opportunity for offensive rebounds because defensive players are positioned closest to the basket. Also, since free throws are sometimes awarded without a field-goal attempt, they are a less effective method of scoring.

Other variables making a substantial contribution to output include of-fensive and defensive rebounds and, in several cases, steals. As expected, personal fouls and turnovers reduce output. The difference in blocked shots and the ratio of assists proved to be insignificant. The difference in blocked shots probably is insignificant because so few occur in the average game. The average frequency of blocked shots is about 10 per game, which could have only a small impact on the ratio of final scores. The assists variable should probably be interpreted jointly with shooting percentage, since as-sists frequently lead to easy shots, which are missed less often. Conse-quently, the absence of an impact of assists separate from shooting percent-age is not so surprising and, furthermore, does not indicate the irrelevance of assists. This is a case like the offensive lineman's blocking assisting the running back in football, where joint production confounds the estimation of separate independent effects. The relatively high coefficient of deter-mination for a cross-sectional regression with so many observations con-firms our belief that the list of included inputs is comprehensive.

Contrary to the hypothesis that the home team has an advantage, the coefficient on the locational variable is consistently insignificant. Does this imply that a home-court advantage does not exist? Not necessarily, since the location variable does not include the effect of playing at home on the level of other inputs.

Differences between teams can be examined by comparing coefficients for the five teams. Buffalo's and Philadelphia's output is a good deal more responsive to field-goal-shooting percentage than is Boston's or either of the New York teams'. On the other hand, the New York Knicks' output is relatively insensitive to offensive rebounds, yet, compared to the other teams, is more responsive to the ratio of defensive rebounds.

Since the Buffalo franchise changed coaches in midseason we estimated separate equations for both coaches. The final two columns of Table 1 report these results. Of particular interest is the hypothesis that performance improves after a coaching change. In fact, a frequent justification for replacing a coach is that the incumbent is not getting as much out of the players as is possible. Team potentials and mean efficiencies are reported in Table 2. An interesting development occurred in the Buffalo case; while team efficiency improved (from .99897 to .99926) with the coaching change, the frontier output declined. Replacing the coach resulted in a decline in expected output for the Buffalo team. In other words, the change actually led to a reduction in team output, contrary to its (presumed) intended purpose.

Efficiencies for the other teams are also reported in Table 2. Buffalo is the most efficient team; even the pre-coaching-change (Buffalo I) efficiency exceeded that of the next most efficient team. Somewhat surprising is the relatively high level of efficiency achieved by the Philadelphia franchise. Many sports commentators have suggested that, while the 76ers are loaded with talented players, they do not play well together. Thus, one expects a rather poor showing by the Philadelphia club in terms of efficiency. One explanation of our result is that, while the combination of Philadelphia players may not be complementary, given the particular personnel, the coach assembled and directed them in an effective manner. In other words, Philadelphia's output might increase if team members were more compatible, but, given that they are not, they are combined in a fairly efficient manner.[5] The lowest level of efficiency is .99849, associated with the New York Knicks.

Compared to other studies estimating production efficiencies, these numbers are extremely large. Two explanations are plausible. First, in a competitive industry one expects inefficient firms to be driven out of business. While the sale of professional sports entertainment is not competitive,[6] the actual athletic contests are probably highly competitive, since the players and coaches have managerial control over strategic decisions

Table 1
Production-Function Estimates for Professional Basketball

Variables	League	Boston	Buffalo	N.Y. Knicks	N.Y. Nets	Philadelphia	Buffalo 1	Buffalo 2
Constant	-.0016	-.0064	-.0040	-.0084	.0011	-.0001	-.0031	-.0012
Field-goal-shooting percentage[a]	.6136*	.5511*	.6562*	.5500*	.5839*	.6634*	.6585*	.6230*
	(20.395)	(8.158)	(10.437)	(8.494)	(8.872)	(8.958)	(8.092)	(4.731)
Free-throw-shooting percentage[a]	.1137*	.0760*	.1677*	.0979*	.1308*	.1260*	.1768*	.1860*
	(8.581)	(2.466)	(6.295)	(3.269)	(4.378)	(4.378)	(4.538)	(4.383)
Offensive rebounds[a]	.0812*	.0847*	.0900*	.0554*	.0873*	.0829*	.0929*	.0789*
	(13.144)	(6.828)	(7.518)	(4.174)	(6.370)	(4.836)	(6.492)	(2.657)
Defensive rebounds[a]	.0610*	.0839*	.0438	.1182*	-.0034	.0354	.0618	.0709
	(3.103)	(1.958)	(1.150)	(2.571)	(-.082)	(.681)	(1.174)	(.977)
Assists[a]	.0116	.0364*	-.0092	.0204	.0333*	.0053	-.0112	-.0078
	(1.289)	(1.727)	(-.509)	(.087)	(1.723)	(.250)	(-.517)	(-.160)

Personal fouls[a]	-.1175* (-12.013)	-.1706* (-7.179)	-.0952* (-5.890)	-.1212* (-4.658)	-.1418* (-5.773)	-.1196* (-4.486)	-.0791* (-3.389)	-.1129* (-4.038)
Steals[a]	.0165* (3.181)	.0138 (1.441)	.0114 (1.234)	.0400* (2.710)	.0268* (1.879)	.0254* (2.199)	.0065 (.422)	.0223* (1.788)
Turnovers[a]	-.1216* (-11.018)	-.0908* (-4.540)	-.1287* (-6.380)	-.1434* (-5.149)	-.0752* (-2.842)	-.1231* (-4.448)	-.1562* (-5.428)	-.0922* (-2.892)
Home court[b]	.0067 (1.276)	.0075 (.690)	.0038 (.379)	.0150 (1.113)	-.0013 (-.117)	.0418 (1.304)	-.0005 (-.036)	.0026 (.152)
Blocked shots[c]	-.0003 (-.388)	-.0024 (-1.357)	.0003 (.310)	-.0015 (-.745)	-.0006 (-.360)	.00004 (.028)	.00004 (.024)	.0001 (.064)
$\bar{R}^2$	.8737	.8640	.9041	.8508	.8550	.8752	.9098	.8578
No. games	357	77	79	81	78	79	51	28

[a]Computed as the log of the ratio of the two teams' efforts in a game.
[b]A binary variable: 1 = home game, 0 = away.
[c]Computed as the difference in blocked shots in a game.
*Significant at the 5 percent level (one-tailed test).

Table 2
Estimated Production Output and Efficiency

Variables	League	Boston	Buffalo	N.Y. Knicks	N.Y. Nets	Philadelphia	Buffalo 1	Buffalo 2
Frontier output	1.0025	1.0049	.9804	1.0190	.9589	1.0486	.9841	.9829
Variance (λ)	.00185	.00177	.00127	.00219	.00201	.00154	.00149	.00106
Efficiency ($2^{-\lambda}$)	.99872	.99877	.99912	.99849	.99861	.99893	.99897	.99926
Frontier output × efficiency	1.0012	1.0037	.9795	1.0175	.9576	1.0475	.9831	.9822
Estimated rank	...	3	4	2	5	1	...	...
Actual rank	...	3	4	2	5	1	...	...

affecting individual contests. Coaches and players that do not perform well are quickly rationed out of the market. Second, previous studies used more aggregate data. Estimates made at the industry level, where outputs are not as homogenous or inputs are measured less accurately than in this study, should exhibit lower estimated efficiency levels.

The estimated production-frontier output of each team is also reported in Table 2. The frontier is calculated using the mean values for all inputs and the estimated coefficients. Of course, a team's actual performance is a combination of its potential (the frontier output) and its efficiency. Only in the case of 100 percent efficiency is performance equal to potential. Multiplying the frontier output by the level of efficiency yields expected output, and teams can be ranked on this basis. Table 2 reveals a ranking identical with one based on actual won/lost records for the 1976 season. Given the extraordinarily high levels of team efficiency, this is to be expected.

The elasticities in Table 1 can easily be transformed to find the marginal productivity of each input. Multiplying the output elasticity by the ratio of the mean of the output to the mean of the input gives the marginal product (MP).

$$(MP)_i = \alpha_i \frac{\overline{Y}}{\overline{X}_i} \tag{4}$$

The result of these calculations is reported in Table 3. Although in most cases a higher output elasticity implies a larger marginal product, this need not be the case. For example, Philadelphia has the second most inelastic output coefficient for offensive rebounds (.0829), yet the marginal product of offensive rebounds for the 76ers exceeds, by a substantial margin, the marginal product of offensive rebounds for all other teams in our study. Apparently the Philadelphia team has a considerable offensive rebounding advantage over its opponents relative to its point margin. The same story applies to comparisons between variables. The Boston team provides an example. Output is more elastic with respect to offensive rebounds than with respect to free-throw percentage, yet the marginal product of free-throw percentage is greater for the Celtics than the marginal product associated with offensive rebounding.

To reconcile our finding against a home-team advantage with the fact that most teams have a better winning percentage at home than on the road, it is necessary to consider two possibilities. First, the production function at home might not be the same as the production function for a basketball team playing on its opponent's court. The other possibility is that, while the production function is the same at home and on the road, the level of some inputs varies systematically with the site of the contest.

Chow tests (Chow 1960) are performed to investigate the possibility that

Table 3
Estimated Marginal Products of Professional Basketball Inputs

Variables	League	Boston	Buffalo	N.Y. Knicks	N.Y. Nets	Philadelphia	Buffalo 1	Buffalo 2
Field-goal-shooting percentage	.6245	.5445	.6637	.5262	.5858	.6449	.6646	.6325
Free-throw-shooting percentage	.1132	.0733	.1600	.0943	.1238	.1307	.1666	.1817
Offensive rebounds	.0737	.0636	.0792	.0565	.0734	.0879	.0781	.0758
Defensive rebounds	.0553	.0753	.0428	.1169	-.0036	.0318	.0594	.0714
Assists	.0121	.0326	-.0100	.0185	.0398	.0054	-.0122	-.0085
Personal fouls	-.1178	-.1590	-.1033	-.1182	-.1182	-.1330	-.0847	-.1254
Steals	.0160	.0156	.0093	.0408	.0211	.0244	.0060	.0149
Turnovers	-.1094	-.0702	-.1129	-.1329	-.0739	-.1140	-.1373	-.0806
Home court	.0135	.0147	.0071	.0298	-.0025	.0300	-.0010	.0044
Blocked shots	.0008	.0022	-.0005	.0011	.0009	.0002	-.00003	.0002

teams have two distinct production functions—one for home games and one for games played in another city. To test this hypothesis, we ran regressions nearly identical with the specification in equation (3) (deleting only the binary locational variable) for three different samples: all games, home games only, and away games only. The hypothesis that home and away production functions are identical is accepted for all five teams at the 5 percent significance level.

The mean values of inputs for home games can be compared to the mean values for away games to determine whether teams employ more inputs at home than in games played on the road. The t-values are presented in Table 4 for differences in mean inputs and output at home and on the road. All teams except the New York Nets performed significantly better as hosts than as visitors. The primary reason for this is traced to relatively better shooting and rebounding by teams when playing in front of hometown fans. In most cases field-goal percentage, and offensive and defensive rebounds, have significantly higher values at home than for away games.

The difference in assists may be misleading. While it may signal a more cooperative attitude by players on the home team, or less effective defense by the visitors, it could well result from padding the statistics of local fa-

Table 4
Significance of Differences in Means of Inputs and Outputs between Home and Away Games[a]

Variables	Boston	Buffalo	N.Y. Knicks	N.Y. Nets	Philadelphia
Points scored[b]	2.4233*	4.2177*	4.0425*	1.2993	3.3251*
Field-goal-shooting percentage[b]	1.1755	3.1358*	2.2685*	.8570	2.3670*
Free-throw-shooting percentage[b]	.2566	.5152	−.3112	−.1385	.5697
Offensive rebounds[b]	.6190	−.1537	.1892	.4771	.5798
Defensive rebounds[b]	1.2182	2.8751*	3.0393*	2.0512*	3.4547*
Assists[b]	2.6541*	4.6799*	4.3995*	2.0102*	5.2479*
Personal fouls[b]	.0590	−1.4311	−1.8036*	−1.3300	−.0248
Steals[b]	1.4198	4.1345*	.5822	−.5207	−.0967
Turnovers[b]	−1.6713*	−2.0116*	−.9351	−.1163	.7177
Blocks[c]	2.1670*	1.3628	3.1956*	1.6538	2.8959*
Degrees of freedom	75	77	79	76	77

[a]Calculated as home-game value minus away-game value.
[b]Measured as the log of the ratio.
[c]Measured as the difference in shots blocked.
*Significant at the 5 percent level.

vorites. Very little discretion is available to a scorekeeper for most of the measures, but whether a pass followed by a basket is counted as an assist or not is highly subjective. Teams also block relatively more shots at home than on the road. Unlike assists, there is little reason to believe measurement error is at fault. Perhaps officials are influenced by the crowd and unwittingly shade close calls (between goaltending and a legal block) in favor of the home team. Or perhaps the adrenalin pumps harder at home in anticipation of local advertising endorsement contracts. At any rate, although statistically significant for three of the teams, blocked shots' contribution to output is so small as to be of no practical importance in determining the source of the home-court advantage.

Lack of a statistically significant difference in the ratio of personal fouls between home and away games, except in the case of the Knicks, provides evidence that officials appear to be unbiased. This, of course, assumes that teams do not play "rougher" at home, in which case they would actually deserve more fouls.

Conclusion

Overall, the empirical results are encouraging. Application of the Richmond technique allows us to estimate the potential output of each team and calculate the efficiency with which inputs are combined. Output is most responsive to field-goal percentage, free-throw percentage, and rebounding. Other inputs significantly affecting output are turnovers and personal fouls. Careful examination of location leads us to believe the observed home-court advantage in professional basketball results from superior performance by the home team and not preferential treatment by officials. We also conclude that the determinants of performance are the same at home as on the road. The marginal products presented here could be of value to professional basketball teams. The same combination of inputs contributes different amounts to different teams; a team can evaluate players on the basis of their contribution to output and choose those players that increase output the most relative to their salary. Finally, the interaction of team potential and efficiency used to evaluate performance and rank teams results in a ranking identical with one based on actual won/lost records; given the extremely high estimates of efficiency, this outcome is to be expected and confirms the reliability of our estimating technique.

Notes

We would like to thank the National Basketball Association, especially Matt Winnick (director of media information), for providing data, and an anonymous referee (not, however, clad in black-and-white-striped shirt) for useful comments on an earlier draft of this paper. Computer time was provided by Vanderbilt University.

1. More recently, Aigner, Lovell, and Schmidt (1977) decomposed the term u into two parts: a random component and a measure of production efficiency. Obviously, this technique is theoretically superior; measurement error may cause observed output to be larger than the frontier. However, in the case of professional basketball, measurement problems are more unlikely than for other data sources so, for simplicity's sake, we employ the Richmond technique in our empirical work.

2. For more on the question whether the individual team or an entire league is analogous to the firm, see Neale (1964) and Demmert (1973, 15–20).

3. Each team faced 19 other teams four times during the season and two opponents three times ($4 \times 19 + 2 \times 3 = 82$).

4. This is to be expected because an increase in shooting percentage substitutes for alternative ways of scoring (e.g., offensive rebounding coupled with poorer shooting).

5. The Philadelphia coach was replaced just a few games into the next season.

6. Indeed, most teams have local monopolies in the output market.

References

Afriat, S. N. 1972. "Efficiency Estimation of Production Functions." *International Economic Review* 13 (October): 568–98.

Aigner, D., C. A. K. Lovell, and P. Schmidt. 1977. "Formulation and Estimation of Statistical Production Function Models." *Journal of Econometrics* 5 (July): 21–37.

Chow, G. L. 1960. "Tests of Equality between Sets of Coefficients in Two Linear Regressions." *Econometrica* 28 (July): 591–605.

Demmert, H. G. 1973. *The Economics of Professional Sports Teams.* Lexington, Mass.: Heath.

Neale, W. C. 1964. "The Peculiar Economics of Professional Sports." *Quarterly Journal of Economics* 78 (February): 1–14.

Richmond, J. 1974. "Estimating the Efficiency of Production." *International Economic Review* 15 (June): 515–21.

Timmer, C. P. 1971. "Using a Probabilistic Frontier Production Function to Measure Technical Efficiency." *Journal of Political Economy* 79 (July–August): 776–94.

IV Sports and the Structure of Competition

Brian L. Goff, William F. Shughart II, and Robert D. Tollison

Homo Basketballus

I.   Introduction

This paper is about comparative economic institutions as they relate to survivorship in professional basketball. The thesis of the argument is simple. We argue that, ceteris paribus, fitter players will last longer in the National Basketball Association (NBA) and that part of the explanation for this differential longevity can be traced to the organization of high school athletics in the states where players played high school basketball. Basically, there are two organizational formats for high school basketball competition: the open or no-classification system where any school, regardless of size, can win the state championship; and the classified system where schools compete on the basis of school size. By analogy we treat the latter system as a cartel and the former as free competition. We argue that the more competitive system, at the margin, adapts and selects players who are fitter for future basketball performance. Thus, professional players from open systems will survive longer in the NBA, all else equal. Property rights and economic organization matter in sports, as they do in all other economic activities.

Section II explains the organizational format of high school athletics and how basic differences in organization affect player development. Section III presents an empirical investigation of the importance of these differences for career lengths in professional basketball. Section IV offers some concluding remarks.

II.   High School Basketball Organization and Player Incentives

High school athletics in the United States are organized at the state level. Most states have systems that segment high schools into divisions on the basis of school size. In these states small, rural high schools compete in a division with schools of comparable size. Likewise, the larger, urban high schools compete with each other. Depending on the dispersion of the population and schools, up to five classifications may exist (e.g., Class 1A through Class 5A). Each division has its own state champion, and schools compete for the title only with those schools in the same classification. A few states have systems that allow open competition among all schools in certain sports. In this case the smaller schools are in direct competition with the larger schools for a single state title.[1] Historically, many states have had open competition in basketball, although today only a few open-competition states remain. As population discrepancies between rural and urban areas became larger, most states abandoned the open system in favor of restricted competition. Table 1 summarizes the history of the two organizational forms in the fifty states and the District of Columbia for the years 1960 through 1978.

The two systems assign property rights differently. In open-competition states, property rights favor the larger schools. They have a larger pool of talent from which to draw, and in an open setting they will have an advantage in the struggle for the state championship. In contrast, property rights favor the smaller schools where competition is restricted. In these states the smaller schools have a better opportunity to win because they compete for the state title with schools that have similar talent pools.

This difference in the assignment of property rights provides different incentives to players. In open-competition states players have an incentive to specialize in the areas in which they hold a comparative advantage relative to the entire population of basketball players. Shorter, lighter players at smaller schools, for example, will specialize in quickness, shooting, passing, and so on, and not in an inside power game.

Players in classified states have a different incentive. Because they compete only with schools of similar size, these players will tend to specialize in those areas in which they have a comparative advantage relative to the teams and players within their classification and not relative to the entire population of basketball players in a state. With classification some small players will play center and specialize in aspects of the game such as inside moves and shots and shot blocking instead of improving their outside shot, ball handling skills, and so on.

Inefficient skills are developed by players relative to the entire population of basketball players in states where competition is classified. A 6'2" player at a small school in a classified state often plays center and develops inside skills that are of less use to him at higher levels of competition. Open competition provides a better incentive for players to develop efficient skills relative to the entire population of players. A 6'2" player at a small school may still have to guard another team's center, but he also has more of an incentive to develop his outside skills and ball handling.

An implication of this analysis is that open competition will enhance the

Table 1
Organization of State High School Basketball, 1960–78

State	Open Competition	Restricted Competition	State	Open Competition	Restricted Competition
Alabama		X	Missouri	X (1962)	X
Alaska	X		Montana		X
Arizona		X	Nebraska		X
Arkansas	X (1977)	X	Nevada		X
California		X	New Hampshire		X
Colorado		X	New Jersey		X
Connecticut		X	New Mexico		X
Delaware	X		New York		X
District of Columbia	X		North Carolina		X
Florida		X	North Dakota		X
Georgia		X	Ohio		X
Hawaii	X (1960–69)	X	Oklahoma		X
Idaho		X	Oregon		X
Illinois	X (1960–71)	X	Pennsylvania		X
Indiana	X		Rhode Island	X (1960–66, 1971–78)	
Iowa		X	South Carolina		X
Kansas		X	South Dakota		X
Kentucky	X		Tennessee	X (1960–72)	X
Louisiana		X	Texas		X
Maine	X (1965–66)	X	Utah		X
Maryland		X	Vermont		X
Massachusetts	X (1960–69)	X	Virginia		X
Michigan		X	Washington		X
Minnesota	X (1960–70)	X	West Virginia		X
Mississippi	X (1960–69, 1973–75, 1977)	X	Wisconsin	X (1960–71)	X
			Wyoming		X

Source: Hollander (1979).
Note: We had difficulty determining the status of competition in certain years for Alaska, Arkansas, Maine, Mississippi, Missouri, and Rhode Island. This affected our sample for only two players, A. Norris and P. Short, both of whom are from Mississippi. At best, we were able to determine that Mississippi had open competition for at least part of the time that these two players were in high school.

survival prospects of shorter players relative to taller players. Taller players play center at all stages of their careers. They develop their skills independently of high school basketball organization. Open competition, however, will have an impact on the survival characteristics of shorter players. For example, the 6'2" players in open-competition states will learn to set more screens to get open shots, to control the tempo of the game, and to be excellent outside shooters. These skills may not translate into more visible output in the NBA, but they nevertheless will be valuable to NBA teams because such players spread the defense and open up the lane for power players.[2]

In short, the efficiency-enhancing organizational form at the high school level will provide players from open-competition states with better survival characteristics. In the NBA, these players will be more strongly suited for finding their niche and filling roles that an NBA franchise finds useful. Playing basketball in open-competition states allows players to survive longer in the NBA, ceteris paribus.

III.   Empirical Model

We estimated a model of player survival in the NBA using variables that measure the type of high school system in which the player participated, his performance in the NBA, complementary inputs to high school basketball, family income in a state, and the sorting of players among teams. We ran this model on professional basketball players who were on NBA rosters during the 1983–84 season and used years played in the NBA as a measure of player longevity.

Our empirical model is given in equation (1).

$$NBA\ YEARS = f\ (DCOMP,\ SCORING,\ REBOUNDS,\ EXP/PUPIL,\ MFI,$$
$$TRADES,\ RELEASE,\ TOTSORT,\ WEIGHT,\ DHARD)\ \ (1)$$

where

DCOMP	=	1 if the player's home state had open competition on his eighteenth birthday and 0 otherwise,
SCORING	=	a player's NBA career scoring average,
REBOUNDS	=	a player's NBA career rebounding average,
EXP/PUPIL	=	1976 state educational expenditures per pupil in a player's home state,
MFI	=	1975 median family income by state,
TRADES	=	the number of times a player has been traded divided by number of seasons in the NBA,
RELEASE	=	the number of times a player has been released, waived, or used free agency divided by number of seasons in the NBA,
TOTSORT	=	the sum of *TRADES* and *RELEASE*,
WEIGHT	=	a player's listed weight,
DHARD	=	1 if a player played less than four years of college basketball and 0 otherwise.

Our dependent variable, *NBA YEARS,* measures basketball survivorship directly. Suppose that the skill levels of basketball players from a state are normally distributed and that NBA teams sign only players whose skills exceed a certain threshold. Suppose further that open competition increases the basketball abilities of players from such states, that is, shifts the skill distribution to the right. Open competition therefore would unambiguously increase the *number of players* whose abilities exceed the NBA threshold. Moreover, if we assume that the variances of the two distributions are the same, then beyond the threshold, the open-competition distribution lies everywhere above and to the right of the restricted-competition distribution. It must be the case, then, that the *average skill level* of those players from open-competition states is greater than that of above-threshold players from closed-competition states.[3] Assuming that average longevity in the league is a proxy for average skills, the implication is that players from states with unrestricted competition ought to have longer professional careers, on average.

The dummy variable, *DCOMP,* is central to our hypothesis. A positive sign would support our theory of property rights and player adaptation and fitness. (A list of NBA players in the 1983–84 season who came from open-competition states is provided in an appendix table.)

The other independent variables control for ceteris paribus conditions. *SCORING* and *REBOUNDS* control for player performance. Better players (measured in terms of output) tend to be retained longer in the league. *EXP/PUPIL* is a proxy for complementary inputs to high school basketball, for example, gymnasiums, outdoor courts, coaches, and so on. *MFI* is an economic variable. The opportunity cost of practicing basketball is lower for children in poor families. Thus, children from poorer families tend to be better players, other things equal. *TRADES, RELEASE,* and *TOTSORT* measure the movement of a player around the league. The number of times a player moves around the league by trade, free agency, waiver, or release will raise his chances of survival. This movement is a type of sorting device that allows the pairing of a player with a team for which his marginal revenue product is the highest and can be seen as overcoming the competitive restraint that the draft system puts on the initial matching of players and teams. *WEIGHT* controls for physiology. Does a heavier player survive longer? Will his knees last? *DHARD* proxies movement into the NBA before the completion of a full four years of college basketball. Do such players survive longer?

The results from estimating equation (1) by ordinary least squares are given in Table 2. All specifications are double-log. Equations (1) through (4) use the natural log of NBA years as the dependent variable.

Table 2
Regression Results: Double-Log Estimation of Years in Professional Basketball

Ln (Variable)	(1)	(2)	(3)	(4)
CONSTANT	−2.88	−4.961	−1.332	−2.012
	(−2.62)**	(−2.29)*	(−1.34)	(−2.02)*
DCOMP	0.284	0.258	0.255	0.301
	(2.22)*	(2.00)*	(2.51)*	(2.60)*
SCORING	0.435	0.502	0.469	0.468
	(6.15)**	(6.19)**	(7.44)**	(7.32)**
REBOUNDS	0.114	0.080	0.155	0.184
	(2.69)**	(1.64)	(3.81)**	(4.73)**
EXP/PUPIL	0.739	0.738	0.530	0.548
	(3.52)**	(3.50)**	(2.82)**	(2.88)**
MFI	−1.044	−1.021	−0.827	−0.871
	(−2.83)**	(−2.76)**	(−2.51)*	(−2.61)*
TRADES			0.298	
			(7.17)**	
RELEASE			0.217	
			(5.13)**	
TOTSORT				0.294
				(8.46)**
WEIGHT		0.391		
		(1.12)		
DHARD		−0.144		
		(−1.48)		
Adjusted R^2	.354	.358	.491	.476
F-statistic (d.f.)	35.11**	25.64**	43.80**	47.96**
	(5,305)	(7,303)	(7,303)	(6,304)
N	311	311	311	311

Source: *NBA YEARS, SCORING, REBOUNDS, TRADES, RELEASE, WEIGHT,* and *DHARD* are
from or are computed from *NBA Register 1984–85* (1984). *DCOMP* is from (Hollander, 1979,
pp. 242–51). *MFI* is from (U.S. Dept. of Commerce, 1979b, p. 456). *EXP/PUPIL* is from (U.S.
Dept. of Commerce 1979a, p. 27).
Note: Dependent Variable = ln (*NBA YEARS*).
t-statistics are in parentheses.
*Significant at .05 level for two-tailed test.
**Significant at .01 level for two-tailed test.

The organizational variable for open competition, *DCOMP*, is positive and significant at the 5 percent level in all specifications. Unfettered competition at the high school level enables players to develop more efficient survival characteristics for future basketball performance. Of the performance statistics, *SCORING* and *REBOUNDS* have the expected positive signs.[4] *SCORING* is significant at the 1 percent level in each specification. The coefficient on *REBOUNDS* is sensitive to specification; it is not significant in equation (2).[5] State expenditures per pupil have a positive and significant influence on career length. More complementary inputs within a state aid young players in sharpening skills that help them survive in the NBA. The higher the opportunity cost to a young player of investing in basketball skills, the fewer years he will survive in the NBA. This result is shown by the negative and significant sign on home state median family income, *MFI*. The three variables that control for the sorting of players among teams, *TRADES*, *RELEASE*, and *TOTSORT*, are all positive and generally significant. Switching teams helps a player find a team on which he can play a role that raises his value and lengthens his career.

In equation (2), we added a dummy variable, *DHARD*, which is equal to unity if a player entered the NBA before finishing four years of college (a so-called hardship case). The estimated coefficient is negative, suggesting that leaving college early shortens professional careers, but the effect is not significantly different from zero. *WEIGHT* also is added in this specification. Extra weight may tear down a player's body more quickly, or it may help him survive in the rough world inside the lane. The coefficient on *WEIGHT* is positive, but it is not significant. Overall, the specifications explain between 35 and 49 percent of the variation in career lengths.[6]

A potential problem with our empirical analysis is that we have omitted consideration of college basketball experience.[7] Some states are recognized for superior college-level programs. Indiana, for instance, is known for high-quality basketball at both the high school and college levels. Also, eleven of the twenty-four players in our open-competition sample played for Indiana high schools, and seven of these played for Indiana colleges. It is possible that our competition variable captures the benefits of college as well as high school basketball training. We tested for this by omitting NBA players from Indiana high schools from our sample. The results essentially are unchanged.[8]

IV. Concluding Remarks

Organizational forms and property rights have been shown by economists to influence the incentives facing decision makers in the marketplace. This paper demonstrates that the incentives provided at the high school level by

Appendix Table I

Player	Home State	High School	Year of 18th Birthday
M. Benson	Indiana	New Castle (Chrysler)	1972
L. Bird	Indiana	French Lick (Springs Valley)	1974
J. Bridgeman	Indiana	East Chicago (Washington)	1971
F. Brown	Wisconsin	Milwaukee (Lincoln)	1966
W. Bryant	Indiana	Gary (Emerson)	1977
D. Buse	Indiana	Holland	1968
H. Catchings	Mississippi	Jackson (Jim Hill)	1969
J. Eaves	Kentucky	Louisville (Ballard)	1977
D. Griffith	Kentucky	Louisville (Male)	1976
D. Issel	Illinois	Bavaria	1966
W. Johnson	Illinois	Chicago (Lindbloom)	1970
E. Jordan	D.C.	Archbishop Carroll	1973
J. Lamp	Kentucky	Louisville (Ballard)	1977
A. Leavell	Indiana	Muncie (Central)	1975
R. Macklin	Kentucky	Louisville (Shawnee)	1976
K. Macy	Indiana	Peru	1975
R. Miller	Kentucky	Louisville (Central)	1974
A. Norris	Mississippi	Jackson (Jim Hill)	1978
D. Robisch	Illinois	Springfield	1967
P. Short	Mississippi	Hattiesburg (Blair)	1975
J. Sichting	Indiana	Martinsville	1974
R. Tolbert	Indiana	Anderson (Madison Heights)	1976
P. Wittman	Indiana	Indianapolis (Ben Davis)	1977
M. Woodson	Indiana	Indianapolis (Broad Ripple)	1976

the organization of high school athletics can influence the subsequent development of athletes at the professional level. Laissez-faire in athletics at the state level helps to promote the development of efficient survival characteristics by high school basketball players. Players from states such as Indiana and Kentucky, which allow open competition in high school basketball, have longer careers in the NBA, controlling for statistical performance and other influential factors. Indeed, our estimates suggest that players from open-competition states can expect their professional careers to last about 1 to 1.5 years longer than players from classified states, all else equal. Moreover, from an economic standpoint, the positive influence that complementary inputs have on career length is interesting, as is the result that higher opportunity costs (measured in terms of family income) to investments in basketball capital by younger players decrease career length. Poorer children practice more and ultimately become better players.

Our result carries no policy implications. States that classify high school competition have very good reasons (e.g., transportation costs) for doing so. Classification is not a free lunch, however; it mutes an interesting form of evolutionary competition at work.

Notes

We benefited from comments by James Buchanan, Mark Crain, Kevin Grier, and William Landes on an earlier version. Any remaining errors are our own.

1. These figures are from Newman (1985). Open competition can lead to significant public interest in high school basketball. In Indiana, where all schools compete for a single state title, over 1 million people turned out for the state championship tournament in 1984. This is compared to a total postseason turnout of 200,000 in the most populous state, California, where competition is restricted.

2. This discussion illustrates that many useful basketball skills cannot be reduced to a single metric. An appendix table lists the players in our sample from open-competition states. On average, these players are slightly in excess of 6′6″ whereas the average height of remaining NBA players is almost 6′7″. The players from open-competition states also are slightly lighter than other NBA players.

3. This result holds even though relative to their own distributions, the average skill level of above-threshold players is lower in open-competition states. The relevant comparison for our purposes is between the two hypothetical skill distributions.

4. We also estimated the effects of blocks, steals, and assists. None of these other performance statistics had a significant influence on career length. In addition, we dropped *SCORING* and *REBOUNDS* from the specifications to test the inference that open competition leads to higher skills. The signs and significance of *DCOMP* and the remaining variables were unaffected by the exclusion of the skill variables. These results have two implications. First, there is no collinearity problem between *DCOMP* and the performance statistics. Second, because of this lack of collinearity, open competition apparently increases survivorship by developing less quantifiable basketball skills such as setting screens, controlling tempo, making passes that lead to assists, and so forth.

5. This is apparently due to collinearity between *REBOUNDS* and *WEIGHT*, that is, heavier players tend to specialize in an inside power game.

6. One problem that we faced is that some players had experience in the ABA (the American Basketball Association dissolved in 1976) before entering the NBA, but all of our performance statistics are for the NBA. We addressed this issue by estimating the same equations that appear in Table 2, adding a dummy variable, *DABA*, equal to 1 if an NBA player in the 1983–84 season had previous ABA experience. The results of this exercise show that ABA experience has a positive and significant influence

on career length and that the other variables in the model, especially *DCOMP,* are unchanged in sign and significance. Largely, the positive coefficient on DABA reflects the obvious fact that an ex-ABA player still playing in 1983–84 has an above-average career length. These results are available on request.

7.   It also is true that all but five players in our sample of open-competition states came from Illinois, Indiana, and Kentucky—three states in the country where basketball arguably dominates football as the sport of preference. Thus, our empirical results do not distinguish the hypothesis that open competition leads players to adopt skills that increase their longevity at the professional level from the hypothesis that states where basketball is popular turn out more NBA-quality players and that these players are longer-lived. Open competition may produce *both* more fan interest (see note 1) and fitter players. In short, the organization of high school athletics and preferences are endogenous to our model. Note the discussion later, however, where we report the results from excluding Indiana from the sample.

8.   We also obtained results for the number of players in the NBA by state (*PLAYERS*) as a function of open or restricted competition. The results are

$$PLAYERS = -5.79 + .85\ DCOMP + 1.75\ POP - .24\ SAL - .72\ EXPP$$
$$(1.89) \qquad (13.73) \qquad (-3.00) \quad (-1.20)$$
$$R^2 = .807 \qquad F(4,46) = 48.24$$

All continuous variables are in natural logarithms and t-statistics are in parentheses. Overall, the equation is significant and explains over 80 percent of the variation in NBA players across states. *DCOMP* equals 1 if a state had open competition between 1965 and 1978 and 0 otherwise. The coefficient is positive and significant at the .07 level. *POP* is 1975 state population and has the expected positive coefficient. *SAL* is 1975 average secondary teacher salary by state. (We also included percent change in home state population 1970–75 as an explanatory variable in some specifications. The estimated coefficient was not significantly different from zero; the other results were unaffected.) Teacher salaries appear to be substitutes for expenditures on athletics. *EXPP* is expenditure per student and has a negative but insignificant sign. The main results presented in the paper suggest that once in the NBA, players from open-competition states survive longer. The results here suggest that players from open-competition states also are more likely to play in the NBA, controlling for population.

References

Douchant, Mike, and Alex Sachare, eds. 1984. *NBA Register 1984–85*. St. Louis: Sporting News.

Hollander, Zander. 1979. *Modern Encyclopedia of Basketball.* Garden City,
	N.Y.: Doubleday and Company.
Newman, Barry. 1985. "Back Home in Indiana." *Sports Illustrated,* February
	18, 38–60.
U.S. Department of Commerce. 1979a. *State and Metropolitan Area Data Book,
	1978.* Washington, D.C.: U.S. Government Printing Office.
———. 1979b. *Statistical Abstract of the United States, 1978.* Washington,
	D.C.: U.S. Government Printing Office.

David N. Laband

How the Structure of Competition Influences Performance in Professional Sports: The Case of Tennis and Golf

I.   Introduction

It is no great secret in the golf world that the most recent 18 major men's golf championship tournaments have been won by 18 different men.[1] Not only do the top professional golfers not consistently win the major tour events, they do not win many tournaments, period. For example, Greg Norman, the top money winner on the PGA tour in 1986, won only two of the 19 PGA tournaments he entered that year. The top woman golfer that year, Pat Bradley, fared little better, winning just five of the 26 LPGA tournaments she entered.[2] By contrast, the world of professional tennis displays a remarkable concentration of winning among the top players. Ivan Lendl, the top money winner among the men in 1986, won 74 of 80 matches and nine of the 15 tournaments he entered. The top women's player, Martina Navratilova, won 89 of 92 matches and 14 of the 17 tournaments she entered.[3] The statistics presented in Table 1 reveal the pronounced difference between golf and tennis with respect to dominance by the top players. Over the 14-year period, 1973–86, 67 percent of the men's Grand Slam tennis tournaments were won by the top four ranked players from the previous year, whereas only 20 percent of the men's Grand Slam golf tournaments were won by the top four ranked golfers from the previous year.[4] Among the women the disparity is consistent: over the 1973–86 period, 85 percent of the ladies' Grand Slam tennis tournaments were won by the top four ranked women from the previous year whereas only 26 percent of the ladies' Grand Slam golf events were won by women ranked in the top four for the previous year.[5] In a nutshell, the four-"firm" concentration ratio measuring dominance in the marketplace reveals that tournament wins are concentrated among the top few players to a much greater extent in tennis than in golf. Moreover, this concentration persists even though membership in the "top player" group changes.

To the casual observer of both tennis and golf, these differences in domi-

Table 1
Concentration of Grand-Slam Tournament Wins among the Top Four Players in Golf and Tennis: 1973–86

	Golf	
Men	11 of 56 tournaments	= .196
Women	14 of 53 tournaments[a]	= .264

[a] I could not positively identify the #4 ranked women golfers for 1973 and 1974, or the #3 ranked woman golfer for 1972. I thus could not with certainty determine the status of 3 tournament winners during those years.

	Tennis	
Men	37 of 55 tournaments[b]	= .673
Women	48 of 56 tournaments[c]	= .857

[b] Wimbledon was boycotted by the top men professionals in 1973 so I have omitted that tournament from the sample.
[c] The Australian Open tournament for both men and women was moved from December, 1986, to January, 1987; I have included these results in both calculations.

nation by the few top players may seem confounding, because both sports seemingly demand the same playing skill to be successful—the ability to correctly hit a small white ball with some form of club. And, indeed, there appears to be substantial amazement within the golfing community that no golfer has won more than one Grand Slam tournament in five years and perhaps equal amazement within the tennis community at how utterly dominating figures such as Martina Navratilova and Ivan Lendl have been.

The point of this paper is to argue that the structure-conduct-performance model employed so fruitfully by industrial organization economists to analyze the behavior and performance of firms in product markets can, to some degree, be applied to the world of professional sports. In the case of tennis and golf, I demonstrate that the marked difference in concentration of tournament wins among the top players (performance) is strictly an artifact of structural differences in the nature of competition between the two sports. Analysis of open versus match play golf results and yearly turnover among the top players is supportive of the theory.

This paper is organized as follows. In Section II, notable differences between golf and tennis are identified and their probable impact on the concentration of tournament wins among the top competitors are discussed. It is demonstrated that the dominance result in tennis can be derived from the match play versus open play form of competition, even when talent is distributed identically across the two sports. In short, the dominance in tennis does not result from the presence of once-in-a-lifetime stars in tennis during the sample period. The theory that the structure of competition has an impact on performance is tested in Section III, by comparing performance of the top players in open events against their performance in match play. As expected, the top players perform more consistently in a match-play setting than they do in an open-competition setting. In addition, yearly turnover among the top players in golf far exceeds turnover among the top players in tennis. Concluding thoughts round out the paper.

II.   Structure and Performance: Tennis versus Golf

Our analysis necessarily begins with a review of structural differences between golf and tennis. The list of differences identified in Table 2 admittedly is not comprehensive, but it does highlight major differences between the two sports that arguably could exert significant influence on outcomes, in terms of player performance.

The first factor listed is playing surface. Unquestionably, the degree of variability of the playing surface, in all dimensions, is substantially greater in golf than in tennis. In theory, the difference in variability of playing surface would lead one to predict the observed difference in concentration of winning among the top players between tennis and golf. Because there are only three basic surface types in tennis, with rigid court dimensions, a top player in tennis needs command over fewer variables to dominate on all surfaces than does a top player in golf. Assuming the distribution of playing talent is identical across sports, the greater variability of playing surface in golf arguably will be reflected in a higher probability of dominance by the top players in tennis.[6] In point of fact, however, this particular structural difference between tennis and golf does not appear to drive the dominance result. If playing surface exerts a strong influence on player performance then we should expect to observe dominance of tournaments by players who specialize in competing on that surface. Although the dimensions of certain golf courses are said to favor "longball hitters," whereas those of other courses emphasize putting skills, tournaments played at these locations are not dominated by individuals who specialize in playing each type of course. Similarly in tennis, clay-court specialists do not always win the French Open and grass-court specialists do not always, or

Table 2
Structural Differences between Golf and Tennis

Aspect	Golf	Tennis
Playing surface	Dimensions variable; surfaces variable. Number and position of playing hazards is highly variable from course to course. Actual playing surface (grass) is relatively constant, but slopes, hole positions, etc., may vary considerably.	Court dimensions constant, with some variation in distance between court and stands. Differences across surfaces (clay, hard court, grass) but relative uniformity from court to court on the same surface. Grass courts can become divoted.
Weather	Once play commences, it must be seen through to completion for that day's round, without regard to weather conditions, except for lightning. Wind, rain, fog, etc., can influence performance.	Matches not played in hard rain; stadium construction may limit interference by wind, although matches are occasionally played in very windy conditions.
Scoring	Cumulative—one mistake is permanently costly.	All or nothing match play; mistakes not necessarily costly.
Competition	A player competes against the entire field; your shot does not directly influence your opponents' performance.	Competition is one-on-one match play, with as many as seven matches making up a run to the finals of a tournament; the quality of play directly affects opponent's performance. Top players seeded to meet lesser players.

even frequently, win Wimbledon or the Australian Open. Björn Borg was a classic baseline player who admittedly won six French Opens, which is not surprising if surface determines results; however, he also won five straight Wimbledon titles, which is surprising if surface determines results. This is not to claim that surface variability has no ultimate impact on the concentration of tournament wins among the top professionals; the claim is that any such effect is not determinate and probably not of great importance as far as explaining the dominance result.

It also is unlikely that structural differences between golf and tennis with respect to the impact of weather conditions on sanctioned competition drive the dominance result. Although rain may interrupt a tennis match, there is no compelling reason to believe that such interruptions systematically favor the top players. Similarly in golf, bad weather is indifferent to tee-off time, which means that the top players and other players are affected equally by vagaries of the weather.

The third structural difference between golf and tennis involves the system of scoring used to determine the tournament victor. In golf, scoring is cumulative; the individual with the lowest stroke total for (normally) four rounds (seventy-two holes) is the winner. Often a single stroke separates the winner from the contenders. Tennis is a match-play sport, with each major tournament consisting of seven rounds of matches, including the final.[7] Each match is determined by a best three of five set format. The tournament winner must triumph in each of the seven matches played.

The scoring differences between the two sports imply that errors in golf are more costly than are errors in tennis. One or two missed shots in golf may easily spell the difference between victory and defeat. On the other hand, one or two missed shots in tennis may result in a lost game or set, but one can play horrid tennis for two sets in each match, yet win the tournament. The top player may make a number of errors, which may have little bearing on results. The fact that errors in golf are more costly than errors in tennis may be responsible, in part, for observed differences in concentration of tournament wins among the top players between the two sports. However, it seems unlikely that all of the difference can be attributed to this factor.

The final difference noted in the structure of golf versus that of tennis concerns the nature of the competition itself. In golf one plays against the entire field of competitors over a four-day period. To win the tournament, a given individual must outplay each and every other competitor in the field—the lowest score over seventy-two holes of golf wins. Moreover, how well or poorly one individual hits the ball in golf has no impact on the performance of the other competitors. By contrast, one plays against specific opponents in tennis, one at a time, and how well or poorly an individual plays directly influences the performance of his opponent. In addition, the top players in tennis are seeded to play the weakest competitors in the early rounds of each tournament.

A good case can be made that these differences in the nature of competition between golf and tennis are largely responsible for the dominance of top players in tennis and the lack thereof in golf. A simple example should suffice to illustrate the basic argument. Suppose that we identify a single individual in each sport as having extraordinary skills relative to all other competitors (e.g., Greg Norman in golf and Ivan Lendl in tennis). To be more specific, suppose that Norman and Lendl are each exactly two standard deviations above the mean level of playing ability in their respective sports; that there is no variation in their own actual performance; and that talent of all competitors, as measured by results, is distributed normally. To simplify the example, let each golf or tennis tournament consist of a field of exactly 100 competitors, including the individuals just described.

In any given golf tournament, since Norman must play against the entire field of competitors, the normal distribution of talent implies that four out of the 99 other players will beat him, because a few individuals will be located in the upper tail of that normal distribution; that is, they are having a "hot" tournament. On the other hand, Lendl plays seven matches, the results of which are each independent of the others. He thus has a .96 probability of winning each match. The cumulative probability that Lendl wins the tournament is thus $(.96)^7 = .75145$; that is, the odds are slightly better than three to one that he will win all seven matches he plays. It is clear that the top golfer is unlikely to win outright any given tournament he enters, whereas it is highly likely that the top-ranked tennis player will win a tournament he enters. Notice that this result does not depend on any unusual difference in assumed playing talent between the sports; indeed, the distributions are identical. Moreover, the result obviously would not change by assuming that the observed distribution of talent has subsumed into it the influence of weather, playing surface, and propensity to commit errors.

To address the issue of seeding in tennis tournaments and the observed dominance chronicled in Table 1, the example must be extended. Suppose the match-play statistics among the top four tennis players and between the top four and the next 124 are as follows:

#1: wins two of three from #2; wins three of four from #3; wins four of five from #4; wins 99/100 against all players ranked below #4;

#2: wins one of three from #1; wins two of three from #3; wins three of four from #4; wins 98/100 against all players ranked below #4;

#3: wins one of four from #1; wins one of three from #2; wins two of three from #4; wins 97/100 against all players ranked below #4;

#4: wins one of five from #1; wins one of four from #2; wins one of three from #3; wins 96/100 against all players ranked below him.

Let us then diagram a typical seven-round tournament (see Table 3). Assuming that match-play results are independent events, each of the top four seeds has a strong probability of advancing to the semifinal round. If the seedings hold true to form, then the probability that one of the top four seeded players will win the tournament, *facing the toughest competition possible,* is equal to the cumulative probabilities calculated for each of those players: $.51 + .20 + .07 + .04 = .82$.[8] Note that the cumulative probability of a top player winning the tournament does not decline if one or more (up to three) of the seeded players gets beaten in a preliminary round. If, for example, the #2 seed loses early on, the probability that the #3 seed wins the tournament triples from .07 to .21, while the probability that the #1 seed wins jumps from .51 to .57 and the probability that #4

Table 3
A Stylized Tennis Tournament with Four Top-seeded Players
(cumulative probabilities in parentheses)

Player	1	2	3	4	5	Semifinal	Final
			Round				
#1	.99	.99	.99	.99	.99	.80	.67
	(.99)	(.98)	(.97)	(.96)	(.95)	(.76)	(.51)
#2	.98	.98	.98	.98	.98	.67	.33
	(.98)	(.96)	(.94)	(.92)	(.90)	(.61)	(.20)
#3	.97	.97	.97	.97	.97	.33	.25
	(.97)	(.94)	(.91)	(.89)	(.86)	(.28)	(.07)
#4	.96	.96	.96	.96	.96	.20	.25
	(.96)	(.92)	(.88)	(.85)	(.82)	(.16)	(.04)

Cumulative probability that
one of the top four seeds $= .51 + .20 + .07 + .04 = .82$.
wins the tournament

wins rises from .04 to .05. Even if the top two seeds get knocked out, the cumulative probability that the tournament is won by either #3 or #4 still equals .82 (.56 + .26).

III. Empirical Evidence that Structure Influences Dominance

The structure of competition in professional golf tournaments, as described earlier, is open. At the master level, during sudden-death playoffs of open tournaments and for a few specific events (e.g., the Ryder Cup, a biennial competition between U.S. and European golfers) the structure of competition is match play as it is in tennis. To the extent one is able to identify higher-versus-lower-ranked competitors in match play, one can investigate whether the match-play format favors the top players in golf, as I have claimed occurs in tennis.

Data limitations curtail my ability to examine amateur results and Ryder Cup results. Although statistics on the Ryder Cup are well known, no world ranking of golfers was assembled prior to 1986.[9] Results of the 1987 Ryder Cup competition held in America and the 1987 World Golf match-play tournament held at Inagi, Japan, in November are presented in Table 4 and discussed below.

Table 4
Ryder Cup and World Golf Match Play Results for 1987

Ryder Cup—Singles Play:

Andy Bean	(21)	def.	Ian Woosnam	(19)
Howard Clark	(38)	def.	Dan Pohl	(22)
Mark Calcavecchia	(32)	def.	Nick Faldo	(44)
Payne Stewart	(5)	def.	Jose-Maria Olazabal	(43)
Scott Simpson	(27)	def.	Jose Rivero	(58)
Tom Kite	(15)	def.	Sandy Lyle	(6)
Eamonn Darcy	(—)	def.	Ben Crenshaw	(17)
Seve Ballesteros	(2)	def.	Curtis Strange	(11)
Lanny Wadkins	(7)	def.	Ken Brown	(72)
Sam Torrance	(35)	tie	Larry Mize	(13)
Bernhard Langer	(3)	tie	Larry Nelson	(85)
Gordon Brand, Jr.	(55)	tie	Hal Sutton	(11)

World Golf:

Payne Stewart	(5)	def.	Ian Woosnam	(19)
Sandy Lyle	(6)	def.	Lanny Wadkins	(7)
Bernhard Langer	(3)	tie	Mark Calcavecchia	(32)
Jose-Maria Olazabal	(43)	def.	Scott Simpson	(27)
Tom Kite	(15)	def.	Ken Brown	(72)
Nick Faldo	(44)	def.	Curtis Strange	(11)
Tateo Ozaki	(40)	def.	Ian Baker-Finch	(29)
Brian Jones	(76)	tie	Hajime Meshiai	(—)
Peter Senior	(39)	def.	Isao Aoki	(9)
Masashi Ozaki	(16)	def.	Graham Marsh	(24)
Rodger Davis	(17)	tie	Tommy Nakajima	(4)
Greg Norman	(1)	def.	Tohru Nakamura	(67)
Payne Stewart	(5)	def.	Brian Jones	(76)
Graham Marsh	(24)	tie	Lanny Wadkins	(7)
Rodger Davis	(17)	def.	Scott Simpson	(27)
Greg Norman	(1)	def.	Curtis Strange	(11)
Tom Kite	(15)	def.	Peter Senior	(39)
Ian Baker-Finch	(29)	def.	Mark Calcavecchia	(32)
Sandy Lyle	(6)	def.	Tohru Nakamura	(67)
Ian Woosnam	(19)	def.	Hajime Meshiai	(—)
Nick Faldo	(44)	def.	Tateo Ozaki	(40)
Bernhard Langer	(3)	def.	Tommy Nakajima	(4)
Masashi Ozaki	(16)	def.	Ken Brown	(72)
Jose-Maria Olazabal	(43)	def.	Isao Aoki	(9)
Payne Stewart	(5)	def.	Ian Woosnam	(19)
Sandy Lyle	(6)	def.	Mark Calcavecchia	(32)
Lanny Wadkins	(7)	def.	Bernhard Langer	(3)
Scott Simpson	(27)	def.	Nick Faldo	(44)

Table 4
(Continued)

World Golf (continued):

Curtis Strange	(11)	def.	Ken Brown	(72)
Tom Kite	(15)	def.	Jose-Maria Olazabal	(43)
Graham Marsh	(24)	def.	Isao Aoki	(9)
Peter Senior	(39)	def.	Tateo Ozaki	(40)
Rodger Davis	(17)	tie	Tohru Nakamura	(67)
Brian Jones	(76)	def.	Masashi Ozaki	(16)
Ian Baker-Finch	(34)	def.	Hajime Meshiai	(—)
Tommy Nakajima	(4)	def.	Greg Norman	(1)

The Ryder Cup play is scored by hole; that is, the lowest score between the two competitors wins that hole. The match is decided by who wins the most holes, and can end prior to playing 18 holes. For example, a score of three and two means that play was stopped after 16 holes, because one person had won three more holes than the other, with only two holes to play. It is impossible for the loser to catch the winner under the system of scoring employed. The World Golf event was played as an 18-hole playoff, with the low score winning the match. Of the 40 matches that resulted in a non-tie decision, twenty-six (65 percent) were won by the higher-seeded player.[10]

Tables 5 and 6 detail the results of sudden-death playoffs in men's and women's golf, respectively, during the 1980s. Recall from Table 1 that dominance of the Grand Slam golf events among the men is less than 20 percent among the top four players. In a match-play environment, however, results hold true to rankings 58 percent of the time (54 of 93 playoffs) for the men and 68 percent of the time (34 of 50 playoffs) among the women. Again, to prevent any simultaneity problems, the rankings listed are taken from the year previous to the playoff. These figures are consistent with the Ryder Cup and World Golf results and are impressive for two reasons. First, the fact that a low-ranked player is even in a playoff implies that he or she is having an unusually good tournament, is "hot" so to speak, whereas the top-ranked golfer may be having merely an average tournament. Seemingly, then, the odds favor the lower-ranked player. Moreover, playoffs are sudden-death, usually lasting only one hole. Random forces undoubtedly exert a much greater influence on results than would be the case for an 18-hole match between the two individuals. The fact that sudden-death match-play results hold true to rankings nearly 60 percent of the time for men and 70 percent of the time for women, both of which are significantly greater than random results, argues in favor of

Table 5
Playoff Records in Men's Golf during the 1980s

Winning Player	Rank	Losing Player	Rank	Year	Tournament
Dave Barr	141	Frank Conner	87	1981	Quad Cities
		Woody Blackburn	166		
		Dan Halldorson	36		
		Victor Regalado	77		
Andy Bean	4	Lee Trevino	2	1981	Memphis
	4	Bill Rogers	23	1981	Western Open
	33	Hubert Green	16	1986	Doral-Eastern
Ronnie Black	191	Sam Torrance	—	1983	Southern
Woody Blackburn	141	Ron Streck	81	1985	San Diego
Phil Blackmar	28	Jodie Mudd	34	1985	Hartford
		Da Pohl	27		
Jim Colbert	50	Fuzzy Zoeller	28	1983	Colonial
John Cook	78	Hale Irwin	38	1981	Crosby
		Bobby Clampett	163		
		Ben Crenshaw	5		
		Barney Thompson	—		
	77	Johnny Miller	20	1983	Canadian
Fred Couples	53	T. C. Chen	—	1983	Kemper
		Barry Jaeckel	70		
		Gil Morgan	26		
		Scott Simpson	24		
Bob Eastwood	24	Payne Stewart	11	1985	Byron Nelson
Danny Edwards	29	Morris Hatalsky	65	1983	Miller High Life
Dave Eichelberger	31	Bob Murphy	41	1981	Tallahassee
		Mark O'Meara	—		
Keith Fergus	21	Ray Floyd	2	1982	Georgia-Pacific
	30	Rex Caldwell	68	1983	Bob Hope Classic
Ed Fiori	36	Tom Kite	1	1982	Bob Hope Classic
Ray Floyd	26	Jack Nicklaus	71	1980	Doral
	10	Barry Jaeckel	116	1981	Tournament Players
		Curtis Strange	3		
	5	Lon Hinkle	76	1986	Walt Disney
		Mike Sullivan	127		
Bob Gilder	6	Rex Caldwell	68	1983	Phoenix
		Johnny Miller	20		
		Mark O'Meara	118		
Jay Haas	15	John Adams	138	1982	Hall of Fame
Donnie Hammond	77	John Cook	106	1986	Bob Hope Classic
Morris Hatalsky	56	George Cadle	99	1983	Milwaukee

Table 5
(Continued)

Winning Player	Rank	Losing Player	Rank	Year	Tournament
Hale Irwin	38	Bobby Clampett	163	1981	Buick Open
		Peter Jacobsen	26		
		Gil Morgan	28		
	13	Jim Nelford	50	1984	Bing Crosby
Peter Jacobsen	29	Payne Stewart	25	1984	Colonial
Tom Kite	1	Jack Nicklaus	16	1982	Bay Hill
		Denis Watson	87		
	14	Fred Couples	38	1986	Western
		David Frost	70		
		Nick Price	80		
Gary Koch	27	Gary Hallberg	45	1984	San Diego
		George Burns	83		Bay Hill
Bernhard Langer	75	Bobby Wadkins	67	1985	Sea Pines
Wayne Levi	20	Gil Morgan	29	1980	Pleasant Valley
	37	Steve Pate	—	1985	Georgia-Pacific
Bruce Lietzke	16	Ray Floyd	10	1981	San Diego
		Tom Jenkins	—		
		Tom Watkins	1	1981	Byron Nelson
	32	Andy Bean	24	1984	Honda
John Mahaffey	44	Jim Simons	89	1984	Bob Hope
	21	Jodie Mudd	114	1985	Texas
Roger Maltbie	8	George Burns	21	1985	Westchester
		Ray Floyd	68		
Gil Morgan	26	Lanny Wadkins	7	1983	Tucson
		Curtis Strange	10		
Larry Nelson	11	Mark Hayes	61	1981	Greensboro
Jack Nicklaus	10	Andy Bean	24	1984	Memorial
Mike Nicolette	106	Greg Norman	—	1983	Bay Hill
Greg Norman	42	Larry Mize	17	1986	Kemper
Mac O'Grady	20	Roger Maltbie	8	1986	Hartford
Corey Pavin	6	Dave Barr	65	1986	Milwaukee
Dan Pohl	27	Payne Stewart	19	1986	Colonial
Jack Renner	41	Wayne Levi	22	1984	Hawaiian
Bill Rogers	23	Ben Crenshaw	5	1981	Texas
Gene Sauers	121	Blaine McCallister	—	1986	Bank of Boston
Craig Stadler	8	Dan Pohl	42	1982	Masters
		Ray Floyd	2		World Series

Table 5
(Continued)

Winning Player	Rank	Losing Player	Rank	Year	Tournament
Curtis Strange	21	Lee Trevino	4	1980	Houston
	14	Peter Jacobsen	10	1985	Honda
	1	Calvin Peete	3	1986	Houston
Hal Sutton	26	David Ogrin	—	1985	Memphis
		Mike Reid	49		Southwest
Doug Tewell	43	Jerry Pate	11	1980	Heritage
Bob Tway	45	Bernhard Langer	13	1986	Andy Williams
Howard Twitty	15	Jim Simons	50	1980	Hartford
Scott Verplank	—	Jim Thorpe	48	1985	Western
Lanny Wadkins	29	Craig Stadler	8	1985	Bob Hope
Tom Watson	1	D. A. Weibring	57	1980	San Diego
		Tommy Valentine	—	1981	Atlanta
	3	Johnny Miller	12	1982	Los Angeles
		Frank Conner	58		Heritage
	12	Greg Norman	74	1984	Western
Mark Wiebe	166	John Mahaffey	21	1985	Anheuser-Busch
Fuzzy Zoeller	2	Greg Norman	74	1984	U.S. Open

Table 6
Playoff Records in Women's Golf during the 1980s

Winning Player	Rank	Losing Player	Rank	Year	Tournament
A. Alcott	5	P. Sheehan	2	1985	Nestle
	4	L. Howe	64	1986	Mazda
P. Bradley	11	B. Daniel	5	1983	Columbia
	4	A. Alcott	5	1985	National Pro-Am
	2	A. Okamoto	23	1986	duMaurier
J. Britz	16	N. Lopez	1	1980	Mary Kay
J. Carner	5	D. Germain	19	1981	S&H
	2	S. Haynie	13	1982	Henredon
	1	C. Montgomery	141	1983	Portland
B. Daniel	1	D. Caponi	2	1981	Florida Citrus
		P. Sheehan	5		
		C. Hill	41		
		P. Rizzo	—		
	2	C. Callison	—	1982	Sun City
	5	J. Carner	1	1983	MacDonalds

Table 6
(Continued)

Winning Player	Rank	Losing Player	Rank	Year	Tournament
J. Geddes	17	S. Little	42	1986	U.S. Open
J. Inkster	30	P. Bradley	3	1984	Dinah Shore
	19	D. Massey	35	1986	Lady Keystone
		C. Hill	118		
B. King	1	P. Sheehan	2	1985	Samaritan
	6	J. Carner	11	1986	Henredon
	6	A. Ritzman	50	1986	Rail
		C. Kratzert	—		
S. Little	7	K. Whitworth	24	1981	CPC
	8	K. Whitworth	10	1982	UVB
N. Lopez	7	L. Garbacz	32	1985	Ping
A. Miller	41	D. Massey	81	1983	W. Virginia
		L. Garbacz	55		
A. Okamoto	76	S. Little	8	1982	Arizona Copper
		K. Whitworth	9		
		D. White	17		
S. Palmer	57	J. Stephenson	10	1986	Mayflower
		C. Johnson	29		
P. Sheehan	4	K. Postlewait	30	1982	Orlando
P. Sheehan	5	A. Alcott	4	1986	San Jose
		B. King	6		
		A. Okamoto	23		
V. Skinner	79	P. Bradley	4	1985	San Jose
B. Solomon	22	J. Blalock	8	1981	Birmingham
H. Stacy	11	A. Alcott	3	1980	CPC
	11	A. Alcott	3	1981	Inamori
	11	A. Ritzman	38	1981	West Virginia
		P. Pulz	32		
		K. Postlewait	36		
		S. McAllister	62		
	9	K. Postlewait	30	1982	West Virginia
	9	J. Carner	2	1982	Whirlpool
D. White	14	D. Massey	17	1980	Coca-Cola
K. Whitworth	24	A. Ritzman	38	1981	Coca-Cola
	5	R. Jones	27	1984	Rochester

Table 7
The World Top Ten Men's Tennis Players and PGA Golfers, 1973–86

Golf:

Rank	1986	1985	1984	1983	1982
1.	G. Norman	C. Strange	T. Watson	H. Sutton	C. Stadler
2.	B. Tway	L. Wadkins	M. O'Meara	F. Zoeller	R. Floyd
3.	P. Stewart	C. Peete	A. Bean	L. Wadkins	T. Kite
4.	A. Bean	J. Thorpe	D. Watson	C. Peete	C. Peete
5.	D. Pohl	R. Floyd	T. Kite	G. Morgan	T. Watson
6.	H. Sutton	C. Pavin	B. Lietzke	R. Caldwell	B. Gilder
7.	T. Kite	H. Sutton	F. Couples	B. Crenshaw	L. Wadkins
8.	B. Crenshaw	R. Maltbie	C. Stadler	M. McCumber	W. Levi
9.	R. Floyd	J. Mahaffey	G. Norman	T. Kite	J. Pate
10.	B. Langer	M. O'Meara	P. Jacobsen	J. Nicklaus	C. Strange

Rank	1981	1980	1979	1978	1977
1.	T. Kite	T. Watson	T. Watson	T. Watson	T. Watson
2.	R. Floyd	L. Trevino	L. Nelson	G. Morgan	J. Nicklaus
3.	T. Watson	C. Strange	L. Hinkle	A. Bean	L. Wadkins
4.	B. Lietzke	A. Bean	L. Trevino	J. Nicklaus	H. Irwin
5.	B. Rogers	B. Crenshaw	B. Crenshaw	H. Green	B. Lietzke
6.	J. Pate	J. Pate	B. Rogers	L. Trevino	T. Weiskopf
7.	H. Irwin	G. Burns	A. Bean	H. Irwin	R. Floyd
8.	C. Stadler	C. Stadler	B. Lietzke	B. Kratzert	M. Barber
9.	C. Strange	M. Reid	F. Zoeller	G. Player	H. Green
10.	L. Nelson	R. Floyd	L. Wadkins	J. Pate	B. Kratzert

Rank	1976	1975	1974	1973	
1.	J. Nicklaus	J. Nicklaus	J. Miller	J. Nicklaus	
2.	B. Crenshaw	J. Miller	J. Nicklaus	B. Crampton	
3.	H. Irwin	T. Weiskopf	H. Green	T. Weiskopf	
4.	H. Green	H. Irwin	L. Trevino	L. Trevino	
5.	A. Geiberger	G. Littler	J. C. Snead	L. Wadkins	
6.	J. C. Snead	A. Geiberger	D. Stockton	M. Barber	
7.	R. Floyd	T. Watson	H. Irwin	H. Irwin	
8.	D. Graham	J. Mahaffey	J. Heard	B. Casper	
9.	D. January	L. Trevino	B. Allin	J. Miller	
10.	J. Pate	B. Crampton	T. Watson	J. Schlee	

Table 7
(Continued)

Tennis:

Rank	1986	1985	1984	1983	1982
1.	I. Lendl	I. Lendl	J. McEnroe	J. McEnroe	J. McEnroe
2.	B. Becker	J. McEnroe	J. Connors	I. Lendl	J. Connors
3.	M. Wilander	M. Wilander	I. Lendl	J. Connors	I. Lendl
4.	Y. Noah	J. Connors	M. Wilander	M. Wilander	G. Vilas
5.	S. Edberg	S. Edberg	A. Gomez	Y. Noah	V. Gerulaitis
6.	H. Leconte	B. Becker	A. Jarryd	J. Arias	J-L. Clerc
7.	J. Nystrom	Y. Noah	H. Sundstrom	J. Higueras	M. Wilander
8.	J. Connors	A. Jarryd	P. Cash	J-L. Clerc	G. Mayer
9.	M. Mecir	M. Mecir	E. Teltscher	K. Curren	Y. Noah
10.	A. Gomez	K. Curren	Y. Noah	G. Mayer	P. McNamara

Rank	1981	1980	1979	1978	1977
1.	J. McEnroe	B. Borg	B. Borg	J. Connors	J. Connors
2.	I. Lendl	J. McEnroe	J. Connors	B. Borg	G. Vilas
3.	J. Connors	J. Connors	J. McEnroe	G. Vilas	B. Borg
4.	B. Borg	G. Mayer	V. Gerulaitis	J. McEnroe	V. Gerulaitis
5.	J-L. Clerc	G. Vilas	R. Tanner	V. Gerulaitis	B. Gottfried
6.	G. Vilas	I. Lendl	G. Vilas	E. Dibbs	E. Dibbs
7.	G. Mayer	H. Solomon	A. Ashe	B. Gottfried	M. Orantes
8.	E. Teltscher	J-L. Clerc	H. Solomon	R. Ramirez	R. Ramirez
9.	V. Gerulaitis	V. Gerulaitis	J. Higueras	H. Solomon	I. Nastase
10.	P. McNamara	E. Teltscher	E. Dibbs	C. Barazzutti	D. Stockton

Rank	1976	1975	1974	1973	
1.	J. Connors	J. Connors	J. Connors	I. Nastase	
2.	B. Borg	G. Vilas	J. Newcombe	J. Newcombe	
3.	I. Nastase	B. Borg	B. Borg	J. Connors	
4.	M. Orantes	A. Ashe	R. Laver	T. Okker	
5.	R. Ramirez	M. Orantes	G. Vilas	S. Smith	
6.	G. Vilas	K. Rosewall	T. Okker	K. Rosewall	
7.	A. Panatta	I. Nastase	A. Ashe	M. Orantes	
8.	H. Solomon	J. Alexander	K. Rosewall	R. Laver	
9.	E. Dibbs	R. Tanner	S. Smith	J. Kodes	
10.	B. Gottfried	R. Laver	I. Nastase	A. Ashe	

Note: In golf, the average number of top-ten players in one year who are top-ten players in the following year = 3.54 with a standard deviation = 1.560737. In tennis, the average number of top-ten players in one year who are top-ten players in the following year = 6.92 with a standard deviation = 1.1875465.

the theory that the structure of competition determines the degree to which a sport is dominated by the top competitors.

The open versus match-play format differences between tennis and golf in conjunction with the practice of seeding the top competitors in tennis against weak opposition in early rounds of tournaments implies yet another difference in performance by competitors in the two sports. The top players should perform well more consistently in tennis than in golf. The data presented in Table 7 testify to the validity of this prediction.

Data available in the Men's International Professional Tennis Council's *Media Guide* (1987) and *PGA Tour Book* (1987), with gaps filled in by the PGA, enabled me to compile a list of the (men's) top-10 golfers and tennis players annually from 1973–86 inclusive. At issue is the number of new faces among the top-ten from one year to the next; I expect less annual turnover in tennis than in golf. The data are unambiguous: an average of nearly 7 out of the top 10 tennis players in any given year return to the top 10 in the following year whereas only roughly 3.5 of the top 10 golfers from one year return to the top 10 in the following year, a difference significant at the .01 level for a one-tailed t-test ($t = 5.97$).[11]

IV.   Concluding Comments

The purpose of this paper was to demonstrate that the structure of competition in professional sports may be largely responsible for determining the short-run and long-run performance of athletes in each respective sport. In the particular case at hand, I have assumed an *identical* distribution of playing talent across tennis and golf and demonstrated that dominance of the sport of tennis by the top players can be explained by the match-play structure of competition and the practice of seeding the top players against weaker players. Lack of dominance in golf is an artifact of the open-field nature of competition. Analysis of match-play results in golf during the 1980s suggests that outcomes run considerably truer to player rankings in match-play than in open play. Although a "superstar" indeed may be beneficial for the game of golf, it seems unlikely that a superstar in golf can ever possibly dominate that sport the way a superstar in tennis, possessing equal talent relative to competitors as the superstar golfer, can dominate the sport of tennis, both in terms of tournament wins in a specific year or over a period of time spanning several years.

Notes

Helpful comments in the formative stages of this analysis were received from Mason Gerety, Dan Benjamin, Mike Spivey, and Charles Diamond. My intellectual debt in this regard is substantial. Errors in the analysis are my sole responsibility.

1. The four tournaments that constitute the so-called Grand Slam of golf on the men's tour are the PGA tournament, the Masters, the U.S. Open, and the British Open.

2. There is some possibility that Bradley played even more than 26 tournaments; the 1986 LPGA media guide does not include data on players failing to make the cut in tournaments.

3. Moreover, Lendl and Navratilova made the finals of the tournaments they entered 12 and 16 times respectively (out of 15 and 17 tournaments), whereas Norman and Bradley finished in first or second place in only six and 11 times, respectively (out of 19 and 26 tournaments).

4. The four tournaments that make up the major tennis championships for both men and women are the French Open, the All-England Championships (Wimbledon), the U.S. Open, and the Australian Open. Because a player's ranking and earnings position in any year t are dependent upon performance in the major tournaments played that year, one cannot examine dominance by looking at an individual's ranking and performance from the same year. However, there is no particular reason to expect an individual's ranking in year $t - 1$ to be associated a priori with that player's performance in year t.

5. The Grand Slam events on the LPGA are the U.S. Open, the LPGA tournament, the Nabisco Dinah Shore tournament, and the duMaurier tournament.

6. The assumption of an equal distribution of talent across sports is not a particularly strong one. Indeed, controlling for differences in payoffs across sports, the playing talent must be distributed identically in the long run, given free entry and exit.

7. This format describes men's tournaments—women's tournaments normally field a smaller draw and thus feature fewer rounds of play. In addition, the women routinely play best two of three matches.

8. That is, if #1 beats #4 in the semifinals, we assume that #1 must play #2 in the finals; #2 and #3 are both assumed to play #1 in the finals, and if #4 beats #1 in the semifinals, #4 is assumed to play #2 in the finals.

9. For this reason, the lack of any uniform world ranking system, it is impossible to analyze previous match-play golf results. In past years the U.S. PGA tournament and the British Open were played under a match-play format. The same is true of golf at the amateur level. Without a system that ranks players by performance, there is no way of knowing ex ante who should win the match. Money winnings are a poor proxy of performance, because many of the world's golf players do not compete on the PGA circuit, which offers money far in excess of that offered elsewhere in the world. Indeed, the Sony World Top 100 ranking of golfers contains many non-Americans and many golfers who do not compete in the United States.

10. The rankings are taken from the Sony World Top 100 ranking, for June 14, 1987. The system is based on tournament placement over a three-year period, adjusting for quality of field.

11.   These results are all the stronger for the fact that they are based only on performance on the PGA tour and thus generally exclude most foreign players, many of whom are top-caliber competitors. Without this foreign competition, which is present in the tennis rankings, one would expect less turnover in the ranking of top golfers. My suspicion is that if the Sony World Top 100 ranking had existed over the 1973–86 period, there would have been even more turnover among the top-ten golfers from year to year than is reflected in the annual PGA top ten.

References

Ladies Professional Golf Association. *1987 Player Guide.*
Men's International Professional Tennis Council. *Official 1987 Media Guide.*
Professional Golf Association Tour. *Official PGA Tour Book 1987.*
Women's International Tennis Association. *1987 Media Guide.*

V Sports and Organizational Economics

Arthur A. Fleisher III, Brian L. Goff,
William F. Shughart II, and Robert D. Tollison

Crime or Punishment?
Enforcement of the NCAA Football Cartel

Saw Varsity's Horns Off
—Texas Aggie War
Hymn

I.   Introduction

The National Collegiate Athletic Association (NCAA) is a private organization that regulates college athletics in the United States. It was founded in 1906 to control violence in college football (Frey 1982). Once the NCAA had been organized to police college sports, it was possible to extend its powers to cartelize certain aspects of intercollegiate athletic competition. The cartel was not instituted overnight; it evolved slowly and assumed its modern form about 1950. The so-called Sanity Rule, which established recruitment and financial aid guidelines for student-athletes, was passed in 1948. This rule was the first step toward a monopsony among member schools. In 1951–52, the NCAA adopted controls over live television appearances by members, extending the cartelization process into the output market. At the same time, member schools also delegated cartel enforcement powers to the NCAA and set up a Committee on Infractions. This committee serves as the enforcement arm of the cartel, investigating rule violations by member schools, assessing the severity of these violations, and meting out penalties.

On the output side of the cartel, the NCAA limited the number of times that a school's football team could appear on television as well as the number and dates of games played during a season. The NCAA's television restrictions lasted until 1984 when the Supreme Court ruled in *NCAA v. The University of Oklahoma and The University of Georgia* that the exclusive television contract of the NCAA and the limitations the NCAA placed on the television appearances of member institutions amounted to a restraint of trade. This decision, in effect, deregulated the television side of the NCAA college football cartel.

The ruling, however, did not interfere with the behavior of the NCAA in its role as a monopsonist with respect to college athletes. Indeed, in the majority opinion, Justice Stevens actually endorsed many of the restrictions of the NCAA designed to "preserve amateurism" and "competitive balance." While the College Football Association (a subset of NCAA institutions) now negotiates its own television agreement, the NCAA maintains exclusive control over the regulation of player recruitment by member schools.

The essence of these rules is that players cannot be paid according to their marginal revenue products (MRPs). Rather, they are paid a uniform wage in-kind, consisting of a scholarship, room and board, an expense allowance, and so on. The problem is that in the era of modern college athletics many (if not most) players have MRPs in excess of the value of their stipulated payments. Seen in this light, the NCAA is a mechanism by which schools capture rents from student-athletes.

That the NCAA promotes a form of monopsony is not controversial (Becker 1985). What is interesting in this case is *how* the cartel is enforced. The NCAA itself is a small organization with a small staff; it does not have the resources to serve as the primary enforcer of the monopsony arrangement. In practice, basic enforcement takes place in the process of competition for players among schools. If a school cheats on the cartel by offering an illegal payment to a recruit, other schools may learn of the offer and turn in the offender. The NCAA may then proceed with an investigation of such allegations and ultimately may impose penalties (such as no television or bowl appearances and loss of scholarships for a specified period) on a cartel breaker.

Our use of the conjectural tense here brings us to the purpose of the paper. Though most economists accept the idea that the NCAA functions as a monopsony, no one has explicitly modeled the process by which it is enforced. As with other cartels, this process must be deduced from the enforcement behavior of the NCAA over time. In other words, in an era when violations of NCAA rules are reported to be widespread, one must pierce the tired rhetoric about the maintenance of amateur athletics in order to perceive what the NCAA enforcement strategy is (Underwood 1978).[1] To this end we develop and test a theory of NCAA enforcement activity. Our theory stresses the indirect and probabilistic ways in which cheating is detected and advances a redistributive hypothesis with respect to who wins and who loses from NCAA enforcement activities. To tell, for example, whether a team is cheating, competitors will observe its on-field performance rather than searching for cancelled checks from illegal payments. Thus, other things equal, the variability of a school's winning percentage will be a signal of the amount of cheating by the school. When a team that has not won the conference championship for years suddenly becomes better and wins, it becomes a suspect for recruiting violations and eventual NCAA probation. In this way the NCAA functions to protect perennial athletic powers.

The paper proceeds as follows. A theory of NCAA enforcement is presented in Section II. The theory is evaluated in Section III based on tests using thirty years of NCAA enforcement data with respect to college football programs. Concluding remarks are offered in Section IV.

II.   The NCAA as a Monopsonist

The NCAA is virtually the sole purchaser of able high school athletes (excluding perhaps baseball and tennis players).[2] Our interest is not in the degree of monopsony power possessed by the NCAA, but in how this cartel is enforced. Suffice it to say that the cartel appears to be effective at capturing rents from players by holding wages below the level of their marginal revenue products. Players at the top NCAA institutions help generate large gate and television receipts for their respective schools.[3] In return, players receive athletic scholarships that include tuition, room and board, and nominal expense allowances. In addition to playing and practicing football during the season, players must maintain their academic eligibility and keep in shape during the off season (which includes several weeks of spring practice). In effect players are required to work at football for as much as ten months a year.[4]

Because the NCAA is an association of many "firms," it encounters problems that a single-firm monopsonist would not face. A single-firm monopsonist finds the equilibrium wage for a factor of production. The NCAA sets the monopsony wage, and then must enforce that wage among member schools. The standard wage rate is established in the various issues of the *NCAA Manual,* which describe the allowable compensation for student-athletes at member institutions. The number, length, and value of academic scholarships are set as well as legal expense allowances. The rules also restrict in-kind payments from institutions to players and recruits in the form of free tickets, T-shirts, transportation, and accommodations.[5]

Alumni are also restricted by the guidelines set out in the *Manual.* They are prohibited from offering cash or in-kind payments to players or recruits. Moreover, limitations are set on the amount of money that an NCAA athlete may earn outside of school. In this way the NCAA curtails the use of "summer jobs" as a means by which alumni can offer higher wages to athletes.

The NCAA takes steps to ensure that the prescribed wage is the effective wage. Sanctions are placed on schools that depart from the regulations. Minor violations bring reprimands and increased attention from the NCAA. Serious violations result in the loss of scholarships, forfeiture of an athlete's eligibility, and loss of television and postseason bowl game revenues. More recently, the NCAA has instituted a "death penalty"—cancellation of a school's football program—for members who repeatedly violate its regulations.[6] Liability for alumni activity is placed on the school that the alumni support.

The basic problem in any cartel is the incentive for individual firms to cheat on the agreement. The NCAA is no exception in this regard; individual coaches, alumni, and schools stand to benefit from violating the NCAA agreement while other schools adhere to it. Winning coaches are wealthier coaches. Higher winning percentages are a signal of higher quality coaching, and raise the coach's opportunity wage in the market. Winning schools are wealthier schools. Successful football teams draw more fans to the stadium, and generate additional revenues from regular season television appearances and from invitations to postseason bowl games. A school may receive increased financial support from public and private sources as a result of increased exposure from a nationally ranked football program. The quality of students who apply for admission may improve (McCormick and Tinsley 1987). Alumni are happier (wealthier?) when their alma mater wins on the gridiron. These rewards provide incentives for coaches, schools, and alumni to offer recruits wages above those set by the cartel as a whole. Any one school can gain an advantage over its competitors by attracting higher quality athletes with the offer of wages above those paid by other cartel members. In deciding whether to engage in such behavior, the agents involved in recruitment of athletes will balance the expected gains from violating the agreement against the sanctions imposed if caught times the probability of detection.

In order to make the sanctions a viable threat to potential violators and to reduce the profitability of cheating, a cartel must be able to detect violators. The NCAA Committee on Infractions polices the recruitment process and tries to detect illegal activities and enforce the monopsonistic wage rules. However, the enforcement staff of the NCAA is small compared with the size of the cartel it polices. In 1978 the enforcement staff consisted of 11 employees; there are over 800 institutions in the NCAA (Underwood 1978). Thus, member institutions must play the basic role in the detection of cartel violations; they must monitor each other for signs of illegal activity. The Committee on Infractions then investigates the allegations brought before it, assesses the extent of violations, and levies penalties.

One method that individual cartel members can use to discourage cheating is to monitor the activities of other schools directly. Direct monitoring reduces the ability of schools to offer illegal inducements to recruits and players without detection. Such evidence may exist in the form of cancelled checks, cosigned loans, travel accounts, letters, and so on, but this evidence is difficult and costly to find. Complete direct monitoring of a rival's recruiting practices would require constant surveillance of its coaches

and alumni as they attempt to recruit potential players. Because this is pro-
hibitively costly, schools will seek more efficient methods to monitor
rivals' recruiting behavior.

More generally, as Stigler (1964) discusses, cartels will use probabilistic
or indirect evidence to spot firms that are violating the cartel agreement. In
the case of secret price cutting, no direct evidence will exist about cheating, so cartel members will resort to the use of probabilistic evidence.
Similarly, NCAA cartel members will use probabilistic or indirect evidence as a guide to the amount of cheating by their rivals. In a word,
NCAA members will monitor outputs rather than inputs (Alchian and
Demsetz 1972).

Perhaps the best indirect evidence of illegal payments to players is given
by a team's competitive performance. Certain aspects of a team's performance offer probabilistic evidence of violations. For example, the variability of a team's won-loss record provides indirect evidence of their compensation practices. A perennial break-even team that begins to attract
consistently higher quality athletes and produce a winning record will
cause rivals to infer illegal practices (higher wage rates). The rivals will
initiate an investigation by the Committee on Infractions to find evidence
of violations leading to a subsequent enforcement and penalty action.

A related method of cartel enforcement resides in the recruitment process. Suppose two schools are bidding for an athlete. The loser knows that
it was outbid, and thus it can turn in its rival to the NCAA. Greater success
in recruiting thus can lead to increased scrutiny by the cartel. This method
of cartel enforcement is closely related to the output monitoring hypothesis
for a simple reason—there is a link between recruiting and winning. Success in the recruiting wars will reveal itself on the playing field. We therefore think that winning variance proxies for recruiting variance.

Returning to the winning variance argument for a moment, note that for
the hypothesis to hold strictly, upward and downward movements in winning percentage must lead to an increased propensity to enforcement and
probation. It would seem that the theory only admits of an improvement
hypothesis; that is, teams start to improve by making illegal payments that,
if detected, ultimately lead to probation. Nevertheless, the hypothesis can
also be consistent with a decline in winning percentage. The enforcement
process may be sufficiently slow to lead, for example, to public revelations
of violations prior to sanctions and probation. In the interim a team may
halt the illegal payments as a way of showing "good-faith" efforts to correct the violations, and start to lose more games as the quality of its inputs
declines.[7] On this interpretation, variance of winning percentage is the appropriate predictor of cartel enforcement activities.

This enforcement process leads to redistribution within the cartel in the sense that NCAA enforcement will favor schools that are consistent winners. The NCAA redistributes wealth by punishing "up and coming" teams that recruit players away from traditional winners. If this is the case, consistently higher winning percentages will not by themselves bring about higher probabilities of enforcement action. Thus, the NCAA functions as an agent for major college athletic programs with long histories of fielding winning teams.

III. Empirical Evidence

A Logit Analysis of Enforcement Actions

As an initial test of the hypothesis of output monitoring among NCAA members, we estimate the following model of NCAA enforcement. (All data are for 1953–83 unless otherwise specified.)

$$ENFORCEMENT = f(CV, CV^2, DC, SCPOP, AGE, STAD), \quad (1)$$

where

ENFORCEMENT	= 1 if a school's football program has been put on probation and 0 otherwise;
CV	= the coefficient of variation of a school's football winning percentage;
CV^2	= the coefficient of variation squared;
DC	= the interaction of *DCONF* and *CCHAM,* where *DCONF* equals 1 if a team has switched conferences and 0 otherwise, and where *CCHAM* is equal to the number of conference championships won by the school (before or after a switch);
SCPOP	= the average number of secondary schools in the state of each institution in 1960, 1970, and 1980, divided by the population of the state in the same years;
AGE	= founding date of each school;
STAD	= the size of a school's football stadium, averaged over 1960, 1970, and 1980.

The dependent variable, *ENFORCEMENT,* designates whether a school's football program was placed on probation over the 1953–83 period.[8] Table 1 lists the eighty-five schools in our sample, classifying them in terms of whether or not they have been on probation.[9]

CV measures the variability of each school's winning percentage. (The mean winning percentages, standard deviations, and coefficients of variation for each school are listed in Appendix Table 1.) *CV* is a measure of

Table 1
NCAA Football Enforcement Actions, 1953–1983

No Probation	No Probation	Probation
Air Force	North Carolina State	Arizona
Alabama	Northwestern	Arizona State
Arkansas	Notre Dame	Auburn
Army	Ohio State	California
Baylor	Oregon State	Clemson
Boston College	Penn State	Colorado
Brigham Young	Pittsburgh	Houston
Cincinnati	Purdue	Illinois
Colorado State	Rice	Kansas
Duke	Rutgers	Kansas State
East Carolina	Stanford	Kentucky
Florida	Syracuse	Miami (Florida)
Florida State	Temple	Michigan State
Georgia	Tennessee	Minnesota
Georgia Tech	Texas	Mississippi State
Indiana	Texas Christian	Oklahoma
Iowa	Texas—El Paso	Oklahoma State
Iowa State	Texas Tech	Oregon
Louisiana State	Tulane	South Carolina
Louisville	UCLA	Southern California
Maryland	Utah	Southern Methodist
Memphis State	Utah State	Southern Mississippi
Michigan	Vanderbilt	Texas A&M
Mississippi	Virginia	Tulsa
Missouri	Virginia Tech	Wyoming
Navy	Wake Forest	
Nebraska	Washington	
New Mexico	Washington State	
New Mexico State	West Virginia	
North Carolina	Wisconsin	

output variability that provides indirect information about a school's compensation practices. Our theory suggests that a higher variability of winning percentage will raise the probability of investigation and probation. For example, take two rival teams, Western U. and Southwestern U. If Western U. has a very low winning percentage for several years and then suddenly has a championship team, it is likely that Southwestern U. will alert the Committee on Infractions to possible violations. Teams that compete for players will turn in teams with improved winning records. As discussed earlier, the enforcement process may hit the violator as its winning record is rising, or with a lag after it has ceased player payments and started to lose. In any event the variance of winning percentage drives enforcement. The square of the coefficient of variation, CV^2, controls for a diminishing effect of winning variability on enforcement actions.[10]

DC controls for teams that have switched conferences and also won conference championships. Both of these events serve as an additional signal that a school is a potential violator. On the one hand, if a switcher previously competed successfully either in some other conference or as an independent football power, its new conference opponents will suspect that the earlier winning records were related to rule violations. This will be especially so if the switcher rapidly achieves success at the expense of its new rivals (the University of Arizona and Arizona State University in the Pacific-10 Conference and the University of Houston in the Southwest Conference are examples of teams that were put on probation soon after changing conferences or becoming conference members). On the other hand, a champion that withdraws from a conference, especially after having been penalized, will be suspected of carrying its illegal behavior to new competitive venue. In both cases the combination of mobility and success raise the probability that the NCAA's "competitive balance" is being disturbed. We therefore expect *DC* to have a positive sign—an increase in *DC* will lead to a higher probability of probation, all else equal.

SCPOP proxies the cost to cartel members of directly monitoring competition for inputs. An obvious way for schools to achieve a higher winning percentage is to recruit the best players from secondary schools. In a state with more secondary schools the difficulty of directly monitoring recruitment practices across universities is increased. Because of this increased monitoring cost, schools in those states will violate the rules more often, other things the same. We thus expect that the coefficient on *SCPOP* will have a positive sign because more cheating will lead to a higher probability of detection.[11]

The variable *STAD* proxies the demand for football under the assumption that stadium sizes have adjusted to the demand for seats. A common problem in cartels is that individual members often have different demand-cost configurations. In the NCAA a school that faces a relatively higher and more inelastic demand for its football program has more incentive to pay athletes above the cartel wage. The higher and the more inelastic the demand for its football program, the more likely a school is to engage in cheating because the gains are higher. We expect that more cheating leads to a higher probability of detection, ceteris paribus; therefore, *STAD* will have a positive sign.

The *AGE* variable is a proxy for the number of alumni of a school. *AGE* is also an indicator of the demand for football and a proxy for the amount of cheating taking place. An older school has more alumni and more football tradition. As the pool of alumni and their loyalty becomes greater, the demand for better football performance increases and becomes more inelastic. One way for a college to increase its chances of establishing or maintaining a winning football program is for a supporter to give payments and other perquisites to recruits and players. We thus expect older schools to be prosecuted more, other things equal.

We estimate equation (1) by means of a logit analysis.[12] This technique constrains the predicted values for the binary dependent variable, *ENFORCEMENT,* to fall between 0 and 1. The results are reported in Table 2. All of the explanatory variables are significant at the 0.05 level for a two-tailed test.[13] Although the coefficient of multiple determination is biased downward in this type of analysis relative to a model with a continuous dependent variable, the logit estimation of equation (1) accounts for 33 percent of the variation in enforcement actions across schools.

The coefficient of variation, *CV,* has a positive and significant sign. Higher variability in a team's winning percentage leads to a greater probability of the NCAA taking action against that school. This result supports the output monitoring hypothesis.

The interaction term, *DC,* is positive and significant. Winning teams

Table 2
Logit Analysis of NCAA Enforcement Actions

Variable	Coefficients (*t*-statistics)	Variable	Coefficients (*t*-statistics)
Constant	−25.60964	SCPOP	0.20829
	(−2.461)[a]		(3.023)[b]
CV	29.08742	STAD	0.01161
	(2.267)[a]		(2.288)[a]
CV[2]	−33.37897	AGE	0.00002
	(−2.273)[a]		(2.417)[a]
DC	0.52742	R[2]	.325
	(2.145)[a]	N	85

Sources: Data on NCAA sanctions are from U.S. House of Representatives, Subcommittee Hearings, *NCAA Enforcement Program* (1978, 1480–1520), and from the *Washington Post* (1978–83, various issues). Data on wins and losses, conference switching, conference championships, and stadium sizes are from *College Football U.S.A. 1869–1971* (1972, 502–508), and from the *World Almanac* (1960, 1970, 1980, various pages). Data on the number of secondary schools are from *Digest of Education Statistics* (National Center for Education Statistics 1962, 7; 1973, 12; 1982, p. 13). Data on age of schools are from *American Universities and Colleges* (1982, various pages).

[a]Significant at 0.05 level for a two-tailed test.
[b]Significant at 0.01 level for a two-tailed test.

that switch conferences face a higher probability of sanction by the NCAA. This result suggests that rival teams use conference switching and quality performance as a signal of illegal activity.

The dispersion of secondary schools, *SCPOP*, also has a positive and significant influence on NCAA sanctions. Fewer high schools allow teams to monitor each other's recruiting activities directly at less cost and thereby to discourage cheating. More high schools increase the cost of monitoring and lead to cheating and more sanctions.

The proxies for demand for a school's football output, *STAD* and *AGE*, are both positive and significant. Other things equal, schools with a higher demand for successful football programs are penalized more than schools with a lower demand for football programs.

In sum, these results support the hypothesis that the NCAA and its member schools use indirect or probabilistic information in order to apprehend violators of the monopsony agreement.[14]

Mean Winning Percentage

We found that when the mean winning percentage of a team is added to equation (1), it does not add significantly to the explanation of NCAA enforcement activity; the other results are basically unchanged.[15] This suggests that NCAA enforcement favors consistently successful teams and does not bother itself with teams that never win. If NCAA enforcement were driven by the desire to detect violations wherever they occur, consistent winning, ceteris paribus, would be an indirect indication of cheating on the cartel agreement. Nonetheless, consistent winners are no more likely to be convicted of violations than are consistent losers. In fact, when mean winning percentage is used in place of the coefficient of variation in equation (1), the sign on winning percentage is negative although the coefficient is not significantly different from zero at standard levels. The negative sign on winning percentage suggests that consistent winners may be prosecuted at a lower rate than other schools. In support of this result, Appendix Table 2 displays the number of times each school in our sample has been in the final top twenty teams over the 1953–83 period, and whether or not they have been put on probation. The teams appearing in the final top twenty the most often are not the most heavily sanctioned. Rather, the teams that have more variable records are sanctioned more, a result that suggests that the NCAA enforcement process favors perennial football powers.

A Closer Look at Probation

The level of aggregation of the logit analysis obscures two features of NCAA enforcement that are of interest. First, does variation in winning

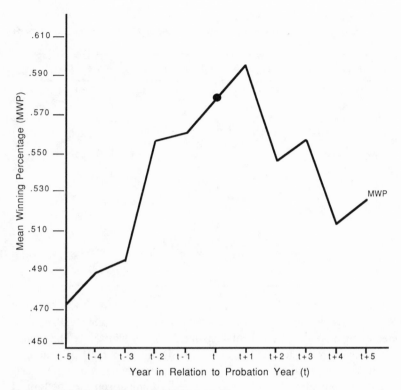

Figure 1. Winning percentage of NCAA violators

percentage lead *directly* to enforcement? Second, is enforcement *effective;* that is, does it cost the school success on the playing field? In other words, what can be said about NCAA enforcement with respect to an improvement hypothesis?

In Figure 1 the mean winning percentage of detected violators, running from five years prior to the start of probation (*t*) to five years after, is plotted. The winning percentages of these schools increased, on average, over the five years prior to probation and one year into probation. The latter result is plausible because illegally acquired recruits will continue to have an impact on team quality during the early part of a probation. One year after probation begins, the average winning percentage of detected violators starts to decline and continues to decline through year *t* + 4. Some recovery from the effects of probation is evident during the fifth season after the sanctions were put into effect.

Table 3 summarizes the changes in mean winning percentages for the teams placed on probation and those that have not been punished by the

Table 3
Changes in Mean Winning Percentages Based on NCAA Enforcement Actions

$t-5$ to $t+1$	Mean	S.D.	$t+1$ to $t+5$	Mean	S.D.
			Probation		
$WINPCT_{t+1}-WINPCT_{t-5}$	.1231	.266	$WINPCT_{t+4}-WINPCT_{t+1}$	−.0795	.290
$WINPCT_{t-4}-WINPCT_{t-5}$	.0163	.231	$WINPCT_{t+2}-WINPCT_{t+1}$	−.0485	.271
$WINPCT_{t-3}-WINPCT_{t-4}$	.0067	.226	$WINPCT_{t+3}-WINPCT_{t+2}$	−.0075	.257
$WINPCT_{t-2}-WINPCT_{t-3}$	.0574	.244	$WINPCT_{t+4}-WINPCT_{t+3}$	−.0313	.133
$WINPCT_{t-1}-WINPCT_{t-2}$	.0063	.229	$WINPCT_{t+5}-WINPCT_{t+4}$	.0295	.208
$WINPCT_{t}-WINPCT_{t-1}$	.0171	.271			
$WINPCT_{t+1}-WINPCT_{t}$	.0204	.186			
			No Probation		
$WINPCT-WINPCT_{-1}$	−.0009	.020	$WINPCT-WINPCT_{-4}$	−.0001	.028
$WINPCT-WINPCT_{-2}$	−.0017	.024	$WINPCT-WINPCT_{-5}$	−.0002	.024
$WINPCT-WINPCT_{-3}$	−.0013	.029	$WINPCT-WINPCT_{-6}$	−.0015	.025

NCAA. Overall, the mean winning percentage of detected violators increased by more than 12 percentage points from $t-5$ to $t+1$. The change in winning percentage over this interval is significant at the 1 percent level and represents approximately a 26 percent increase in the winning percentage of the probation teams. Crime pays. By comparison (see bottom of Table 3), the average six-year change in mean winning percentage for schools not placed on probation is −0.0015 percent.[16] The difference between the six-year change in mean winning percentage for the two groups of schools is significant at the 5 percent level.

The data for the postsanction years ($t+1$ to $t+4$) suggest that enforcement actions decrease the mean winning percentages of detected violators. Over this period the mean winning percentage of detected violators falls by almost 8 percentage points. This decrease is significant at the 5 percent level. It is also different from the mean of the three-year change in winning percentage for no-probation schools at the 5 percent level. Thus, for a team that goes 8–3 in year $t+1$, probation will, on average, lead to a 7–4 record in subsequent seasons. The addition of one game to a team's loss column may not seem important, but the difference between 8–3 and 7–4 is substantial.

Recidivists

Three schools were repeat offenders in our data (Houston, Kansas, and Southern Methodist). In general, the results for recidivists (not reported here but available upon request) are the same as before. Upward variability leads to probation and then to poorer performance with a lag. Such cycles in NCAA enforcement against schools are predictable. One-time offenders will be watched more closely than other schools, especially if they start to win again. The recent discussion and enactment by the NCAA of radical and crippling penalties for repeat offenders (cancelling athletic programs for specified periods) indicate the degree to which the cartel is willing to suppress the rise of new football powers. Indeed, there has been more than discussion. The NCAA literally dismantled the SMU football program.

IV. Concluding Remarks

This paper derives and tests a theory concerning the methods that the NCAA and its member schools use to detect violations of its monopsony agreement. This process is guided by the use of probabilistic evidence. The cartel infers and investigates illegal practices at individual schools by looking at their athletic performance on the field. Greater variability of performance leads to suspicion and to enforcement. Our results also suggest that the enforcement of NCAA rules and regulations have a redistributive impact. Teams with consistently high winning records are not prosecuted more than other teams even though consistent winning could also be interpreted as an indirect signal that violations are taking place. This fact, coupled with the result that teams with volatile winning records are prosecuted more heavily, suggests that up and coming teams (new entrants) are turned in and set up for probation by consistent winners.

In drawing the inference that NCAA enforcement activities benefit the perennial football powers at the expense of up and coming teams, we are not necessarily suggesting that most, if not all, of the member schools engage in illegal recruiting practices but that only a few are ever penalized. An alternative interpretation is that the major college football programs, such as those of Alabama, Michigan, Notre Dame, Ohio State, and Penn State, have developed such strong winning traditions over the years that cheating may not be required for them to maintain their dominant position. These schools are able to attract superior high school athletes season after season at the cartel wage with the offer of a package of complementary inputs—well-equipped training facilities, high-quality coaching staffs, talented teammates, national exposure, and so on—that increases the present value of an amateur football player's future professional income relative to the value added by historically weaker programs. Given this factor, along with NCAA rules that mandate a uniform wage across member schools, the traditional football powers have a built-in competitive advantage in recruiting the best athletes. Accordingly, traditional nonpowers—Clemson,

Colorado, Texas A & M, Texas Christian, and Minnesota, for instance—have an incentive to break the cartel rules if they are ever to achieve gridiron success.

Although our empirical analysis does not distinguish between these two alternative views of the world, it is worth pointing out that NCAA enforcement activities have the same effect in both cases. Whether the observed pattern of sanctions is due to the fact that the NCAA has turned a blind eye to the violations of some of its members but not others, or that only some members have actually violated the rules, is irrelevant to the conclusion that NCAA enforcement activities have served to maintain the status quo, benefiting the perennial football powers at the expense of their rivals.

Notes

We thank Robert McCormick, James Buchanan, Matt Lindsay, and John Siegfried for helpful comments. The usual caveat applies.

1. Like any cartel, the NCAA maintains secrecy with regard to its enforcement strategy. This is evidenced in the U.S. House of Representatives (1978) subcommittee hearings on NCAA enforcement. Moreover, we attempted to obtain a list of enforcement actions from the NCAA. Although this information is widely publicized at the time of the imposition of sanctions, the NCAA refused our request. We ultimately found the data in public sources.

2. The National Association of Intercollegiate Athletics (NAIA) is another association of college athletic programs. However, the NAIA does not have a network television contract and, in general, is an association of schools with small athletic programs.

3. For attendance and television revenue figures, see *1984 NCAA Football Television Committee Report* (1985).

4. The student-athlete monopsony is more rigid than other classical sports monopsonies such as the old reserve clause system of major league baseball. The stipulated payment to college athletes is uniform across member schools (the value of the in-kind benefits, such as the quality of education across schools, obviously can vary). Under the reserve clause baseball players could at least be compensated with respect to differences in ability (Scully 1974).

5. Clearly, the high school athlete does not select a school based only upon sub rosa payments for his services. Expected lifetime wage is the relevant consideration, and in this case a school may be selected because it offers a chance for better football training and for subsequent employment as a professional football player. We return to this issue in the last part of the paper.

6. The Southern Methodist University football program was suspended for the 1987 and 1988 seasons under this provision.

Appendix Table I
All Teams

Team	Winning Percentage*	S.D.	Coefficient of Variation	Team	Winning Percentage*	S.D.	Coefficient of Variation
Air Force	.403	.261	.647	New Mexico State	.438	.218	.498
Alabama	.746	.250	.335	North Carolina	.533	.217	.407
Arizona	.525	.187	.356	North Carolina State	.493	.222	.450
Arizona State	.745	.169	.227	Northwestern	.314	.216	.688
Arkansas	.693	.178	.257	Notre Dame	.701	.223	.318
Army	.504	.256	.508	Ohio State	.781	.162	.207
Auburn	.677	.187	.276	Oklahoma	.782	.188	.240
Baylor	.464	.222	.478	Oklahoma State	.468	.164	.350
Boston College	.598	.182	.304	Oregon	.447	.195	.436
Brigham Young	.511	.260	.509	Oregon State	.455	.250	.549
California	.416	.187	.449	Penn State	.758	.138	.182
Cincinnati	.484	.201	.415	Pittsburgh	.541	.261	.482
Clemson	.589	.201	.341	Purdue	.580	.187	.322
Colorado	.548	.224	.409	Rice	.359	.226	.629
Colorado State	.389	.210	.540	Rutgers	.587	.208	.354
Duke	.510	.173	.339	South Carolina	.486	.157	.323
East Carolina	.600	.218	.363	Southern California	.717	.214	.303
Florida	.612	.174	.284	Southern Methodist	.479	.227	.474
Florida State	.566	.213	.376	Southern Mississippi	.533	.208	.390
Georgia	.636	.223	.351	Stanford	.505	.188	.372
Georgia Tech	.560	.203	.363	Syracuse	.562	.201	.358
Houston	.601	.197	.328	Temple	.475	.246	.518
Illinois	.470	.252	.536	Tennessee	.642	.163	.254
Indiana	.343	.184	.536	Texas	.746	.192	.257
Iowa	.451	.250	.554	Texas A&M	.468	.231	.494
Iowa State	.430	.176	.409	Texas Christian	.367	.225	.613
Kansas	.422	.207	.490	Texas—El Paso	.361	.259	.717
Kansas State	.309	.189	.612	Texas Tech	.516	.229	.443
Kentucky	.430	.202	.470	Tulane	.368	.193	.524
Louisiana State	.648	.191	.295	Tulsa	.524	.226	.431
Louisville	.514	.210	.409	UCLA	.662	.212	.320
Maryland	.538	.234	.435	Utah	.490	.197	.402
Memphis State	.558	.216	.387	Utah State	.572	.187	.327
Miami (Florida)	.539	.203	.377	Vanderbilt	.359	.206	.574
Michigan	.694	.200	.288	Virginia	.306	.181	.592
Michigan State	.576	.219	.380	Virginia Tech	.580	.182	.314
Minnesota	.493	.202	.410	Wake Forest	.306	.178	.582
Mississippi	.664	.217	.327	Washington	.568	.216	.380
Mississippi State	.446	.231	.525	Washington State	.393	.181	.461
Missouri	.598	.190	.318	West Virginia	.581	.214	.368
Navy	.537	.223	.415	Wisconsin	.466	.216	.464
Nebraska	.688	.235	.342	Wyoming	.582	.227	.390
New Mexico	.479	.211	.441				

*Winning percentage is computed by dividing total wins by total wins plus losses; ties are ignored. The winning percentages and standard deviations for Southern Mississippi are at the mean of the other schools.

Appendix Table 2
Number of Top Twenty Finishes, 1953–1983

Team	Times in Top Twenty	Team	Times in Top Twenty
Ohio State	26	North Carolina State	6
*Oklahoma	25	Oregon State	6
*Southern California	25	Wisconsin	6
Alabama	23	Brigham Young	5
Texas	21	*Illinois	5
Penn State	20	Rice	5
Notre Dame	20	Air Force	4
Michigan	18	Texas Christian	4
*Auburn	18	Texas Tech	4
Nebraska	17	*Kentucky	3
UCLA	16	*Kansas	3
Arkansas	16	Rutgers	3
Louisiana State	15	*Wyoming	3
Mississippi	14	*Arizona	2
Georgia	13	*California	2
Pittsburgh	12	Indiana	2
Tennessee	12	*Oklahoma State	2
*Arizona State	11	Tulane	2
*Michigan State	11	Virginia Tech	2
Washington	11	Boston College	1
Georgia Tech	10	East Carolina	1
*Houston	10	*Iowa State	1
Missouri	10	Louisville	1
Purdue	10	Memphis State	1
Syracuse	10	New Mexico State	1
*Florida	9	Northwestern	1
*Clemson	8	*Oregon	1
*Colorado	8	*South Carolina	1
Maryland	8	Texas—El Paso	1
*Miami (Florida)	8	*Tulsa	1
West Virginia	8	Utah State	1
Army	7	Utah	1
Iowa	7	Washington State	1
North Carolina	7	Colorado State	0
*Southern Methodist	7	Cincinnati	0
Stanford	7	*Kansas State	0
*Texas A&M	7	New Mexico	0
Baylor	6	*Southern Mississippi	0
Duke	6	Temple	0
Florida State	6	Vanderbilt	0
*Minnesota	6	Virginia	0
*Mississippi State	6	Wake Forest	0
Navy	6		

*Designates NCAA probation.

7. In 1985, for instance, Texas Christian University unilaterally disclosed evidence that some of its athletes had received illegal payments and dismissed these players in mid-season. The team's record during its remaining games was dismal. At the end of the season, the school was placed on probation by the NCAA.

8. The basic data source is U.S. House of Representatives (1978). We supplemented these data for the 1978–83 period with information from various United Press International (UPI) polls which identify teams that have been placed on NCAA probation (see *Washington Post*, 1978–83, various issues). For the 1953–78 period teams were defined as violators if their football program was placed on probation and if the probation included television sanctions. For 1978–83, the violators were those schools identified by the UPI poll.

9. We restricted our data set to schools which play in major conferences and to major independent schools, i.e., cases where cartel monitoring and potential cheating on the cartel represent a real problem. Beginning with the membership of what is now known as Division I-A, our final sample size was determined by eliminating those schools for which observations on one or more of the independent variables were missing.

10. Our results are sensitive to the inclusion of CV^2.

11. Schools obviously recruit across state borders, blurring the effect captured by this variable. We think it is nonetheless useful to try in some fashion to control for the costs of directly monitoring rivals, and this is the best proxy that we could devise.

12. We used the *LOGIT* procedure of $SPSS^X$, which transforms the log odds ratio to produce values similar to those derived from the probit model. The response function is given by $\ln [p/(1 - p)]2 + 5$. See $SPSS^X$ *User's Guide* (1986, 605).

13. We also estimated equation (1) with a probit model. The results are nearly identical to those reported in Table 2.

14. Independent schools are not members of conferences. Notre Dame, for example, is an independent school that recruits nationally rather than regionally. This makes it more costly for regional schools to monitor Notre Dame's recruiting behavior in other parts of the country. Moreover, conference schools have less of an incentive to monitor independents because they do not compete directly against them in conference play. Thus, independents may be less likely to be convicted of violations. We estimated the logit model in equation (1), including a dummy variable, *IND*, equal to 1 if a school is an independent and 0 otherwise. The results were:

$$ENFORCEMENT = -24.45 + 29.27CV - 33.74CV^2 + 0.52DC$$
$$(-2.38) \quad (2.16) \quad (-2.15) \quad (2.14)$$
$$+ 8.13SCPOP + 0.01AGE + 0.2e - 4STAD$$
$$(2.94) \quad (2.17) \quad (2.36)$$
$$- 0.03IND.$$
$$(-0.06)$$

IND has a negative but insignificant coefficient. This suggests that independents are monitored carefully in recruiting competition by schools in the areas where they recruit; that is, being an independent adds no useful information to the cartel enforcement process.

15.   These results are available on request.

16.   The calculations for the no-probation schools are derived as follows. *WINPCT* is the average winning percentage of all schools in the sample not placed on NCAA probation. $WINPCT_1$ is generated by taking the average of the one-year lag of year-to-year winning percentages for each of these schools. $WINPCT_2$ and so on are derived in the same way, and thus $(WINPCT-WINPCT_1)$ and so on are self-explanatory.

References

Alchian, Armen A., and Harold Demsetz. 1972. "Production, Information Costs and Economic Organization." *American Economic Review* 62:775–95.

American Council on Education. 1983. *American Universities and Colleges.* New York: Walter de Gruyter.

Becker, Gary S. 1985. "College Athletes Should Get Paid What They Are Worth." *Business Week* (September 30): 18.

Frey, James H. 1982. *The Governance of Collegiate Athletics.* West Point, N.Y.: Leisure Press.

McCallum, John D., and Charles Pearson. 1972. *College Football U.S.A. 1869–1971.* New York: McGraw-Hill.

McCormick, Robert E., and Maurice Tinsley. 1987. "Athletics versus Academics? Evidence from SAT Scores." *Journal of Political Economy* 95: 1103–16.

National Center for Education Statistics. 1983. *Digest of Education Statistics 1982.* Washington, D.C.: U.S. Government Printing Office.

National Collegiate Athletic Association. 1985. *1984 NCAA Football Television Committee Report* (Shawnee Mission, Kans.: National Collegiate Athletic Association).

Scully, Gerald W. 1974. "Pay and Performance in Major League Basketball." *American Economic Review* 64:915–30.

SPSSx User's Guide. 1986. 2d ed. New York: McGraw-Hill.

Stigler, George J. 1964. "A Theory of Oligopoly." *Journal of Political Economy* 72:44–61.

Underwood, John. 1978. "The NCAA Goes on Defense." *Sports Illustrated* (October 9): 2029.

United Press International Poll. 1978–1983. Washington, D.C.: Washington Post Co.

U.S. Department of Health, Education and Welfare. 1973. *Digest of Education Statistics.* Washington, D.C.: U.S. Government Printing Office.

U.S. House of Representatives. 1978. *NCAA Enforcement Program, Hearings before the Subcommittee on Oversight and Investigation of the Committee on Interstate and Foreign Commerce, 96th Congress.* Washington, D.C.: U.S. Government Printing Office.

The World Almanac and Book of Facts. Annual. New York: Newspaper Enterprise Association.

Arthur A. Fleisher III, Brian L. Goff, and Robert D. Tollison

NCAA Voting on Academic Requirements: Public or Private Interest?

I.   Introduction

Many economists have argued that the National Collegiate Athletic Association (NCAA) is a buyers' cartel with respect to high school athletes (see, for example, Becker 1985). Recent work in this tradition has focused on the methods by which the NCAA enforces its cartel, stressing the comparative efficiency of monitoring competitor performance on the field rather than the purchase of inputs beyond the allowable guidelines (Fleisher et al. 1988a) as the least costly means of detecting cheating on the cartel. During a period of time when its policies have drawn increasing scrutiny, the NCAA has moved to adopt even more stringent measures to maintain its monopsony position. For example, the so-called death penalty makes complete suspension of a school's athletic program a possibility (in the case of SMU, a reality), where the cartel rules are repeatedly violated. One of the more controversial rules passed by the NCAA in recent times is the requirement of minimum scores on college entrance examinations by potential college athletes, known originally as Proposition 48. Strongest criticism of Proposition 48 has centered on the racially biased consequences of the academic requirements: blacks have failed to meet the minimum scores at a much higher rate than whites.[1]

There are essentially two competing explanations of a rule such as Proposition 48. NCAA executives and the representatives of member schools claim that this type of rule promotes the academic life of athletes both at the high school and college levels; that is, the rule has a public-interest rationale. Some have questioned this explanation on the basis that disqualified athletes lose a year of eligibility even if they demonstrate the ability to pass college course work. We seek an alternative explanation of such eligibility rules: Is there a self-interest explanation of the requirements? Clearly, this would not be the first historical instance of eligibility requirements that benefited some athletes and teams at the expense of others.

The history of amateur eligibility rules is replete with instances of inter-athlete or interorganizational rent seeking. Baker (1982) and Goff, Shu-ghart, and Tollison (1988) survey this history. In fact, many of the early codes of amateurism explicitly revealed their entry-barring intent. A clear example of exclusion is seen in a British footracing rule of 1866, which excluded any individual who played for direct reimbursement or who made his living through manual labor. From the inception of the modern Olym-pics, some "professionals" have competed in upper-class events such as fencing, whereas other events have maintained strict amateur rules, as in the famous Jim Thorpe episode.

Our purpose in this paper is to present and test a self-interest model of support for stricter eligibility requirements by NCAA member schools. We attempt to step beyond the rhetoric about academics and ask, Are the votes of schools in favor of stricter academic rules a direct outcome of variables related to those schools' self-interest on the playing field and hence in the box office? Specifically, we analyze a vote by the NCAA concerning a pro-posal to trade off college entrance examination scores against an athlete's grade point average in high school.

II.   Empirical Model

In 1986 NCAA members voted on a proposition to implement a Scholastic Aptitude Test (SAT) requirement for freshman eligibility, but with a provi-sion that an athlete's high school grade point average (GPA) could offset a lower SAT score. For instance, a student with a C average in high school had to obtain at least a 700 on the SAT, whereas an athlete with a higher GPA and lower SAT score also would have been permitted to play in his or her freshman year. The provision would have relaxed an earlier proposition that called for the exclusive use of the SAT (or ACT) score in determining freshman eligibility. Thus, a vote for the provision supported looser re-strictions, and a vote against the provision favored tighter restrictions on incoming freshman players.

Several factors influence whether a school is more likely to vote for stricter eligibility rules. First, higher-quality schools would be more likely to vote for stricter academic rules because such schools have a comparative advantage in recruiting academically talented athletes. The eligibility rules allow the more academically inclined schools to impose stricter entrance requirements on other schools.[2] Tighter rules thus increase the competi-tiveness of higher quality schools and conferences on the playing field. Second, the level of demand for athletics at a school will influence the sup-port for tighter eligibility rules. Schools with a high demand for sports will suffer significant revenue losses if athletic success is diminished by stricter eligibility rules. A low-demand school, therefore, would have a relatively higher demand for stricter rules and be more likely to vote accordingly. Third, some schools historically have engaged in more cartel rule-breaking behavior than other schools (or at least they have been caught and penalized more frequently). Schools that act independently in this respect will not demand stricter rules that make such behavior even more difficult to conduct. Overt cartel violators will not favor tighter eligibility requirements. Fourth, a school without a conference affiliation (an independent) stands to gain relatively more from athletic success on the playing field; these schools do not have to share athletic revenues with other conference members. Because of this, independent schools, other things equal, will not desire stricter rules that infringe on their possibility of athletic success.

What we have, then, is an intracartel struggle for the rents from athletic success. This particular struggle pits academically successful schools and conferences against schools and conferences where football is a powerful economic enterprise. This is not the only form that intracartel struggles take in the NCAA (see Fleisher et al. 1988a; Fleisher, Goff, and Tollison 1988b), but it is an interesting new competition that is worthy of analysis.

The earlier general self-interest incentives lead to the following empirical model of votes for and against stricter eligibility rules:

$$VOTE = f(SAT, ENROLLMENT, PROBATION, INDEPENDENT)$$

where

VOTE	= 1 if a school votes for SAT-GPA tradeoff and 0 if a school votes against such a tradeoff,
SAT (school)	= average SAT score of all enrolling freshmen in 1986 by school,
SAT (conference)	= average SAT score for the schools in a conference in 1986 (for independents, it is the average of all independents),
ENROLLMENT	= enrollment by school of full- and parttime students in 1986;
PROBATION	= 1 if school has been on NCAA probation over the 1953–83 period and 0 otherwise,
INDEPENDENT	= 1 if school is not aligned to a conference in football and 0 otherwise.

Our sample includes 82 of the 800 member schools in the NCAA. These 82 schools are all Division I-A schools in football. We limit the sample to this group because our main interest lies in self-interest differences among major athletic programs.[3]

The dependent variable, *VOTE*, is the vote by NCAA members in 1986 on an SAT-GPA tradeoff proposal. Higher-quality schools are proxied by higher SAT scores. Other things equal, we expect schools with higher SAT scores to oppose the SAT-GPA tradeoff and to push for the stricter rule; *SAT* is expected to have a negative sign. *ENROLLMENT* is used as a proxy for the demand for athletics. As this demand increases, the school is more likely to vote for the SAT-GPA sliding scale. *ENROLLMENT* is expected to have a positive sign. As an alternative measure of demand, we estimate one specification with stadium size in place of *ENROLLMENT*. *PROBA-TION* is a measure of the relative amount of detected cartel breaking by a school. As noted earlier, cartel breakers will not favor stricter rules. We expect a positive sign on *PROBATION*. Finally, independent schools will benefit relatively more from looser eligibility requirements because these schools do not share football revenues with members of a conference. We expect independents to favor the SAT-GPA scale and a positive sign on *INDEPENDENT*, other things equal. Table 1 presents the descriptive statistics for the data set.

Table 2 presents three estimations of this model. Specification I includes school *SAT* without conference *SAT*; Specification II includes conference *SAT* without school *SAT*. This is necessary because of collinearity between these two regressors. Specification III uses stadium size as the measure of the demand for athletics rather than enrollment. The estimates are generated with the general linear model procedure of SAS. Overall, the specifications explain between 20 and 39 percent of the likelihood of a vote for or against the SAT-GPA scale, and each specification is significant at the 1 percent level according to the f-test criterion.

Specifically, the estimates indicate that *SAT* scores have a negative impact on likelihood of support for a looser rule. Of the two, the conference *SAT* score has a stronger and more significant coefficient (1 percent level). Higher-quality academics lead to support for stricter rules. The coefficient on *ENROLLMENT* is positive and significant at the 1 percent level. Higher demand as measured by enrollment leads to support for looser rules. In Specification III, the alternative measure of demand, *STADIUM* size, is positive and significant at the 6 percent level. *PROBATION* has a positive coefficient that is significant at the 10 percent level in Specification II and at the 5 percent level in Specification III. Cartel breakers appear to vote against stricter rules. *INDEPENDENT* has a positive coefficient, significant at the 5 percent level in Specifications I and III and at the 1 percent level in Specification II. Independent schools are more likely to vote for looser restrictions, other things equal.

We also estimated the effects of other regressors. An alternative measure of school quality, the number of periodicals in the school's library, has a

Table 1
Descriptive Statistics

Variable	Mean
VOTE	0.62
SAT (school)	1,036
SAT (conference)	1,035
ENROLLMENT	23,244
PROBATION	0.54
INDEPENDENT	0.24
STADIUM	50,881

Table 2
Votes for SAT-GPA Sliding Scale

Variable	Coefficient/(t-statistic)		
Intercept	0.54	3.37	3.62
	(1.11)	(3.50)	(3.27)
SAT (school)	−4.0e−4		
	(1.11)		
SAT (conference)		−0.003	−0.003
		(3.51)	(3.08)
ENROLLMENT	1.9e−5	2.0e−5	
	(4.41)	(5.28)	
PROBATION	0.12	0.16	0.23
	(1.23)	(1.75)	(2.22)
INDEPENDENT	0.26	0.33	0.29
	(2.31)	(3.10)	(2.36)
STADIUM			5.0e−6
			(1.93)
R^2	.285	.387	.192
F-statistic	7.37	11.38	4.27

negative coefficient but is correlated with enrollment. The volatility of winning record, an alternative measure of cartel breaking (Fleisher et al. 1988a) has a positive effect on the support for looser rules. Also, the interaction of conference and school SAT scores has a negative and significant effect on votes.

III. Concluding Remarks

The use of eligibility rules to obtain a competitive advantage on the playing field is not a new form of behavior. We suggest and present some evidence in support of the idea that NCAA votes on academic rules such as Proposition 48 are not guided entirely by the idea of improving the educational quality of student-athletes, but by the competitive self-interest of schools. Proposition 48 works like an entry barrier whether it was conceived as such or not. The evidence in this paper attests to this theory, as well as to the simple fact that virtually *all* of the athletes declared ineligible by Proposition 48 subsequently qualified to play for their respective schools. This means they could have played anyway.

Notes

1. For example, in 1986–87, out of 80 men's basketball players that fell short of the test score mark, 73 were black.
2. In fact, if the general student population were required to maintain the Proposition 48 standards, almost 30 percent of the freshman classes at some institutions would not be eligible.
3. We were unable to obtain SAT or ACT data for the University of Texas— El Paso, Texas Christian University, Washington State University, and New Mexico State University. Also, ACT scores are multiplied by 44 to make them comparable in magnitude to SAT scores.

References

Baker, W. J. 1982. *Sports in the Western World*. Totowa, N.J.: Rowman and Littlefield.

Becker, G. 1985. "College Athletes Should Get Paid What They Are Worth." *Business Week* (September 30): 18.

Fleisher, A. A., B. L. Goff, W. F. Shughart, and R. D. Tollison. 1988a. "Crime or Punishment?: Enforcement of the NCAA Football Cartel." *Journal of Economic Behavior and Organization* 10 (December): 433–51.

Fleisher, A. A., B. L. Goff, and R. D. Tollison. 1988b. "A Capture Theory of the NCAA." Unpublished manuscript.

Goff, B. L., W. F. Shughart, and R. D. Tollison. 1988. "Disqualification by Decree: Amateur Rules as Barriers to Entry." *Journal of Institutional and Theoretical Economics* 144 (June): 515–23.

Robert E. McCormick and Maurice Tinsley

Athletics versus Academics?
Evidence from SAT Scores

I. Introduction

It is common in faculty discussions to degrade the value of athletics on campus. To many, athletics represents the worst side of academia. However, many institutions voluntarily continue a long tradition of intercollegiate competition on a large scale. This survivorship suggests that athletics must be contributing something to academics. On April 3, 1985, *USA Today,* reporting the added prestige that Villanova would enjoy following its National Collegiate Athletic Association (NCAA) basketball championship, cited the fact that North Carolina State University had received a 40 percent increase in applications in the wake of its championship victory in 1983. Further reinforcement of this point came when Boston College received 16,200 freshman applications in 1985 compared with 12,500 applications the previous year. Boston College admissions director, Charles Nolan, gave much of the credit for this increase to Heisman Trophy winner Doug Flutie, his 1984 teammates, and the attention they brought the school (*Newsweek,* April 8, 1985 ["On Campus" insert], 14). The University of South Carolina, a school not known for its exploits on the football field, reported a 23 percent increase in applications in 1985 following the best year in its football history.

The preceding stories suggest a symbiosis between athletics and academics very different from the adversary relation common in faculty club discussions. If, as these stories suggest, athletic success breeds increases in applications, then there is a link between athletic success one year and the quality of the incoming freshmen in the future. This is not to say that athletic success necessarily attracts brighter students; instead it advertises the school and increases the number of applicants. Then, even if the average quality of applicants is unchanged, a school with a fixed enrollment policy can sample from a larger number of applicants. Alternatively, administrators can maintain admissions standards and increase enrollment. In the first case average quality increases. In the second case enrollment grows. In both cases it is a direct result of athletic success, and the ultimate effect is a policy decision likely to vary across schools.

II.   Empirical Analysis

We subject the argument that athletics boosts academics through advertising to empirical scrutiny. First, we see if the presence of big-time athletics has an impact on academic quality using freshman Scholastic Aptitude Test (SAT) scores as a measure of quality. Our model of SAT scores is a simple hedonic one. These scores are a function of the quality of university inputs and the environment at the institution, specifically, the number of volumes in the library, the student/faculty ratio, the age of the university, the tuition, the endowment of the university, the salary of the faculty at the school, and so forth. The central hypothesis is tested by including a dummy variable for schools that engage in major college athletics. It is arguable how to measure this, but we chose a criterion that is simple and easy to delineate. If the school is a member of one of the big-time athletic conferences—Atlantic Coast Conference (ACC), Southwestern Conference (SWC), Southeastern Conference (SEC), Big Ten, Big Eight, Pacific Athletic Conference (PAC Ten), or a major independent—we let the dummy take the value one; otherwise it is zero.[1] We collected data on approximately 150 schools for 1971.[2] Of these, we count 63 as big-time athletic schools. Using ordinary least squares, we regressed the SAT scores of the entering freshmen on the variables listed above with the dummy for membership in a major conference.[3] The results are listed in Table 1, where several different specifications are reported.

The results support the advertising view of athletics, and they are not sensitive to model specification.[4] The coefficient on the athletic dummy is positive and significant in all specifications. We interpret this to mean that, other things the same, a school that participates in major college athletics has a better undergraduate student body than one that does not.[5]

The coefficients on the other variables have signs consistent with economic theory.[6] Schools that pay their faculty more have better students (or schools with better students pay the faculty more). Schools that charge higher tuition have better students. Older schools have better reputations, have survived longer, and attract students with higher SAT scores. Schools with lower student/faculty ratios offer more individual attention to students, and they have better students as a consequence. The larger a school's endowment, the higher are the SAT scores of its entering freshmen. Larger schools have poorer students, other things the same.[7]

For a second look at the relation between athletics and academics, we collected data on in-conference football winning percentages for all members of the major athletic conferences annually from 1971 through 1984.[8] We used only members of athletic conferences to control for differences in scheduling and quality of opposition across time. Next, we calculated the average SAT scores for the entering freshmen in 1981 and 1984 (the latest year for which data were available). From these we computed the change in the SAT scores for each school in our sample. Then we regressed this change in SAT scores for 1981–84 on variables that we expect affect academic quality (changes in the student/faculty ratio, changes in tuition, changes in enrollment, and changes in the size of the library), and we included the 15-year trend of in-conference football winning percentage.[9] If the advertising theory is correct, then the trend coefficient will be positive. If, on the other hand, athletics degrades academics, the effect of the football winning trend will be negative. The results of several different model specifications are reported in Table 2. The coefficient on trend is positive and marginally significant in each specification.[10] This is additional evidence that athletic success is associated with academic quality. Taken together, these results, in our minds, cast serious doubt on the question of athletics versus academics. Instead, they suggest a different view, that is, athletics *and* academics.

III.   Conclusions

Universities are understudied organizations, but this is not because they do not present an interesting variety of questions concerning their composition. The question of whether athletic success comes at the expense of academic quality is particularly intriguing because of the supposed competition between rival departments of the same institution.

The evidence presented here is consistent with the view that some students get more than one education while enrolled in college; intercollegiate athletic competition is a natural consequence and by-product of undergraduate education. This implies that athletic success can often go hand in hand with academic success, and, insofar as this study goes, critics of athletic success are misguided if their motive is the academic improvement of the university.

We conclude that there is evidence of a symbiotic relation between athletics and academics on many college campuses, and the elimination of large-scale athletic participation could, for any particular school, have detrimental effects on its enrollment and academic standards. Last, in many ways this study leaves unanswered more questions than it answers. For instance, why do some universities invest in top-quality athletic programs and others choose not to? The Ivy League institutions, among

Table 1
SAT Scores and Big-Time Athletics (Dependent Variable: Average SAT Scores of Entering Freshmen)

Independent Variable	Coefficient									
	(1)	(2)	(3)	(4)	(5)	(6)	(7)	(8)	(9)	(10)
Intercept	543.69 (10.32)	511.71 (9.61)	512.39 (9.58)	596.25 (9.49)	518.22 (10.08)	629.20 (10.86)	609.00 (12.19)	628.90 (12.16)	598.37 (10.58)	643.44 (13.74)
Sports dummy	25.73 (1.83)	30.58 (2.19)	29.70 (2.09)	28.00 (2.00)	43.48 (3.11)	35.05 (2.66)	35.95 (2.75)	31.39 (2.28)	36.20 (2.52)	31.14 (2.41)
Tuition	.11 (12.83)	.10 (12.56)	.11 (7.31)	.11 (7.07)	.09 (9.59)	.08 (8.48)	.08 (9.05)	.08 (9.18)	.09 (8.22)	.08 (8.88)
Volumes in library $\times 10^6$	5.03 (.77)	-1.78 (.26)	-1.97 (.28)	-2.42 (.35)	6.66 (.94)	-1.37 (1.90)	-1.34 (1.86)	-1.32 (1.83)	-1.41 (1.89)	...
Salary of full professors $\times 10^2$	1.76 (6.43)	1.76 (6.53)	1.74 (6.39)	1.65 (6.12)	1.97 (7.39)	1.45 (5.52)	1.47 (5.69)	1.36 (4.97)	1.35 (4.37)	1.36 (5.35)
Age of the university	...	.37 (2.54)	.38 (2.53)	.33 (2.21)	.34 (2.34)	.42 (3.09)	.43 (3.16)	.43 (3.14)	.42 (2.81)	.33 (2.63)

	(1)	(2)	(3)	(4)	(5)	(6)	(7)	(8)	(9)	(10)
Private school dummy	...	...	-8.90 (.37)	-22.67 (.94)	...	...	...	...	...	...
Student/faculty ratio	...	...	...	-3.29 (2.44)	...	-.86 (.69)	...	...	...	...
Total enrollment × 10^3	...	...	...	...	-2.49 (3.49)	-1.08 (1.48)	-1.22 (1.75)	-1.33 (1.88)	-1.02 (1.39)	-1.73 (2.67)
Endowment per student × 10^3	...	...	...	...	...	2.17 (4.34)	2.21 (4.46)	2.05 (3.88)	2.20 (4.27)	1.91 (4.04)
Number of Ph.D.'s awarded per faculty	...	...	...	...	...	...	...	6.90 (.78)	...	...
Male proportion of undergraduate enrollment	...	...	...	...	...	...	...	...	45.63 (1.38)	...
F-ratio	96.70	81.44	67.50	60.63	74.95	66.58	76.32	66.88	59.05	86.84
R^2	.7192	.7308	.7311	.7415	.7511	.8038	.8031	.8057	.8015	.7979
Number of observations	156	156	156	156	156	139	139	138	126	139

Source: *American Universities and Colleges* (1971).
Note: t-ratios are in parentheses.

Table 2
Change in SAT Scores and Football Records (Dependent Variable: Change in SAT Scores of Entering Freshmen, 1981–84)

Independent Variable	Coefficient			
Intercept	14.25	8.58	7.67	7.21
	(3.14)	(1.22)	(1.10)	(1.04)
Trend in football winning percentage (1971–84)	278.71	286.52	255.94	302.37
	(1.50)	(1.49)	(1.34)	(1.55)
Change in student/faculty ratio (1981–84)	3.56	3.47	3.18	3.88
	(2.00)	(1.92)	(1.78)	(2.04)
Private school dummy (1981–84)	9.29	14.17	18.76	26.23
	(.78)	(.62)	(.84)	(1.12)
Change in in-state tuition (1981–84)	. . .	−.01	−.01	−.02
		(.54)	(.77)	(1.06)
Change in out-of-state tuition (1981–84)	. . .	.01	.01	.01
		(1.15)	(1.08)	(1.34)
Change in library volumes $\times 10^6$ (1981–84)	. . .	. . .	9.00	8.63
			(1.45)	(1.40)
Change in enrollment (1981–84)	. . .	. . .	. . .	−.003
				(1.05)
F-ratio	2.69	1.88	1.96	1.84
R^2	.168	.200	.241	.264
Number of observations	44	44	44	44

Note: t-ratios are in parentheses.

others, have not recently placed great emphasis on big-time athletic success possibly because their unrivaled academic tradition does not require the low-cost advertising provided by a nationally competitive athletic program. One wonders whether old, rich, and privately endowed schools, stuffed with academic heritage, are the only ones that do not find athletics important to survival.

Notes

We are grateful to the Clemson University Athletic Department and the Clemson University Alumni Association for help in this project. We also thank Bill Mc-Lellan, Rex Cottle, a referee, and the editor for their suggestions. We acknowledge the financial support of Thomas C. Breazeale and the Center for Policy Studies, Clemson University. We alone are responsible for the final product.

1. We included Notre Dame, Pitt, Penn State, and others as major independents. See Appendix Table A1 for a complete listing.

2. The choice of 1971 was arbitrary and was based on the fact that a large portion of the data were already available as a by-product of other research.

3. For some schools we have American College Test (ACT) scores instead of SAT scores. Using an algorithm developed by Langston and Watkins (1980), we converted the ACT scores to SAT scores. Apparently there is no widely employed conversion formula used by either testing service.

4. We examined the residuals for heteroscedasticity. Depending on specification, there is evidence that the residual variance declines with the age of the university or the size of the library. Hence, we also estimated the 10 model specifications in Table 1 by weighted least squares first using age and then library as weighting devices. The only statistically meaningful difference is that the coefficient on library volumes is positive in some specifications but only significant in a subset. We will supply these tables on request.

5. The average SAT score of the entering freshmen at the schools in our sample in 1971 was 1,106. Averaged across the 10 model coefficients, the coefficient on the sports dummy is 33. Hence, major sports participation is associated with approximately a 3 percent increase in SAT scores.

6. The only exception is that the coefficient on library volumes is negative in all specifications but the first. In part this may be due to multicollinearity, but more likely it is due to heteroscedasticity of the residual variance. Correcting for this possibility reverses the sign on the library coefficient (see n. 4). We also estimated the coefficients in logs. These results closely mirror the estimates in Table 1. We will supply these tables on request. The variables are self-explanatory with a couple of exceptions. Tuition is the simple average of in-state and out-of-state tuition for public schools. Salary is the average salary of the full professors at the institution, and Ph.D.s awarded is the total earned degrees awarded from 1961 to 1970 adjusted for the faculty size in 1971.

7. The reason for this result may be that large schools can afford the risk of students with low SAT scores but other less quantifiable skills that make them attractive, i.e., students with high variance estimates of scholastic success. In the case of all these independent variables, our discussion is not meant to imply empirical causality but instead our intuition about the causal link.

8. They are the ACC, the SEC, the SWC, the Big Ten, the Big Eight, and the PAC Ten. The data were supplied to us by the sports information office of the Athletic Department at Clemson.

9. The trend variable was obtained by regressing annual in-conference football winning records on time. The coefficient on time is the trend variable. The data are reported in Appendix Table A2.

Appendix Table A1
SAT Scores and University Data, 1971

School	SAT	Sports Dummy	Library	Salary	Student/ Faculty Ratio	Tuition
American Univ.	1,050	0	318,578	22,000	24.338	2,220
Arizona State	925	1	1,300,000	18,800	25.433	770
Auburn	1,047	1	762,750	17,100	17.206	675
Bates Coll.	1,230	0	154,716	18,500	12.856	2,750
Baylor	955	1	510,680	15,500	12.906	900
Beloit Coll.	1,180	0	216,401	19,300	11.960	3,100
Boston Univ.	1,139	0	829,046	21,300	9.764	2,090
Bowling Green State	941	0	701,209	19,800	18.670	900
Brandeis	1,257	0	457,065	24,900	7.757	2,900
Briar Cliff Coll.	983	0	57,000	16,700	8.191	2,125
Brown	1,285	0	1,312,842	24,200	9.551	2,850
Bucknell	1,259	0	365,000	19,400	12.428	2,700
California Inst. Tech.	1,429	0	230,000	26,000	5.875	2,565
Carnegie-Mellon	1,229	0	363,081	23,400	8.217	2,500
Catholic Univ.	1,100	0	849,723	21,100	10.839	2,000
Clark Coll. (Atlanta)	1,243	0	3,000,000	22,300	11.900	2,600
Clemson	1,005	1	487,405	17,400	12.329	925
Colby Coll.	1,243	0	310,000	21,600	12.389	2,500
Colgate	1,257	0	265,000	24,800	12.250	2,800
Coll. Holy Cross	1,163	0	285,000	19,000	12.917	2,480
Colorado Coll.	1,186	0	243,490	19,700	11.414	2,400
Colorado State	1,013	0	765,477	19,000	15.453	1,026
Columbia	1,333	0	4,241,130	25,800	4.215	2,800
Connecticut Coll.	1,200	0	267,279	19,200	9.983	2,700
Cornell Univ.	1,285	0	3,779,990	25,100	5.649	2,175
Creighton	963	0	297,851	16,800	6.163	1,700
Dartmouth Coll.	1,350	0	1,008,048	23,200	8.393	2,820
Davidson Coll.	1,244	0	173,000	19,900	10.660	2,050
Duke	1,268	1	2,225,000	23,900	6.554	2,300
Earlham Coll.	1,173	0	177,069	17,600	10.136	2,600
Emory	1,221	0	927,542	21,300	6.406	2,400
Florida State	1,035	1	918,351	20,600	14.958	1,095
George Washington	1,135	0	547,339	23,900	7.173	2,050
Georgetown Univ.	1,213	0	624,256	20,900	14.417	2,350
Georgia Inst. Tech.	1,187	1	483,563	19,000	9.804	1,000
Georgia State	952	0	332,796	18,400	19.730	468
Goucher Coll.	1,169	0	154,777	20,000	8.760	2,000
Grinnell Coll.	1,260	0	196,500	18,700	10.597	2,495
Harvard	1,392	0	8,500,000	27,200	2.722	2,800
Howard Univ.	850	0	664,391	22,200	6.495	700
Illinois State	937	0	487,139	20,200	18.590	755
Indiana	1,010	1	2,150,567	22,900	33.445	1,070
Iowa State	1,175	1	831,034	21,600	13.411	915
Jacksonville Univ.	983	0	151,822	14,600	18.133	1,375
Johns Hopkins	1,291	0	1,985,075	26,900	4.225	2,700
Kalamazoo Coll.	1,190	0	160,000	20,600	9.773	1,380

School	SAT	Sports Dummy	Library	Salary	Student/ Faculty Ratio	Tuition
Kansas State	934	1	600,000	18,300	15.472	655
Knox Coll.	1,167	0	145,840	23,500	13.491	2,606
Lake Forest Coll.	1,160	0	120,200	24,000	11.667	2,795
Lehigh	1,248	0	547,320	21,400	13.709	2,450
Louisiana State	896	1	1,348,290	19,200	20.200	635
Macalester Coll.	1,185	0	193,588	25,400	10.112	2,250
Marquette	1,064	0	550,184	19,300	14.684	1,835
Massachusetts Inst. Tech.	1,398	0	1,313,212	25,900	7.748	2,650
Miami (Ohio)	1,165	0	597,192	20,600	21.099	850
Michigan State	1,140	1	1,500,000	21,300	21.783	990
Mississippi State	941	1	361,544	17,000	14.329	718
Morgan State	719	0	150,000	17,100	16.279	350
Mount Holyoke Coll.	1,255	0	331,900	21,100	8.967	2,450
New York Univ.	1,160	0	1,813,612	24,000	7.323	2,700
North Carolina State	1,085	1	570,993	19,300	11.812	1,800
Northwestern	1,250	1	2,374,913	25,700	11.154	2,700
Ohio State	927	1	2,507,126	21,000	18.718	1,245
Ohio Univ.	1,016	0	460,026	20,700	21.435	1,185
Oklahoma State	920	1	997,000	18,100	17.838	810
Oregon State	1,009	1	643,189	18,200	13.970	907
Pennsylvania State	1,145	1	1,547,742	19,600	18.165	1,200
Princeton	1,319	0	2,726,087	25,500	6.641	2,800
Purdue	1,063	1	1,089,478	23,500	14.719	900
Rensselaer Polytechnic Inst.	1,300	0	207,800	21,100	10.514	2,475
Rice	1,341	1	657,000	22,700	7.842	2,100
Rutgers	1,069	0	1,941,500	25,600	17.321	600
St. Bonaventure	1,066	0	156,181	18,700	18.856	1,600
St. Lawrence	1,185	0	120,600	22,200	16.310	2,675
St. Louis	1,038	0	698,192	18,300	6.394	950
Smith Coll.	1,273	0	793,067	21,700	9.296	2,450
South Carolina	993	1	1,050,000	18,600	21.624	905
South Dakota State	950	0	230,000	14,500	13.339	585
Southern Illinois (Carbondale)	920	0	1,403,535	20,500	18.833	858
Southern Methodist	1,089	1	1,109,692	19,500	10.818	1,800
Stanford	1,320	1	3,447,372	25,000	9.957	2,610
State Univ. New York (Buffalo)	1,163	0	263,103	26,900	19.132	900
State Univ. New York (Stony Brook)	1,194	0	500,000	26,900	17.028	900
Sweet Briar Coll.	1,102	0	146,134	16,900	9.662	2,800
Syracuse	1,157	1	1,548,733	22,400	18.226	2,600
Temple	1,051	0	1,055,893	23,800	10.938	1,420
Texas A&M	1,063	1	711,710	19,700	12.406	660
Texas Christian	1,040	1	638,221	15,600	16.123	1,500
Texas Tech.	935	1	1,242,842	18,900	18.509	660
Trinity Coll. (Hartford)	1,267	0	482,675	19,600	14.471	2,500

School	SAT	Sports Dummy	Library	Salary	Student/ Faculty Ratio	Tuition
Tufts	1,255	0	450,000	22,900	2.581	2,850
Tulane	1,148	1	1,089,915	19,700	5.565	2,100
Univ. Alabama	952	1	1,168,277	17,400	18.920	765
Univ. Arizona	930	1	1,164,834	18,600	20.176	795
Univ. Arkansas	969	1	628,412	17,300	14.079	660
Univ. California (Berkeley)	1,350	1	4,009,595	23,300	14.919	1,000
Univ. California (Los Angeles)	1,140	1	3,042,550	23,300	15.933	1,350
Univ. Chicago	1,308	0	3,072,200	26,600	6.140	2,625
Univ. Cincinnati	1,046	0	1,164,683	22,400	14.962	910
Univ. Colorado	1,103	1	1,300,000	19,600	23.882	1,057
Univ. Connecticut	1,076	0	1,083,694	24,900	15.574	640
Univ. Delaware	1,097	0	912,782	21,200	18.395	762
Univ. Denver	1,056	0	838,728	19,100	13.802	2,400
Univ. Florida	1,155	1	1,112,719	19,000	11.354	1,095
Univ. Georgia	1,043	1	1,158,047	20,300	13.482	675
Univ. Hartford	1,008	0	170,000	19,000	18.567	1,875
Univ. Hawaii	1,011	0	1,125,542	24,400	15.820	549
Univ. Houston	1,011	1	746,752	19,800	31.779	832
Univ. Illinois (Urbana-Champaign)	1,120	1	4,416,330	22,200	14.158	825
Univ. Iowa	1,047	1	1,651,805	22,400	14.571	935
Univ. Kansas	979	1	1,568,807	19,100	10.069	950
Univ. Kentucky	920	1	1,153,774	20,800	12.192	680
Univ. Maryland	1,040	1	1,299,520	21,000	13.630	950
Univ. Miami (Florida)	980	1	995,797	22,200	13.956	2,000
Univ. Michigan	1,203	1	4,256,597	23,800	12.394	650
Univ. Minnesota	995	1	3,112,526	22,300	25.045	1,018
Univ. Mississippi	920	1	456,583	16,100	20.364	806
Univ. Montana	913	0	550,537	18,000	17.658	625
Univ. Nebraska	994	1	1,101,475	19,400	12.128	898
Univ. Nevada (Reno)	889	0	413,075	19,200	17.043	600
Univ. New Hampshire	1,070	0	583,640	20,500	15.645	1,500
Univ. New Mexico	878	0	758,574	18,000	18.987	840
Univ. North Carolina	1,126	1	1,819,669	22,400	10.566	1,300
Univ. Notre Dame	1,193	1	1,042,000	20,300	13.337	2,300
Univ. Oklahoma	955	1	1,335,000	17,900	19.694	755
Univ. Oregon	1,029	1	1,104,320	20,600	12.107	1,413
Univ. Pennsylvania	1,264	0	2,350,000	24,800	5.035	2,450
Univ. Pittsburgh	1,046	1	1,551,109	22,200	10.727	1,960
Univ. Rhode Island	1,048	0	435,000	21,100	14.594	775
Univ. Rochester	1,242	0	1,333,333	25,500	4.694	2,600
Univ. San Francisco	1,048	0	366,400	19,900	16.100	1,530
Univ. South Florida	1,000	0	295,691	18,700	19.376	1,095
Univ. Southern California	1,083	1	1,393,161	21,000	9.430	2,150
Univ. Texas	1,081	1	2,269,700	22,400	27.183	740
Univ. Tulsa	1,011	0	411,524	17,400	23.996	1,000
Univ. Utah	917	0	1,378,479	19,600	16.758	817

Appendix Table A1
(Continued)

School	SAT	Sports Dummy	Library	Salary	Student/ Faculty Ratio	Tuition
Univ. Vermont	1,077	0	538,928	19,500	10.326	1,675
Univ. Virginia	1,213	1	1,697,919	25,000	8.439	745
Univ. Washington	1,109	1	1,878,700	21,000	11.654	1,038
Univ. Wisconsin (Madison)	1,138	1	2,878,615	21,200	14.577	1,832
Univ. Wyoming	927	0	486,000	17,800	14.065	871
Utah State	861	0	419,166	17,200	20.484	693
Vanderbilt	1,223	1	1,256,386	23,100	5.373	2,200
Vassar Coll.	1,278	0	415,426	20,800	8.155	2,500
Villanova	1,083	0	415,235	17,600	18.644	2,050
Virginia Polytechnic Inst.	1,084	1	623,405	19,200	14.202	780
Wake Forest	1,150	1	450,190	18,600	5.918	1,650
Washington and Lee	1,184	0	225,263	20,700	10.242	2,200
Washington State	1,023	1	851,162	19,500	16.176	809
Washington Univ. (St. Louis)	1,232	0	1,421,349	22,400	5.621	2,650
Wayne State Univ.	955	0	1,367,553	22,300	17.444	1,168
Wells Coll.	1,168	0	171,845	17,300	7.707	2,570
West Virginia	934	1	722,091	18,400	13.670	707
Wichita State	890	0	319,281	18,000	20.220	655
Williams Coll.	1,296	0	378,111	21,700	7.221	2,450
Yale	1,385	0	5,829,035	28,500	4.328	2,900

Source: *American Universities and Colleges* (1971).

Appendix Table A2
Football Records, 1971–84, and University Data, 1981–84

School	Change in SAT Score (1981–84)	Trend in Football (1971–84)	Change in Library (1981–84)	Change in Student/Faculty Ratio (1981–84)	Change in Enrollment (1981–84)
Alabama	−79	−.02264	300,000	−.781986	−1,079
Arizona State	4	−.03084	0	−3.203609	2,176
Auburn	26	.00752	200,000	−.423028	130
Baylor	13	.02120	118,433	−2.128292	452
California (Berkeley)	−5	−.01978	300,000	−.025678	910
California (Los Angeles)	8	.01299	900,000	−.920580	284
Clemson	7	.04698	298,977	.405970	408
Colorado	−21	−.03543	100,000	−.772881	−112
Colorado State	55	.00401	0	−.360967	−418
Duke	8	−.00742	300,000	−.522183	116
Florida	26	.02275	0	−2.044191	−823
Georgia	3	.01919	200,000	.116969	−148
Georgia Tech.	18	−.10000	600,000	.581224	−431
Illinois	83	.02062	4,400,000	.683499	−485

Appendix Table A2
(Continued)

School	Change in SAT Score (1981–84)	Trend in Football (1971–84)	Change in Library (1981–84)	Change in Student/Faculty Ratio (1981–84)	Change in Enrollment (1981–84)
Indiana	32	.00344	0	.972285	720
Iowa	25	.05596	200,000	4.422518	3,882
Iowa State	10	−.01592	100,000	.723796	1,894
Kentucky	64	.00206	0	−1.212812	−2,234
Louisiana State	−6	−.01100	200,000	1.298267	136
Maryland	34	.02400	100,000	−.284136	229
Michigan	26	−.01948	300,000	−1.154211	−452
Michigan State	12	−.02890	200,000	−.061443	−1,818
Minnesota	−9	−.02435	−200,000	−4.610345	−5,451
Mississippi State	4	.00498	344,563	−.702887	−87
Missouri	0	.01228	0	−4.674407	−1,114
Nebraska	11	.01335	200,000	1.113134	180
New Mexico	19	−.01068	200,000	−.610303	1,373
North Carolina	−20	−.00873	1,000,000	−2.449271	−959
North Carolina State	29	−.03275	0	−.346426	2,325
Northwestern	15	−.02154	300,000	.201567	28
Ohio State	36	−.00645	300,000	−.782364	−170
Oklahoma	6	−.01005	200,000	−2.722107	−1,271
Oklahoma State	7	.01445	0	−.437839	−1,232
Oregon State	−11	−.02570	46,024	−4.836829	−1,804
Purdue	12	−.00090	200,000	−.349355	−1,083
Rice	24	−.03118	100,000	.131133	178
Southern California	−5	−.00548	200,000	. . .	1,317
Southern Methodist	16	.03701	1,149,049	−.594538	−20
Tennessee	21	.00060	−200,000	−.619006	−3,172
Texas A&M	−6	−.00887	200,000	−.569768	771
Texas Christian	70	−.11837	200,000	.223644	250
Utah	−68	.01391	0	−7.026273	892
Virginia	39	.01262	0	−.053832	−85
Wake Forest	20	.00425	103,995	−9.975589	210
Washington	45	.03525	100,000	.024859	−194
Wisconsin	22	.01988	0	.886294	2,011

Source: *Peterson's Annual Guide to Undergraduate Study* (1982, 1985).

10.   Again the control variables perform as expected. For example, larger increases in the library are associated with larger increases in freshman SAT scores.

References

American Universities and Colleges. 1971. Edited by W. Todd Furniss. Washington, D.C.: American Council Educ.

Langston, Ira W., and Thomas B. Watkins. 1980. "SAT-ACT Equivalents." Research Memorandum no. 80-5. Champaign: Univ. Illinois, Office of School and College Relations.

Peterson's Annual Guide to Undergraduate Study. 1983 Edition. 1982. 13th ed. Princeton, N.J.: Peterson's Guides.

Peterson's Annual Guide to Undergraduate Study: Four Year Colleges, 1986. 1985. 16th ed. Princeton, N.J.: Peterson's Guides.

Robert E. McCormick and Maurice Tinsley

Athletics and Academics:
A Model of University Contributions

I.   Introduction

What is the impact of big-time athletics on the welfare of higher education? Many people believe there is no room in the academy for large-scale inter-collegiate athletic competition; others take a more liberal view of educa-tion. A common complaint is that athletic fundraisers capture donations that would otherwise accrue to the academic endowment of the school. Our purpose here is to determine if this argument has any empirical basis.

We develop a model of the demand for college that incorporates con-sumption *and* the pursuit of human capital. Students attend school to get a multifaceted education, part of which is the accumulation of production human capital. The value added of a college education to lifetime earnings is well documented. But, we speculate, another aspect to the human capital story also plays an important role in the analysis: consumption human capi-tal. Students learn these latter skills more or less as a free by-product of getting production human capital; collegial relations often spill out of the classroom into the dorm room, the dining hall, the fraternity or sorority house, the local bar, the intramural field, and the football stadium; and the maintenance of this stock of consumption capital is important. That is, in-tercollegiate athletics can be a prominent input in the acquisition of a stu-dent's consumption capital. In this context, college athletic contests attract viewers and media attention, which lure prospective students, faculty, and donors, and maintain contact between alumni and alma mater. In this view, athletics makes two major contributions to higher education: maintenance and continued consumption of skills acquired while in undergraduate school, and advertising.[1]

The paper proceeds as follows. First, we develop our model of a college education, Section II, and then we use it to assay the relation between ath-letics and academics. The test is designed to determine if contributions to athletic booster organizations affect philanthropic contributions for general academic operations, Section III. Finally, Section IV offers a summary and conclusions.

II.   A Human Capital Theory of College Education

A university education is an investment in human production capital; a calculated gamble that the marginal increase in future salary more than offsets the opportunity cost. But college provides at least two products: production capital and consumption capital. This is confirmed by the regular empirical finding that the return to education typically is less than the market interest rate.[2] Students are getting more out of college than just higher lifetime earnings.

To earn these higher wages, individuals must not only obtain an increase in production capital, but they must be able to convince others that they have the requisite skills to warrant a higher salary. Thus, a diploma signals the purchase of some capital, the quality of which is partly a function of the degree granting institution.[3] The college name, in part, is a warranty on the quality of the degree, which helps explain why colleges have entrance rules, degree requirements, and academic standards. They must protect the brand name of the alumni and the prospective graduates. As a consequence, students can use diplomas as signals of their human capital stock. For such services, the university extracts a fee. This remuneration, and the prospect of future rewards, prompts the school to maintain quality; the college of record provides information to current and prospective employers.[4]

Because the diploma provides a continuing flow of services, the graduate has an incentive to ensure the continued academic quality of his or her alma mater. Lower standards and poor performance by future graduates adversely affect the wage earning capacity of alumni, declining with age and experience. Over time other signals, most important recent job performance, become better instruments for judging future ability, and employers become less concerned with the degree-granting institution. Nevertheless, the nameplate on a person's college diploma always identifies the graduate with an institution and is a source of information, albeit of diminishing value, for a lifetime. Whether alumni choose to protect that investment is a dynamic capital-budgeting problem depending on a number of factors: quality of the institution, number of graduates, career choice, and other relative prices. This is the basis for our model of alumni contributions to the academic side of campus, and the genesis of our empirical test.

Additional Considerations

A college diploma sends at least three signals to the job market: the grade point average, the degree curriculum, and the alma mater. To the extent that the reputation of the graduate's university is perhaps the strongest signal to a prospective employer, the first-year alumnus has the most incentive to make a contribution to the academic scholarship fund of his or her alma mater.[5] A decline in the quality of education at any institution devalues the degrees of all graduates, but clearly has the greatest effect on those graduates relying most heavily on this signal. On this count, we expect that philanthropic participation rates to colleges *decline* (income-adjusted) with age. On the other hand, as time elapses the greater is the probability that quality deterioration takes place. For graduates just out of school, there is very little opportunity for the school to change in ways that substantially alter the value of the diploma, at least in the near future. However, the graduate knows the reputation of the diploma could seriously depreciate years from now if the university is not well managed. On this count, participation rates (the number of donors) should increase with age.[6] To ensure continued quality, recent graduates are more likely to insist that their contributions go into a trust fund, allowing only the interest to be consumed. By contrast, the old donor is less concerned with this problem and is more likely to make an unrestricted grant.[7]

Consumption Capital

Students learn many things while in school, but not all of this learning is marketable. Part of it is used directly for consumption in a household production sense. For example, some students learn social skills, others beer drinking, and others physical education (tennis, racquetball, softball, and jogging). Others fine tune their tastes for music, dance, or opera. Whole departments exist at some institutions to teach students these consumption skills.

One desirable recreational vocation available to many college students is intercollegiate athletics. Sports competition between schools is available in football, basketball, baseball, soccer, tennis, track, golf, hockey, swimming, wrestling, and others. Of these football and basketball are big spectator sports. On some campuses, football weekends are the single largest social events of the school year. Students spend a lot of time acquiring school-specific consumption capital here, including names of great heroes, school records, location of the appropriate facilities, memorable moments or great plays, and recognition of coaches and players. This consumption capital depreciates,[8] especially when poor athletic performance demotes the school to the back pages of the sports section, stadium seats are empty, or the team is seldom on television or radio. Consequently, former students having acquired this capital in the school have an incentive to maintain the flow through contributions to the athletic booster club.

In this view, athletic contributions foster success on the field of play. Success, in turn, keeps the value of the alumni's consumption capital stock high. In sum, graduates of a college or university have an incentive to protect its academic credentials with donations to the alumni fund; and to the extent that the school provides intercollegiate athletic contests, they have an independent incentive to contribute to the athletic fund to ensure continued or improved success there.

Intramural Competition for Donations

The various academic colleges and departments within a university are in direct and intense competition for alumni dollars. Competition comes not only from other charitable organizations but also from peer colleges and departments on campus. Relative to undergraduates, students earning advanced degrees are generally inclined to make donations to their specific school and not to the general academic endowment. MBA graduates like to see their dollars go for scholarships, buildings, and faculty in the business school. Likewise, medical graduates prefer their donations support the hospital and medical center. But, to the extent that they participated in intercollegiate athletic events as players or spectators and acquired consumption capital there, medical school and MBA graduates alike are inclined to donate to the athletic department. In this view, fundraisers at the medical school compete with the business school for alumni contributions, but neither vies with the athletic booster club for donations. In all instances however, the empirical question is the same: Does an increase in the contributions made to support athletics have an impact on donations to the academic endowment?

The Role of Athletic Advertising

Universities have an incentive to degrade the quality of diplomas already issued. Money saved on the library, faculty, staff, and grounds will not, in all likelihood, show up immediately in lower admissions or starting salaries for graduates. School administrators, if they choose, can consume their brand names. Of course, students and employers are aware of this incentive, too, and all parties are inclined to seek solutions to the problem. Private firms frequently address this problem by offering a bond through advertising as a means of ensuring continued quality.[9] Luxurious buildings and elaborate grounds also are bonding devices, the value of which is maintained only by a continuing commitment to academic quality. Perhaps this helps to explain the often observed beauty of many college campuses and the extra care that commonly goes towards planning, construction, and maintenance there.

Athletic investment and success also may bond the university. A high-quality athletic program is expensive, $1–10 million annually. Just as large expenditures on advertising signal an investment protected only by maintaining product quality, large expenditures on athletics are recouped only by attracting fans and students in the future. Hence, expenditures in one year become sunk, inducing the administration to maintain academic standards for fear of losing the investment in the future. Interpreted in this light, large expenditures on athletic stadiums and teams have a comparable quality-assuring effect on education as investments in a new chemistry building or a refurbished administration hall.

Summary

The popular belief holds that gifts to the athletic department represent dollars lost by the academic endowment. In this view, people give pathologically to their alma mater without regard to its effect. Donations to the athletic department satisfy this urge, leaving academic coffers bare, and vice versa. The alternative view developed here is that graduates have two different investments to protect with contributions—production and consumption.[10] Intercollegiate athletic events maintain the graduate's stock of consumption capital, expenditures on these events bond the administration to continued academic quality, and publicity about these events advertises the university; a three-hour telecast of the football team carried nationwide at prime time reminds alumni of their alma mater. It also attracts new students, professors, and outside donors. In the next section, we subject these arguments to empirical scrutiny.

III. Empirical Analysis

The theory detailed in the last section suggests a two-equation model of alumni gift giving. The first describes contributions for the academic endowment, the second, gifts to the athletic department.[11] Academic donations are a function of the quality of the diploma. Contributions to the athletic department are determined by athletic success.[12] Both groups must cope with free-rider problems. The controversy over the link between academic and athletic gift giving is addressed by including athletic gift giving in the academic equations. If, as so many claim, a dollar of athletic support supplants a dollar of academic support, the relation will be negative.

We obtained cross-sectional data on alumni gift giving at Clemson University annually from 1979 to 1983. We also collected contributions to IPTAY, the Clemson University Athletic Department fundraising organization, for the same period. The data are available by county in South Carolina, for the states of Georgia and North Carolina, and for the rest of the country as a whole.[13]

Equation (1), the human capital, brand-name equation, identifies contributions to the academic side of campus:

$$G_e = \alpha_1 + \alpha_2 G_a + \alpha_3 D + \alpha_4 T + \alpha_5 A + \alpha_6 Y + \alpha_7 S + \alpha_8 N$$
$$+ \alpha_9 C + \alpha_{10} W \tag{1}$$

Equation (2), the consumption capital equation, explains donations to the athletic department:

$$G_a = \beta_1 + \beta_2 D + \beta_3 M + \beta_4 F + \beta_5 Y + \beta_6 P + \beta_7 W \tag{2}$$

where

G_e = dollar contributions to the academic endowment per alumnus,
G_a = dollar contributions to athletics per alumnus,
D = road miles from county seat or state capital to school,
T = tuition and fees per semester,
A = alumni per region,
Y = per capita income per region,
S = university enrollment by region,
N = total population of each region,
C = cash receipts from farm marketing of crops by county,
W = a proxy for wealth (school expenditures per pupil),
M = number of members in athletic booster club per region,
F = football winning percentage, lagged one year,
P = price of a football ticket divided by stadium capacity.

The model was estimated in logs by the methods of ordinary least squares (OLS) and three-stage least squares (3SLS).[14] A sample of specifications for equation (1) are reported in Table 1.[15]

The coefficient on distance is positive and significant. Alumni living a considerable distance from the university find it increasingly expensive to obtain information about their alma mater, and they receive fewer benefits. This makes it less likely that they will contribute to the academic endowment; alumni are less inclined to contribute the farther they live from campus. However, those that do choose to donate will have a tendency to contribute more per person (the Alchian and Allen theorem); hence $\alpha_3 > 0$.

The coefficient on tuition is negative and significant. Apparently, when tuition is high the alumni sense the brand name of the university is being protected in some fashion, and hence, contributions are less useful (to them) in serving that purpose.

The positive and significant coefficient of the alumni census variable is a surprising result given the free-rider problems clubs usually encounter. A 10 percent increase in the number of alumni in a region is associated with a 5.5 percent increase in contributions per person, ceteris paribus. Presumably, the feeling of pleasure alumni get from belonging to a larger group more than offsets the desire for a free ride on the upkeep of the

Table 1
Parameter Estimates—Model 1 (dependent variable is contributions to the academic endowment per alumnus; all variables in logs)

Independent Variable	Coefficient Estimate/($|t$-ratio$|$)					
	OLS			3SLS		
Intercept	−1.668	−2.013	−2.286	−0.026	−2.072	−2.256
	(0.75)	(0.83)	(0.95)	(0.01)	(0.85)	(0.94)
Athletic contributions	0.410	0.556	0.525	0.623	0.596	0.500
per alumnus	(4.02)	(4.97)	(4.73)	(5.52)	(5.33)	(4.50)
Distance from campus	0.306	0.304	0.244	0.461	0.307	0.241
	(4.03)	(2.43)	(1.94)	(4.24)	(2.45)	(1.92)
Tuition and fees per	−0.448	−0.659	−1.245	−0.551	−0.678	−1.248
semester	(1.71)	(2.23)	(3.37)	(1.87)	(2.29)	(3.38)
Number of alumni	0.501	0.687	0.577	0.739	0.682	0.577
	(3.38)	(3.67)	(3.04)	(3.94)	(3.65)	(3.04)
Income per capita	0.460	0.645	0.285	0.368	0.641	0.278
	(1.45)	(1.93)	(0.79)	(1.16)	(1.91)	(0.77)
Population	−0.181	−0.413	−0.350	−0.501	−0.411	−0.349
	(2.47)	(2.43)	(2.06)	(2.99)	(2.42)	(2.06)
Student enrollment	−0.252	−0.281	−0.202	−0.200	−0.278	−0.202
	(1.64)	(1.79)	(1.28)	(1.28)	(1.77)	(1.28)
Agricultural production		0.109	0.098		0.109	0.098
		(2.42)	(2.19)		(2.41)	(2.19)
Local expenditures on			0.989			1.013
education per pupil			(2.58)			(2.65)
f ratio	6.39	6.94	7.07			
R^2	.1598	.201	.224			
Sample size	245	230	230	230	230	230

university's brand name. Moreover, larger alumni groups are capable of providing larger local benefits, such as meetings, picnics, and information, further increasing the willingness to donate. In spite of this solidarity, we are surprised.

The income elasticity of demand is approximately 0.5, but its significance is dependent on model specification. When the wealth proxy, local school expenditures per pupil, is included, the income variable loses significance. The population coefficient is negative and significant. In small locales a person is better known to others through family, friends, and business associates; and hence, the demand for a diploma signal is weaker, reducing contributions. Whereas, in large communities more market substitutes for human capital signaling are available. However, it is in large communities where signaling has the most value. On the first count, fewer donations are expected; on the second, more. Apparently, the first effect dominates; alternatives for job signaling are more available in large communities than in small ones.

The enrollment variable has a negative coefficient, significant in some specifications. Communities with a large number of students enrolled at a particular college have a stronger feel for the quality of diplomas from that institution, and hence, the incentive to contribute to the alumni fund is muted for any individual student or graduate.[16]

The agricultural production variable has a positive coefficient of about 0.1, significant at the 1 percent level. There is a relation between the academic programs of the school and the careers of the alumni; for an agriculturally oriented school, alumni living in predominantly farming areas have a propensity to contribute more per person than alumni living in urban areas, ceteris paribus. This phenomenon also reinforces the results of the population coefficient, reported earlier. Agricultural counties presumably are more homogenous, helping to eliminate the free-rider problem. On all counts, $\alpha_9 > 0$.

The wealth variable, local school expenditures per pupil, is positive and significant. Richer communities give more per alumni to support academics.[17]

There is no evidence that athletic booster club fundraising crowds out philanthropic donations to the academic endowment. The coefficient on G_a, contributions to the athletic fund, is positive, the elasticity is about 0.5, and it is significant at the 1 percent level. A 10 percent increase per alumnus in donations to the athletic booster club is associated with a 5.0 percent increase in donations to the alumni fund. Clearly, this is bad news for the notion that the athletic department is robbing the alumni fund of contributions. The opposite is true; at least according to these numbers, the two go hand in hand.[18]

IV.   Conclusions

Universities are understudied organizations, but this is not because they do not present an interesting variety of questions concerning their composition. The question of whether athletic success comes at the expense of academic quality is particularly intriguing because of the supposed competition between rival departments of the same institution.

The thesis maintained here is that many students get more than one education while enrolled in college; intercollegiate athletic competition is a natural consequence and by-product of undergraduate education for many students. This implies that athletic success goes hand in hand with academic success and that critics of athletic success, insofar as this study goes, are misguided if their motive is the academic improvement of the university.

Empirically, we find a positive, significant relation between academic philanthropy and gift giving to support athletics; athletic fundraising does not appear to crowd out gifts to academics. We conclude there is a symbiotic relation between athletics and academics on many campuses and the elimination of athletics and athletic fundraising could have deleterious effects on both academic contributions and academic standards. All told, the two-tiered, human capital approach to university attendance, production and consumption, appears to be a rich analytical framework ripe for continued study.

Notes

We are grateful to the Clemson University Athletic Department and the Clemson University Alumni Association for help on this project. We also thank Bill McLellan and Rex Cottle for their counsel. We alone are responsible for the final product.

1.   See McCormick and Tinsley (1987) for evidence on the relation between undergraduate SAT scores and athletic competition.
2.   See Taubman (1976), for example.
3.   See Spence (1973).
4.   See Klein and Leffler (1981) and Shapiro (1983) for a general discussion.
5.   See Ireland and Johnson (1970) for a discussion of the economics of charitable contributions, although in our model altruism is not the motive for donating.
6.   We expect the academic funds donated per graduate to fall over time and to be dependent on the other signals produced by the student. Grade point average also transmits information to prospective employers. However, it is not clear how differences in the grade point average will affect the contributions made by new alumni. If the student has very high grades, contributions will be small—the less the dependence on the reputation of the alma mater, the less the incentive to donate funds. On the other hand, because a student with a high grade point average usually has invested more in his or her education, ceteris paribus, than a student with low grades, there is more to lose by a drop in the academic standard of the

alma mater. In this instance, a graduate with high grades could be expected to contribute more than a graduate with low grades. The net effect is ambiguous.

7. Hall and Lindsay (1980) argue that "medical school admission processes give the clearest picture of donors' intentions . . . administrators do not consider all demanders to be appropriately qualified to receive the benefits of donor-sponsored medical training" (60). Donors in essence are buying a specific quality student, who will reinforce the reputation of the university which, in turn, confers benefits on the donor. The university is more than willing to search for an appropriate student in return for continuing financial support.

8. Likewise, the value of friendship capital also decays, prompting universities to foster reunions.

9. See Klein, Crawford, and Alchian (1978) and Klein and Leffler (1981).

10. It is here that athletic success may be detrimental to academic quality. If athletics are prominent on campus, prospective students, parents, and donors may fear that *too much* time is devoted to consumption there and not enough to production (studying). In the arguments that follow we assume that the advertising, brand-name effect dominates. It remains an empirical question, an on which we shed some light in Section IV.

11. There is a complication that impedes both athletic and academic fundraising groups; the classic problem of the free rider. Honors students or abnormally successful graduates exert external benefits on fellow alumni. Furthermore, alumni can attempt to free ride on the contributions of fellow graduates. A supporter of the varsity football team, meanwhile, can share in the enjoyment of victory every Saturday without contributing, free riding the contributions of others, unless administrators uncover ways to shield the fan from athletic success. In both cases, the group members—alumni and athletic fans—have an incentive to disguise their demand for the product they consume. If the managers in charge of the respective organizations can find demand-revealing schemes, financial benefits accrue. Brevity demands that we simply note a variety of devices used by fundraisers to cope with this problem: (1) bundled and multipart pricing schemes; (2) naming buildings, benches, or component schools after donors; and (3) the publication of donor lists. In spite of these and other efforts, we expect that any group will have less of a donation per person as the size of the group increases, ceteris paribus.

12. Coughlin and Erekson (1984) examined the cross-sectional variation in contributions to athletic departments. They found that football attendance, population, bowl appearances, and winning boosted philanthropy. They also discovered that professional sports competition detracted from giving to support intercollegiate athletics.

13. There are forty-six counties in South Carolina; each year is a cross-section of forty-nine localities. In total, we have 245 observations.

14. 3SLS is employed because the error terms may be correlated across equations given the cross-sectional nature of the data and the structure of the

        model. If this problem is serious, then OLS estimates of the two equations will be biased and misleading. 3SLS estimation takes into account any correlation of error terms across equations.

15.   The estimates of equation (2) are not reported for brevity's sake. They are available on request.

16.   We also estimated a specification of equation (1) including the lagged SAT scores of the entering freshmen. The variable was insignificant and including it did not alter other estimates.

17.   We used other measures of wealth; specifically, automobiles per capita, boats per capita, and population density. In all cases the central result is unaltered: there is a positive, significant relation between contributions to athletics and gifts to academics. We will supply the alternate specifications on request.

18.   Due to the pooled nature of the data, neither ordinary least squares nor seemingly unrelated regressions may be efficient ways to estimate the parameters of the model. The error terms over the cross-sectional units, the counties, very easily could be different from the time-series error terms within a county. To account for this possibility we also estimated the two gift equations assuming a heteroscedastic error structure across counties and an autoregressive error structure within counties (but note, there is no evidence of heteroscedasticity or autocorrelation). The basic result is unaltered. There is a positive and significant association between academic contributions and athletic donations. Using this estimation technique, the coefficient estimate on G_a in the academic contributions equation is slightly larger.

References

Becker, Gary S. 1981. *A Treatise on the Family*. Cambridge: Harvard University Press.

Coughlin, Cletus C., and O. Homer Erekson. 1984. "An Examination of Contributions to Support Intercollegiate Athletics." *Southern Economic Journal* 51, no. 1 (July): 180–95.

Hall, Thomas D., and Cotton M. Lindsay. 1980. "Medical Schools: Producers of What, Sellers to Whom?" *Journal of Law and Economics* 23 (April): 55–80.

Ireland, Thomas R., and David B. Johnson. 1970. *Economics of Charity*. Blacksburg, Va.: Center for the Study of Public Choice.

Klein, Benjamin, and Keith B. Leffler. 1981. "The Role of Market Forces in Assuring Contractual Performance." *Journal of Political Economy* 89 (August): 615–41.

Klein, Benjamin, Robert G. Crawford, and Armen A. Alchian. 1978. "Vertical Integration, Appropriable Rents, and the Competitive Contracting Process." *Journal of Law and Economics* 21 (October): 297–326.

McCormick, Robert, and Maurice Tinsley. 1987. "Athletics versus Academics?

Evidence from SAT Scores." *Journal of Political Economy* 95 (October): 1103–16.

Shapiro, Carl. 1983. "Premiums for High Quality Products as Returns to Reputations." *Quarterly Journal of Economics* 98 (November): 659–79.

Spence, Michael T. 1973. "Job Market Signaling." *Quarterly Journal of Economics* 87 (August): 355–74.

Taubman, Paul. 1976. "Earnings, Education, Genetics and Environment." *Journal of Human Resources* 11 (Fall): 447–61.

VI Sports and the Efficient Markets Hypothesis

Richard A. Zuber, John M. Gandar, and Benny D. Bowers

Beating the Spread: Testing the Efficiency of the Gambling Market for National Football League Games

I.   Introduction

In recent years a number of studies, employing tests of efficiency developed for analyzing securities markets, have examined the efficiency of racetrack gambling. Results are mixed: certain studies have found these markets to be efficient (Snyder 1978; Ali 1979; Figlewski 1979); others have found inefficiencies that allow for profitable wagering (Hausch, Ziemba, and Rubinstein 1981; Asch, Malkiel, and Quandt 1984). In this paper we extend the examination of gambling market efficiency to the gambling market for National Football League (NFL) games. The only previous work in this area, the study of Vergin and Scriabin (1978), investigated biases in the setting of point spreads for NFL games and developed betting strategies based on these biases that allowed for profitable wagering. The intent of the present paper is to test for efficiency in this gambling market more directly than do Vergin and Scriabin. We conduct both a "weak" test of efficiency, the ability of the Las Vegas gambling "line" to predict point spreads, and a stronger test, the ability of an explanatory model of actual point spreads to predict game outcomes and earn speculative profits.

II.   Initial Efficiency Tests

The conventional test of market efficiency is often presented in the form of the hypothesis that forward prices are the best unbiased forecast of future spot prices.[1] The direct equivalent of this efficiency test for the NFL gambling market is to estimate the equation

$$PS_{it} = b + b_1 VL_{it} + u_{it}, \tag{1}$$

where PS_{it} is the actual point spread on the ith game in the tth week, VL_{it} is the Las Vegas gambling line,[2] and u_{it} is the error term. It should be understood that VL_{it} is not the bookmaker's prediction of the game's outcome.

While the initial line is based on an expert's opinion of the game's outcome, thereafter the bookmaker adjusts the line as gambles are made in order to avoid exposure to unnecessary risk. Thus the line on a game moves to reflect the collective judgment of gamblers about its outcome. If gamblers are using the available information efficiently, then we might expect the final point spread to be the best unbiased forecast of the game's outcome. In terms of equation (1) the efficient markets test is the null hypothesis that jointly $b_0 = 0$ and $b_1 = 1$.

To obtain F-values for this test, equation (1) was estimated by ordinary least squares (OLS) for each week of the 1983 NFL regular season. For 13 of the 16 weeks the null hypothesis cannot be rejected at conventional levels of significance. However, before concluding that efficiency prevails, consider the alternative hypothesis that the Las Vegas line is unrelated to the actual game point spread. In terms of equation (1) this is the joint test that $b_0 = 0$ and $b_1 = 1$. This alternative hypothesis cannot be rejected for 15 of the 16 weeks. That is, the extreme alternative hypothesis is as consistent with the sample data as is the efficiency hypothesis.[3] An alternative testing strategy is required.

To initiate this, consider the following definition of efficiency in a gambling market (see Asch et al. 1984). Such a market is efficient when the rate of return to any gambling strategy based on publicly available information approximates the bookmaker's *vigorish* (or track take). For point spread gambling this commission is approximately 5 percent. That is, in an efficient football gambling market gamblers pursuing any strategy should earn a negative rate of return close to 5 percent. While efficiency in this sense is difficult to establish, it is possible to examine whether there exists sufficient divergence from efficiency in the gambling market to permit profitable gambling strategies. If such gambling opportunities exist we could conclude that inefficiencies exist. The remainder of this paper is concerned with constructing this alternative test of inefficiency for NFL gambling.

III.   Explanatory Model Specification and Results

In this section we develop a plausible explanatory model systematically utilizing publicly available information on NFL games. We see this as a necessary first step for the prediction of game point spreads required for the gambling simulations carried out in the next section.

The actual result of any football game, as measured by the point spread, can be viewed as the net outcome of the simultaneous efforts of the two teams involved. Thus the game point spread is viewed here as the dependent variable in a reduced-form equation, while the independent variables are the net efforts of the two teams. These net efforts, in turn, can be represented by the game statistics and the teams' characteristics. More formally, let PS_{it} be the point spread (measured as the home team's score minus the visiting team's score) of the ith game in the tth week. Then the argument above sees PS_{it} as the dependent variable in the equation

$$PS_{it} = \mathbf{B}'X_{it} + u_{it}, \tag{2}$$

where $\mathbf{B}'$ is a vector of coefficients to be estimated, X_{it} a matrix of observable variables, and u_{it} an error term. Each of the game and team variables in the matrix X_{it} is defined in the same fashion as PS_{it}; that is, each consists of the first difference between the value of the variable for the home team and its value for the visiting team. The explanatory variables used in the estimation of equation (2) for this paper include yards rushed (YR_{it}), yards passed (YP_{it}), number of wins previous to the game (W_{it}), fumbles (F_{it}), interceptions (IN_{it}), number of penalties (PN_{it}), proportion of passing plays attempted to total offensive plays (PP_{it}), and number of rookies (R).[4] A priori expectations are for positive signs on the first three explanatory variables and negative signs on the remainder. Data for all of these variables for the 1983 season were gathered entirely from publicly available information.[5]

While equation (2) was estimated by OLS for a number of subdivisions of the 1983 season, because of the similarity of results Table 1 presents

Table 1
OLS Estimates of Equation (2): 1983 Regular NFL Season

	First 8 Weeks	Entire 16 Weeks		First 8 Weeks	Entire 16 Weeks
Constant	1.547	1.625	IN	−2.619	−2.788
	(.581)**	(.514)**		(.344)**	(.308)**
YR	.047	.041	PN	−.424	−.309
	(.010)**	(.009)**		(.171)*	(.146)*
YP	.044	.045	PP	−.217	−.244
	(.007)**	(.006)**		(.050)*	(.046)**
W	.697	.574	R	−.319	−.309
	(.300)*	(.216)**		(.130)*	(.117)**
F	−2.299	−2.036	R^2	.733	.727
	(.418)**	(.362)**	F	37.28	71.63
			Df	103	215

Note: Standard errors are in parentheses.
*Significant at the 5 percent level.
**Significant at the 1 percent level.

only those for the first half of the season as well as the entire season. The results are gratifyingly neat and clear. All of the explanatory variables are significant and have their expected sign. As measured by the R^2 value, this simple model explains nearly three-fourths of the squared variation in actual point spreads. Finally, estimation of equation (2) sequentially over the last 8 weeks of the season shows that conventional F-tests are unable to reject the null hypothesis of parameter stability. That is, our explanatory model can be utilized for predicting point spreads in the latter part of the season.

IV.   Prediction and Gambling Simulation

Predicted point spreads (PPS_{it}) for the second half of the 1983 NFL regular season ($t = 9, \ldots, 16$) were obtained using the form of the explanatory model developed above. This equation was estimated using the data for week 1 to week $t - 1$. The resulting parameter estimates were then applied to team-specific averages (similarly computed through week $t - 1$) of the relevant home and visiting team explanatory variables. The point spread predictions for the tth week thus represent ex ante predictions utilizing only information available prior to the games in that week.

The predicted point spreads were then used in a number of gambling simulations. In these simulations a bet was made on a game if $|PPS_{it} - VL_{it}| \geq \lambda$, where λ took on the values of 0.5, 1, 2, and 3. Conditional on a bet's being made, the team to bet on is determined by the sign of ($PPS_{it} - VL_{it}$): if this expression is positive, the gamble is made on the home team; if negative, the gamble is made on the visiting team. Finally, the bet is won if the team gambled on beats the spread. This requires that the sign of ($PS_{it} - VL_{it}$) coincide with the sign of ($PPS_{it} - VL_{it}$).[6]

The results of the simulation using $\lambda = 0.5$ are summarized in Table 2. With this filter 102 bets were placed over the eight weeks of simulated gambling, 60 of which won for a winning percentage of 59 percent. This occurred despite 2 comparatively poor weeks, weeks 12 and 13, when the winning percentage fell to 46 and 38 percent, respectively. While Table 2 contains only the results for $\lambda = 0.5$, it should be noted that all four strategies produced winning percentages greater than the 52.4 percent needed to break even.[7]

To further illustrate the potential profitability of the simulation for $\lambda = 0.5$ assume \$110 is bet on each game in the ninth week that meets the criterion of $|PPS_{it} - VL_{it}| \geq 0.5$. Since all 14 games meet this criterion in week nine, \$1,540 is laid out in bets. The net return in this week is \$140 (the eight winning bets produce \$800 in winnings; the six losing bets cost the

Table 2
Gambling Simulations (λ = 0.5), Final 8 Weeks of 1983 Season

Week	Number of Bets	Number of Wins	Wins/Bets (%)	Sum Gambled ($)	Net Return ($)	Rate of Return (%)	Final Wealth ($)
9	14	8	57.1	1,540	140	9.1	1,680
10	13	8	61.5	1,430	250	17.5	1,930
11	13	8	61.5	1,430	250	17.5	2,180
12	13	6	46.2	1,430	−170	−11.5	2,010
13	13	5	38.5	1,430	−380	−26.6	1,630
14	12	8	66.7	1,320	360	27.3	1,990
15	11	10	90.9	1,210	890	73.6	2,880
16	13	7	53.8	1,430	40	2.8	2,920

gambler $660). Continuing the process for the remaining seven weeks of the season results in a final wealth position of $2,920 representing net winnings of $1,380.

One important question remains: Are these results true exploitations of market inefficiencies, or could they be obtained simply by chance? The probability of randomly selecting a winning gamble is .5. When the normal approximation to the binomial distribution is used, the probability of randomly selecting 60 winning bets in 102 gambles is less than 5 percent. Thus it is reasonable to suppose that the profitable gambling simulations developed above represent true exploitations of inefficiencies in the NFL gambling market.

V.   Conclusions

The purpose of this paper was to investigate the speculative efficiency of the gambling market for NFL games. Since we can show that profitable gambling opportunities exist, speculative inefficiencies appear to be present in this market. These results are consistent with the findings of Vergin and Scriabin (1978) for the 1969–74 NFL seasons.

Finally, several points of caution are warranted. First our study was conducted over a single NFL season. Simulations over additional seasons are required before confidence in these results can be assured. Second, there is a considerable difference between the demonstration that our predictive mechanism could have made money in the past and its ability to produce profitable returns in the future. Third, while our results suggest that speculative inefficiencies exist in this market, this does not necessarily imply market inefficiency. There are considerable information costs involved in assembling and processing the required data. Also, because gambling is illegal in most states, there may be large transactions costs involved.

Notes

We would like to thank Jim Marsden, Paul E. Smith, and an anonymous referee for valuable comments.

1. For a convenient summary of this and other tests see de Leeuw and McKelvey (1984).

2. The Las Vegas line used throughout the paper was the last one publicly available, the line published in the media on Fridays over the season. For consistency both PS_{it} and VL_{it} are defined from the home team's perspective. In this paper when $VL_{it} > 0$ (< 0), the home team is the favorite (underdog).

3. Complete results of these tests are available on request from the authors.

4. These explanatory variables were found significant in all models examined over all subdivisions of the 1983 season. Of them perhaps only PV_{it} requires elucidation: this variable was introduced into the model to capture the added risks of the passing-based offenses frequently employed by trailing teams in their efforts to catch up.

5. The data set used in this study was gathered from the *Sporting News*, the *Charlotte Observer*, the *1983 NFL Media Information Book*, and individual 1983 team media guides.

6. The VL_{it} that determines whether a bet is won or lost is the line at the time the bet is made. This represents a major difference between football and racetrack gambling.

7. Gambling on an NFL game is carried out on the "11 for 10" rule: the gambler must lay out \$11 for every \$10 he or she wishes to win. The percentage of winning bets (WP) necessary to break even, 52.4 percent, is obtained by setting the expected value of the random variable, a gamble $WP(10) + (1 - WP)(-11)$, equal to zero.

References

Ali, Mukhtar M. 1979. "Some Evidence of the Efficiency of a Speculative Market." *Econometrica* 47 (March): 387–92.

Asch, Peter, Burton G. Malkiel, and Richard E. Quandt. 1984. "Market Efficiency in Racetrack Betting." *Journal of Business* 57 (April): 165–75.

de Leeuw, Frank, and Michael J. McKelvey. 1984. "Price Expectations of Business Firms: Bias in the Short and Long Run." *American Economic Review* 74 (March): 99–110.

Figlewski, Stephen. 1979. "Subjective Information and Market Efficiency in a Betting Market." *Journal of Political Economy* 87 (February): 75–88.

Hausch, Donald B., William T. Ziemba, and Mark Rubinstein. 1981. "Efficiency of the Market for Racetrack Betting." *Management Science* 27 (December): 1435–52.

Snyder, Wayne W. 1978. "Horse Racing: Testing the Efficient Markets Model." *Journal of Finance* 33 (September): 1109–18.

Vergin, Roger C., and Michael Scriabin. 1978. "Winning Strategies for Wagering on National Football League Games." *Management Science* 24 (April): 809–18.

John L. Dobra, Thomas F. Cargill, and Robert A. Meyer

Efficient Markets for Wagers:
The Case of Professional Basketball Wagering

I.   Introduction: Efficient Markets for Wagers

The proposition that markets efficiently incorporate all available information into current prices and generally are accurate predictors of future value is a commonly understood precept of price theory. In the context of current empirical analyses of financial markets, this precept generally is put in terms of the efficient markets hypothesis (EMH) or the theory of rational expectations. The "random walk" is a special type of efficiency hypothesis put forward as an explanation of the behavior of commodity future and spot prices by Working (1934). The theoretical formulation and implications of the general hypothesis of efficient or rational markets were provided by Muth (1961), Samuelson (1965), Sargent and Wallace (1975), and others.

Fama (1970) provided a convenient three-part classification for the hypothesis that current market prices are accurate predictors of future values based on the information set available to market participants. The "weak form" of the hypothesis assumes that only past price information is available; the "semistrong" form assumes that all publicly available information including past prices are available; and the "strong" form assumes that some market participants have access to "insider" information. Rejection of the strong form of the hypothesis, of course, does not necessarily imply that markets are inefficient. Insiders' trading should anticipate future values of assets more accurately and, therefore, improve market forecast efficiency. In addition, rejection of the "strong form" can reflect improper specification of the econometric model used to test the EMH.

The past two decades have witnessed a significant volume of empirical research on the EMH in the context of commodity and financial asset markets.[1] In spite of this volume of work, there is no clear consensus that specific commodity or financial markets are efficient. Recent work by Schiller (1981) on the volatility of stock and bond yields suggests that such volatility is inconsistent with the EMH. Several studies (Cargill and Rausser 1975; Cootner 1967; and Stevenson and Bear 1970) of the stochastic characteristics of commodity futures have tended to reject several variations of the EMH.

On the other hand, researchers have not rejected the EMH given the well-known statistical and methodological problems encountered in testing the hypothesis. Yet, they have been reluctant to accept the view expressed by Keynes in the *General Theory* (1964) that financial markets are dominated by unstable psychological factors (i.e., "animal spirits") and hence, in the current terminology, are inefficient even in the "weak" form.

This paper investigates the EMH in the context of markets for wagers on National Basketball Association (NBA) contests where intuition suggests Keynes's claim that markets are dominated by unstable and irrational "animal spirits" might hold sway. Indeed, media attention to professional sports often resembles Keynes's "beauty contest." This paper examines whether markets for wagers on these contests exhibit biases that would be observed in markets dominated by such unstable psychological factors.

As a theoretical and practical matter, bookmaking does not differ substantially from brokering stocks, bonds, commodities, or futures contracts. The bookmaker accepts wagers on uncertain events and, in doing so, creates markets for assets that are the bookmaker's promises to pay if particular uncertain events occur; that is, a futures or options contract. The nature of these activities and their strong similarity with activities in financial markets makes sports wagering an interesting phenomenon from an economic perspective.

Bookmaking on basketball games and most other sporting events, of course, is illegal in most political jurisdictions but thrives nonetheless (Reuter and Rubinstein 1982; Merchant 1973). As a consequence of this legal status, economic inquiries into bookmaking have been restricted to types that are legal such as horse and dog racing where pari-mutuel systems are used. Related research includes Losey and Talbott (1980), Figlewski (1979), Snyder (1978), Ali (1977), and Gruen (1976). In addition, there have been a number of purely theoretical studies of markets for wagers, such as Bassett (1981) and Smith (1971).

The first set of authors cited earlier have examined *pari-mutuel* odds wagering where the bookmaker's payout is limited by law to the total amount wagered, less taxes and a brokerage fee known as "breakage." Bassett (1981) has shown the equivalence between odds wagering and point-spread wagering. In "odds" wagering the bookmaker offers to pay a ratio of the amount wagered if an event occurs. In point-spread wagering, bookmakers offer bettors "even-money" odds that a team will win by more than a stated number of points known as the "line" or predicted point spread.

Point-spread wagering is the dominant form of wagering on football and basketball contests and has drawn increasing attention in recent years from the media, in the law enforcement community, and from the organized professional sports leagues, who maintain that the large volume of wagering on their respective contests may damage the leagues. Opponents of sports wagering maintain that it raises the possibility of "fixes," "point shaving," and so on. Others maintain that it heightens interest in the leagues' contests and increases their television ratings and, hence, improves the value of sports franchises.

The lines used in the following analysis come primarily from Nevada casinos but, in some cases in the 1983–84 season, were taken from a newspaper column syndicated by the *New York Daily News*. This differential information set allows us to examine issues similar to those raised by Figlewski's (1979) discussion of the impact of differential information on off-track versus on-track betting on horse races.

An important issue to consider in using casino lines is whether the sums wagered against them are of sufficient magnitude to create strong incentives to make the lines accurate. The sums wagered are indeed significant. In 1983 and 1984, approximately $852 million and $929 million, respectively, were wagered against these lines for all sports in Nevada (*Gaming Business*, 1984 and 1985). It also should be noted that for every dollar wagered legally in Nevada, it is estimated that anywhere from $20 to $300 are wagered illegally outside of the state (Ignatin 1984)!

Football betting undoubtedly accounts for a majority of these sums; however, an exact breakdown by sport is not available. The size of the "handle," or the total amount wagered, in Nevada and nationwide depends upon the event and its national appeal. However, even if basketball wagering is only 10 percent of the total bookmakers' "handle" in Nevada, the amount wagered on these contests nationwide would have easily exceeded $1.7 billion in 1983 and probably amounted to considerably more.[2]

The remainder of this paper comprises three sections. Section II presents a basic theory of bookmaking to formalize "strong" and "semistrong" hypotheses of market efficiency. Section III presents a series of econometric tests of these hypotheses investigating markets for sports wagers in Nevada. Section IV summarizes the empirical findings and examines their implications for theories of market efficiency and the rationality of publicly held expectations. In general, the results cannot refute the EMH, but they do reveal some anomalies in the operations of markets for sports wagers that are similar in nature to findings of other researchers in the fields of sports wagering and financial market analysis.

II. Some Economics of Bookmaking

The outcome of sports contests where point spreads are used is represented in the following by the difference between the respective team's scores.

Hence, for teams h and v (for home and visitor) scoring z_h and z_v, respectively, the spread is simply

$$s = z_v - z_h \qquad (1)$$

Each potential "public" trader, i, forms an expectation of the spread, $\hat{s}_i \ E_i(s)$, based on all available information. Hence, the following model examining the efficiency of markets for wagers is at least a "semistrong" test by Fama's (1970) definition if this information is publicly available. In this case, "all available information" consists of observed spreads from past contests between the two teams, spreads in contests between the two teams and common opponents, as well as other information on teams and players commonly available in the sports sections of major newspapers and other publications. If wagerers have inside information, including possibilities of "fixing" outcomes of NBA games [3] or, possibly, superior ability to predict spreads, the model provides a setting that is very analogous to futures and options markets.

In general, the public's assessment of the relative strengths of the two teams can be aggregated in a probability density function:

$$\int_B^T f(\hat{s}_i)ds \qquad (2)$$

where T and B simply are the highest and lowest expectations of s held by members of the public.

The role of the bookmaker in this market is to set a "line," λ, and accept wagers that the actual spread will be greater or less than λ. Suppose, for example, a trader wagers $\$X$ that the spread is greater than λ. If it turns out that this is the case, the bookmaker returns the wagerer's $\$X$ and pays $\$0.909$ per dollar wagered (i.e., $\$21$ is returned on an $\$11$ wager). Alternatively, if $s < \lambda$ for the wager just described, the bookmaker simply keeps the trader's wager.

The bookmaker can profit from these transactions in two ways. First, by "balancing the books" so that equal amounts are wagered on each side of the line, the bookmaker can keep one-eleventh of losers' wagers (10/11 of the losers' wagers are paid to winners), or one–twenty-second of the total handle. This 4.55 percent is known as "vigorish" and amounts to a brokerage fee. Second, the bookmaker can wager against the public and win (or lose).

From the trader's perspective, the probability of winning the wager is an increasing function of the absolute difference $|\hat{s}_i - \lambda|$. Consequently, the probability that a trader will enter the market also is an increasing function of this absolute difference. Hence, the "handle" (H) can be defined as

Figure 1

$$H = \int_B^T g(|\hat{s}_i - \lambda|) \, ds \tag{3}$$

As an illustration, assume $f(s)$ is unimodal as shown on the upper panel of Figure 1. In this case, $g(|\hat{s}_i - \lambda|)$ will be bimodal.

Applying standard microeconomic analysis, we first assume that the bookmaker seeks to maximize profits. We also assume that the book-maker's costs are relatively constant so that profit maximization for any level of firm output amounts to maximizing the sum of the bookmaker's vigorish and winnings against the public. Because the brokerage fee is not guaranteed, as in pari-mutuel wagering, profit maximization amounts to maximizing the bookmaker's winnings out of the handle.

In setting the line, the bookmaker, in effect, is announcing a price. The bookmaker recognizes both the potential revenues generated on each side of λ, and the bookmaker's own $\hat{s}_b$ relative to λ. For the bookmaker to maximize winnings in the positioning of λ, the bookmaker must formulate some subjective a priori estimate of the probability that the spread will be greater than the line, or $\hat{s}_b > \lambda$. This probability is clearly a function of λ and is represented in the following by $p(\lambda)$.

With these considerations, we can write the mathematical expectation of the bookmaker's expected winnings out of the handle as

$$E(W) = H - \{p(\lambda) \int_\lambda^T g(|\hat{s}_i - \lambda|) \, ds$$

$$+ [1 - p(\lambda)] \int_B^\lambda g(|\hat{s}_i - \lambda|) \, ds\} \tag{4}$$

Evaluating these integrals over the limits, B, λ, and T allows us to define a function $G(-)$, which is assumed to be twice differentiable, and such that

$$H = \int_B^T g(|\hat{s}_i - \lambda|) \, ds = G(|\hat{s}_i - \lambda|)_\lambda^T|$$

$$+ G(|\hat{s}_i - \lambda|)_B^\lambda| = G(T - \lambda) + G(\lambda - B) \tag{5}$$

With these definitions, (4) can be simplified by substituting the right-hand side of (5) into (4) and collecting terms to

$$E(W) = G(T - \lambda)[1 - 10/11 \, p(\lambda)]$$

$$+ G[(\lambda - B)(1/11 + 10/11 \, p(\lambda)] \tag{6}$$

Differentiating (6) with respect to λ yields the bookmaker's first-order conditions for profit maximization with respect to setting the line:

$$\frac{\partial E(W)}{\partial \lambda} = \frac{\partial G(T - \lambda)}{\partial \lambda}[1 - 10/11 \, p(\lambda)] - 10/11 \frac{\partial p(\lambda)}{\partial \lambda} G(T - \lambda)$$

$$+ \frac{\partial G(\lambda - B)}{\partial \lambda}[1/11 + 10/11 \, p(\lambda)] \tag{7}$$

$$+ 10/11 \frac{\partial p(\lambda)}{\partial \lambda} G(\lambda - B) = 0$$

These first-order conditions imply

$$\frac{\partial G(T - \lambda)}{\partial \lambda}[1/11 + 10/11 \, p(\lambda)] + 10/11 \frac{\partial p(\lambda)}{\partial \lambda} G(\lambda - B)$$

$$= 10/11 \frac{\partial p(\lambda)}{\partial \lambda} G(T - \lambda) - \frac{\partial G(T - \lambda)}{\partial \lambda}[1 - 10/11 \, p(\lambda)] \tag{8}$$

which carries the standard implication that marginal revenues (LHS) equal marginal costs (RHS) in equilibrium assuming that the second-order conditions for maximization hold.

As can be seen from (8), the marginal costs and revenues faced by the bookmaker each have two components. On the left-hand side of (8) the marginal revenue obtained from increasing λ is increased wagering at the lower end of the distribution; that is, an increase in $G(\lambda - B)$ because $\partial G(\lambda - B)/\partial \lambda > 0$. This is offset, however, by a decrease in the probability that the spread will be greater than λ, which implies a lower probability that the bookmaker would get to keep $G(\lambda - B)$. On the right-hand side of (8), increases in λ impose the marginal cost of decreases in the wagering at the upper end of the distribution. This cost is offset by the decreasing probability that the bookmaker will have to pay $G(T - \lambda)$.

Further interpretation of these analytics raises a dilemma. On one hand, the bookmaker appears to simply broker between segments of the public with diverse expectations. This, of course, is precisely the role of the investment broker in markets for financial assets. Yet, both kinds of brokers have the opportunity to take net wagering-investment positions in their respective markets. Such cases would arise, however, only if brokers trade on the basis of information not available to the public, or if the public has "irrational" expectations. An indicator of irrational expectations in the Muthian (1961) sense that they are not based on the best reduced form model of the game would be if we observed deviations from the conditions:

$$p(\lambda^*) = 0.5 \quad \text{and} \quad G(\lambda - B) = G(T - \lambda)$$

To pursue the implications of these latter possibilities, consider the consequences if the public's expectations were biased in some manner, for example, in favor of the home team or a popular team like the previous year's champion. In this case, setting the line to "balance the books"—that is, so that $G(T - \lambda) = G(\lambda - B)$, implies $p(\lambda) \neq 0.5$.

Also note that balancing the books is a risk-minimizing strategy for the bookmaker because, if the books are "balanced," the worst the bookmaker can do is win $H/22$ (see Figure 2). On the other hand, if the public's expectations are biased, balancing the books involves forgoing the opportunity of betting against the public and, possibly, winning more than $H/22$. Inspection of the first-order conditions in (8) indicates that a risk-neutral

PUBLIC (nature)

BOOKMAKER'S STRATEGIES	WIN	LOSE
Balance Books	$W = (H / 22)$	$W = (H / 22)$
Wager Against Public	$W < (H / 22)$	$W > (H / 22)$

Figure 2

bookmaker would wager against the public if, on average, the bookmaker's forecast of the spread were more accurate than that of the trader wagering the median dollar.

As can be seen, balancing the books avoids the worst-case situation of betting against the public and losing. Hence, the bookmaker's dilemma is similar to that posed by Newcomb's Problem (Frydman, O'Driscoll, and Schotter 1982) in that two equally valid decision rules disagree. In this case, the analytics are indeterminate and we are left with empirical questions.

In spite of this indeterminacy, these models provide a basis for formalizing several hypotheses on market efficiency and the rationality of public expectations that can be tested empirically. To state these hypotheses, consider the equation to be estimated in Section III:

$$s_j = \alpha + \beta\lambda_j + e_j \qquad (9)$$

where s_j is the observed spread in the jth game, $j = 1, \ldots, J$ games, as defined in (1); λ_j is the line or market forecast of s_j; α and β are regression coefficients to be estimated; and e_j is the regression error term.

If the public's expectations are "rational," in the Muthian (1961) sense that they are based on the best reduced form model of the contest and consequently provide the best ex ante forecast of s_j, the bookmaker's dilemma becomes irrelevant. In this case, $\alpha = 0$, $\beta = 1$, $G(T - \lambda) = G(\lambda - B)$, and the bookmaker's winnings will be $H/22$, or 4.54 percent of the handle.

Alternatively, if the public's expectations display some detectable bias, the bookmaker has the two strategies noted earlier. First, the bookmaker can take a net wagering position against the public by setting λ such that $p(\lambda) = 0.5$. If the bookmaker has better information, then this strategy will lead to observing $\alpha = 0$, $\beta = 1$, $G(T - \lambda) \neq G(\lambda - B)$, and the bookmaker's winnings will be greater than $H/22$.

The third possibility is for the bookmaker to adopt a minimax strategy of balancing the books while the public's expectations are biased. In this event, the estimated values of α and β could diverge from 0 and 1, respectively, according to the nature of the public's bias, and the bookmaker's winnings would still be $H/22$.

However, if this were the case, it would open up opportunities for other "insiders" to trade at the margins to move the line to the hypothesized values and capture wealth transfers from segments of the public with biased expectations. Hence, the first and third hypotheses are distinguishable without extremely detailed information on the market activities of all traders.

The first two hypotheses are distinguishable by the bookmaker's level of winnings, as the forecast accuracy of λ will be the same in either case. If all market participants share the same information and the same reduced form model of the game, α and β will take their hypothesized values. However, this also will be the case if the public's expectations are biased and at least one marginal trader, such as the bookmaker or other market observer-analyst-trader, brings the market into an equilibrium that will transfer wealth in favor of those with superior information or analytical ability. Hence, the second hypothesis can only determine if the public's expectations are biased and if bookmakers win more than 4.54 percent from the public.

The latter is equivalent to a "strong form" of the EMH, whereas the first hypothesis, by comparison, implies that either a "semistrong" or "strong" form of the efficient market hypothesis holds. The first hypothesis could not be rejected if either (1) all members of the public possess the best reduced form model of the game or (2) only some members of the (nonbookmaker) public possess the best reduced form model of the game. In the latter case wealth transfers will occur between members of the public with the bookmaker simply serving as an intermediary broker. This latter case seems somewhat unlikely, however, because common sense suggests that the bookmakers will possess information and a reduced form model of the game as good as anyone's. But, in any event, sports book winnings data provides the basis for a limited "strong-form" test of the EMH.

III. Empirical Evidence

These two principal hypotheses can be tested using data on lines, point spreads, and bookmaker profitability for the 1982–83 and 1983–84 NBA seasons. The major focus of the discussion will be on the 1982–83 season, as the results for the 1983–84 season parallel these. However, results from the latter season are of interest because they can provide evidence on the consistency of results and insight into issues related to differential information.

The results are divided into two parts. The first part consists of estimates of expression (9) for samples of all teams in both seasons, and each individual team in each season for home and away games. Regression results cannot distinguish between the first and second hypotheses, however, because failure to reject the model is consistent with either the "semistrong" or "strong" form. Further, analysis of regression residuals is presented to investigate the normality of regression residuals that would indicate "streakish" behavior against the line. The second part consists of analysis of the winnings of bookmakers that can distinguish between the first and second hypotheses and, hence, constitutes a direct test of the "strong" form of the hypothesis.

Tables 1 and 2 report estimates for expression (9) and the results of an

Table 1
Regression Analysis of Market Forecast (λ)—All Cases

Sample/Statistic	α ($|t|$)	β ($|t|$)	R^2	DW	n
1982–83 Season	0.444 (1.02)	0.948 (0.85)	.232	2.07	810
1983–84 Season	−1.32** (2.58)	0.859* (1.64)	.102	1.87	870

Note: Absolute t-statistic is in parentheses for the tests. $H_0: \alpha = 0$, $H_0: \beta = 1$. A single (double) asterisk indicates significance at the .10 (0.05) level. The notation a indicates that the Durbin-Watson statistic is significant at the .05 (0.01) level.

Table 2
Theil Inequality Coefficient (U) Analysis of Market Forecast (λ)—All Cases

Sample/Statistic	Bias	Dev. Unit	Resid.	Max. Dev.	n
1982–83 Season	.0006	.0009	.9985	.0493	810
1983–Season	.0046	.0030	.9923	.0764	870

Note: A single asterisk under Max. Dev. indicates a significant deviation from nonnormal residuals under the Durbin periodogram test at the .10 level.

analysis of regression residuals, respectively, for all observations available for the 1982–83 and the 1983–84 seasons. The Durbin-Watson statistics suggest the absence of first-order serial correlation in the residuals. The R^2 values are low but the analyses are statistically significant nonetheless. Note that the t-statistics for β shown on Table 1 and in the text provide the test statistic for the hypothesis that $\beta = 1$. It can be determined by inspection that $\beta = 0$, so the equations in Table 1, and the text, are properly specified in that λ_j is a nonrandom predictor of s_j.

Interpretation of the regression analysis on Table 1 and those that follow it estimating (9) can be aided by recalling from (1) that $\lambda = E(z_v - z_h)$. Hence, because $\lambda < 0$ implies that the home team is favored, $\alpha < 0$ implies that the home team should be favored by more than indicated by the line. In other words, $\alpha < 0$ implies that the home team is underrated by the line. The opposite reasoning applies for positive values of the constant, which indicates that the home team is overrated by the line.

Hence, the positive coefficient for the constant in the 1982–83 season indicates that the home team, on average, is overrated. In the 1983–84 season, the estimated constant is significant and indicates that the home team was underrated by an average of 1.32 points. Although this result is interesting for its implications for the EMH, the practical implications of the results are suspect because they may not be particularly useful in wagering on individual contests.

Similar interpretations for deviations from the hypothesized value of β are complicated by whether the team being evaluated is playing at home or away, and on whether it is favored going into the contest by the line. Hence, more detailed analysis generally requires breaking down the sample into smaller subsamples or altering the basic specification provided by (9).

Interpretation of the results of the estimation of the slope coefficient, β, can be aided by reference to Figure 3, illustrating an interpretation of the slope coefficient. The vertical axis represents the observed spread, with the positive values of s indicating the visiting team's winning margin and the negative values the home team's winning margin. The horizontal axis represents the line, λ, with positive values indicating the number of points that the visiting team is favored by, and the negative values indicating the home team's predicted winning margin.

The 45° line indicating $\beta = 1$ bisects the space into a northwestern region where the visiting team beats the line (hence, the home team loses

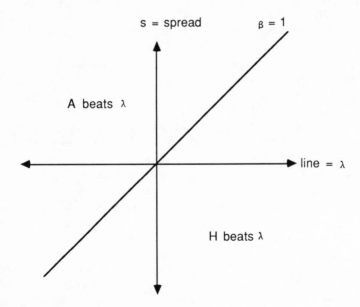

Figure 3. Interpretation of the slope coefficient

against the line), and a southeastern region where the home team beats the line. Note that beating the line has nothing to do with winning the contest because the area bounded above by the $\beta = 1$ line and below by the horizontal axis represents an area where the home team beats the line but loses the game. Similarly, the area above the $\beta = 1$ line and below the horizontal axis represents an area where the away team beats the line but loses the game.

The results shown in Table 1 include all available cases for each respective season. The β coefficients of less than one in Table 1 indicate that when home teams are favored, they tend to be overrated; and when they are underdogs, they tend to be underrated. Hence, against the line, the home-court advantage tends to only work for underdogs. A slope coefficient greater than one, on the other hand, would indicate a strong home team, where it tends to beat the line, but a team that's weak on the road where it tends to lose by more (win by less) than predicted by the line.

Potential differences between home and away performance are explored further later. With respect to the results presented on Table 1, both slope coefficients are less than the hypothesized value but only the coefficient for the 1983–84 is (marginally) significantly different than the hypothesized unit slope at the 0.10 level. This slope coefficient indicates that home teams tended to beat the line when they were favored by fewer points. That is, they tend to lose against the line when they are favored by a relatively large margin against the competition.

In spite of these deviations from hypothesized values, further analysis indicates that the implications of the estimates for the 1983–84 season are generally ambiguous and dependent upon the sample. In short, further analysis is needed to examine details of team, opponent, and home-away specific performance against the line.

The regression results are suggestive, but a more detailed analysis of the residuals would substantiate the adequacy of the model. Although the Durbin-Watson values in Table 1 do not reveal obvious sources of concern, a more detailed analysis of residuals is prudent.

Analyzing the well-known Theil procedure for decomposing the mean squared error of forecasts allows for isolation of the proportion of the MSE of the forecast attributable to two types of systematic error, and to simple "random noise." Table 2 (first three columns) shows these decomposition results for the two pooled samples. Notice that over 99 percent of the MSE is attributable to the residual (i.e., random) component in both cases, with very little evidence that the average value of actual versus predicted spread differed much (i.e., "bias"). In addition, there is little evidence of systematic over- or underestimation of actual point spreads for different magnitudes of spread (i.e., deviation from unit slope).

The foregoing provides strong evidence of market efficiency, yet an even stronger test of randomness based on spectral analysis can search for subtler forms of nonrandomness. The Durbin periodogram test is based on the maximum difference between the periodogram for a purely random process and the observed one. Overall, the analyses in Table 2 (all based on substantial sample sizes) lend even stronger credence to the efficiency implications emerging for these markets. In addition, similar analyses of subsamples (i.e., team data) yield similar results. The Appendix presents the results for sixty-nine subsamples, and none of these cases indicates nonrandomness by the Durbin periodogram test.

Table 3 provides results similar to those presented in Table 1 for the 1982–83 season with games at home and away subsamples for each team. In relatively few cases the estimated coefficients differ from their hypothesized values. Only nine of the ninety-two coefficients shown on Table 3 deviate from these values at the .10 level of significance. Five of these cases involve β coefficients and four of these cases (Boston away, Indiana at home, Portland away, and Washington at home) have slope coefficients less than the hypothesized value. As indicated earlier, an estimated value less than 1.0 suggests that these teams tend to be overrated when they are favored and underrated when they are underdogs.

The one case where the estimated value of β is greater than the hypothesized value (Atlanta away) shows a pattern of beating the line when it was favored but losing when it was the underdog. However, Atlanta was not a strong team in that season and, consequently, was not generally favored in many away games. Hence, the coefficient probably indicates that Atlanta was overrated by the line in the 1982–83 season in contests played away. Note that this conclusion is supported by the negative estimated constant.

This issue can be explored in greater detail by further breaking down the subsamples used in Table 3 by whether the team is the favorite or underdog going into the contest according to the line. Based simply on generalizations about the records of the four teams noted earlier with estimated β coefficients less than unit slope, which would indicate whether these teams generally were favored or underdogs in their subsamples, it would appear that Boston and Portland most likely were overrated by the line. Because Indiana was not a strong team in that season, it is likely that it tended to be an underdog in most contests and, therefore, the findings would indicate that it probably was overrated in home contests. The implications for Washington are more ambiguous and require further analysis.

Three additional factors should be considered in evaluating these results. First, in some cases (e.g., Portland), the implications of the slope and constant terms conflict. Hence, in these cases, the implications drawn from the coefficients are suspect. Also note that, in many cases, coefficients deviate

Table 3
Regression Analysis of Market Forecast (λ)—Home and Away, 1982–83

Sample/Statistic	α ($|t|$)	β ($|t|$)	R^2	DW	n
Atlanta					
HOME	−3.93	1.59	.259	1.57	35
	(1.36)	(1.26)			
AWAY	−2.10	1.97**	.419	2.15	36
	(0.86)	(2.45)			
Boston					
HOME	3.61	0.712	.060	2.04	36
	(0.69)	(0.60)			
AWAY	1.06	0.074*	.001	1.63	33
	(0.44)	(1.92)			
Chicago					
HOME	−0.531	0.914	.114	1.75	36
	(0.25)	(0.20)			
AWAY	3.77	0.673	.060	2.43	33
	(1.00)	(0.71)			
Cleveland					
HOME	−3.55	0.436	.030	1.99	34
	(1.22)	(1.28)			
AWAY	−1.80	0.999	.145	2.44	36
	(0.39)	(0.00)			
Dallas					
HOME	1.75	0.523	.048	2.01	37
	(0.82)	(1.21)			
AWAY	−0.38	0.862	.155	1.52	37
	(0.19)	(0.41)			
Denver					
HOME	−2.97	1.49	.313	2.25	36
	(1.16)	(1.29)			
AWAY	2.05	0.907	.076	2.26	34
	(0.63)	(0.17)			
Detroit					
HOME	0.037	0.531	.056	1.68	36
	(0.02)	(1.25)			
AWAY	−0.882	0.845	.1502	2.09	33
	(0.38)	(0.43)			
Golden State					
HOME	−1.76	0.405	.034	2.64a	35
	(0.94)	(1.57)			
AWAY	4.14	0.428	.025	1.67	36
	(1.14)	(1.24)			
Houston					
HOME	−4.53	0.528	.032	1.75	35
	(1.46)	(0.93)			
AWAY	14.2*	0.145	.001	2.06	35
	(1.81)	(1.25)			

Table 3
(Continued)

Sample/Statistic	α ($|t|$)	β ($|t|$)	R^2	DW	n
Indiana					
HOME	−1.96	0.197**	.001	1.80	35
	(1.18)	(2.33)			
AWAY	4.30	0.511	.061	2.29	34
	(1.35)	(1.39)			
Kansas City					
HOME	2.38	1.04	.151	1.95	36
	(0.92)	(0.09)			
AWAY	0.677	1.02	.275	1.63	33
	(0.34)	(0.07)			
Los Angeles					
HOME	−9.21	1.63	.161	1.80	34
	(1.21)	(0.96)			
AWAY	−0.831	0.606	.047	2.43	40
	(0.32)	(0.88)			
Milwaukee					
HOME	−0.37	1.20	.243	2.22	34
	(0.12)	(0.53)			
AWAY	−0.733	0.827	.146	2.96b	33
	(0.44)	(0.48)			
New Jersey					
HOME	0.904	1.14	.203	2.07	36
	(0.34)	(0.36)			
AWAY	1.01	0.643	.106	2.02	34
	(0.60)	(1.08)			
New York					
HOME	2.81	1.45	.248	2.55	32
	(1.27)	(0.98)			
AWAY	−2.93	0.800	.139	1.73	37
	(1.23)	(0.60)			
Philadelphia					
HOME	1.77	0.946	.093	2.03	37
	(0.325)	(0.11)			
AWAY	0.499	1.24	.250	1.58	38
	(0.22)	(0.67)			
Phoenix					
HOME	2.86	0.761	.102	2.24	36
	(0.91)	(0.62)			
AWAY	−3.28*	1.28	.305	2.15	33
	(1.94)	(0.81)			
Portland					
HOME	2.44	0.658	.083	1.98	38
	(1.28)	(0.94)			
AWAY	4.37*	0.259*	.017	2.78a	31
	(1.69)	(2.01)			

Table 3
(Continued)

Sample/Statistic	α ($|t|$)	β ($|t|$)	R^2	DW	n
San Antonio					
HOME	0.138	1.12	.223	2.24	36
	(0.05)	(0.34)			
AWAY	−1.06	0.593	.073	2.54	35
	(0.60)	(1.11)			
San Diego					
HOME	3.00*	1.02	.214	2.17	34
	(1.75)	(0.06)			
AWAY	0.600	0.971	.170	1.35a	37
	(0.18)	(0.08)			
Seattle					
HOME	1.08	0.820	.117	2.09	40
	(0.36)	(0.49)			
AWAY	−0.411	1.04	.224	1.74	31
	(0.22)	(0.11)			
Utah					
HOME	2.26	1.31	.272	2.22	33
	(1.21)	(0.81)			
AWAY	−2.14	1.36	.209	2.30	36
	(0.48)	(0.80)			
Washington					
HOME	1.26	0.358*	.034	1.48	36
	(1.50)	(1.97)			
AWAY	2.20	0.682	.073	1.94	34
	(0.85)	(0.74)			

Note: Absolute t-statistic is in parentheses for the tests. H_0: $\alpha = 0$, H_0: $\beta = 1$. A single (double) asterisk indicates significance at the .10 (0.05) level. The notation a indicates that the Durbin-Watson statistic is significant at the .05 (.01) level.

in opposite directions in terms of their implications for a team being over- or underrated by the line.

Second, in most cases where significant deviations from the hypothesized values are found, the R^2 value is extremely small. The exception is the equation noted for Atlanta with an R^2 of .419, the highest observed in any subsample. Excluding this case, the highest R^2 observed among the equations noted is .034 for Washington. Hence, in these cases, the equations serve as relatively poor predictors of performance against the line.

Finally, Durbin-Watson statistics and analysis of regression residuals provide another evaluation of market efficiency. Note that in four cases in

Table 3 the Durbin-Watson statistic indicates the presence of first-order serial correlation (Golden State at home, Milwaukee away, Portland away, and San Diego away). These results can be interpreted as indicating significant "streakish" behavior against the line.

Except for the case of San Diego, these cases show negative serial correlation of regression errors. This would suggest an overreaction of the line to short-run changes in performance. This also suggests that tests of significance are biased under these conditions and should be evaluated with caution.

Overall, it seems fair to say that the results indicate that the market is *approximately* efficient, and the EMH is a useful first approximation. There are apparent margins of market forecast error that could have been exploited in the season examined. However, in most cases these biases are ambiguous or weak.

In addition, inspection of Tables 4 and 5, which present similar analyses for the 1983–84 season for all cases (including newspaper lines) and casino lines only, respectively, suggests that the implications of the results favoring inefficiency in the previous tables also are *transitory*. Note that in the regression results in Table 4, five equations produced estimates of β different from the hypothesized value (Atlanta at home, Houston at home and away, Philadelphia away, and San Diego away). Hence, in no case did the bias noted in the previous season carry over to the next.

A comparison of the results presented on Tables 4 and 5 also can be used to investigate an issue similar to that of subjective and differential information examined by Figlewski (1979). That is, the estimated coefficients presented in Table 4 present the results for a sample of all cases for the 1983–84 season whereas Table 5 presents the results for casino lines only. The difference between these samples is that the all-cases sample includes lines from the *New York Daily News* syndicated column, "Latest Line." These newspaper lines differ from those listed in casinos in that they are prepared at least one day in advance of the game and, of course, are not the basis for bookmaking.

A comparison of the results from these tables reveals very little systematic bias. In some cases, like the estimates for Cleveland on Table 5, casino lines are more biased because adding newspaper lines to the sample improves the accuracy of the overall forecast. Similarly, Philadelphia is strongly overrated by both sets of data but including newspaper lines in the sample on Table 4 reduces the bias of the forecast. On the other hand, estimates for Indiana in Table 4 are more biased than those in Table 5, which uses casino lines only, so that, in this case, allowing the public to wager against newspaper lines improves their accuracy. Here, once again, there is very little systematic bias.

Table 4
Regression Analysis of Market Forecast (λ)—All Cases, Home and Away, 1983–84

Sample/Statistic	α ($|t|$)	β ($|t|$)	R^2	DW	n
Atlanta					
HOME	2.07	1.82**	.367	1.52	38
	(1.16)	(2.06)			
AWAY	−5.11	0.518	.032	2.11	38
	(1.64)	(1.02)			
Boston					
HOME	5.91	1.50	.125	2.00	37
	(0.93)	(0.74)			
AWAY	3.89*	0.596	.026	2.22	38
	(1.72)	(0.67)			
Chicago					
HOME	3.19*	1.29	.200	1.29a	37
	(1.86)	(0.67)			
AWAY	−4.91	0.471	.012	2.08	40
	(0.94)	(0.76)			
Cleveland					
HOME	−1.62	0.700	.041	1.69	38
	(0.82)	(0.53)			
AWAY	1.24	1.14	.111	2.02	35
	(0.25)	(0.25)			
Dallas					
HOME	−1.13	1.03	.155	1.82	39
	(0.57)	(0.08)			
AWAY	−3.40	0.415	.015	2.25	36
	(1.08)	(1.02)			
Denver					
HOME	0.354	1.08	.116	1.93	40
	(0.132)	(0.17)			
AWAY	−2.89	0.710	.029	2.20	37
	(0.67)	(0.42)			
Detroit					
HOME	−3.41	0.914	.073	2.23	38
	(0.93)	(0.16)			
AWAY	1.55	1.03	.147	1.47	36
	(0.81)	(0.07)			
Golden State					
HOME	0.059	0.540	.044	2.16	38
	(0.04)	(1.10)			
AWAY	−3.54	0.862	.046	2.36	38
	(0.79)	(0.21)			
Houston					
HOME	−2.47	−0.387**	.010	1.93	38
	(1.09)	(2.15)			
AWAY	−9.75**	−0.334**	.010	2.06	37
	(2.37)	(2.42)			

Table 4
(Continued)

Sample/Statistic	α ($|t|$)	β ($|t|$)	R^2	DW	n
Indiana					
HOME	−0.665	0.824	.099	1.60	39
	(0.45)	(0.43)			
AWAY	−4.86	0.548	.018	2.01	38
	(0.76)	(0.67)			
Kansas City					
HOME	−1.76	0.439	.028	1.85	38
	(0.88)	(1.30)			
AWAY	4.26	1.75	.170	2.12	38
	(1.06)	(1.16)			
Los Angeles					
HOME	−8.16	−0.167	.001	2.00	37
	(1.06)	(1.43)			
AWAY	−0.002	0.710	.043	2.61a	39
	(0.00)	(0.52)			
Milwaukee					
HOME	−1.19	1.21	.143	1.43	39
	(0.34)	(0.43)			
AWAY	0.905	1.004	.080	1.78	39
	(0.427)	(0.01)			
New Jersey					
HOME	−0.857	0.655	.087	2.01	38
	(0.41)	(0.97)			
AWAY	−0.690	0.727	.066	2.22	37
	(0.32)	(0.59)			
New York					
HOME	−5.27	0.478	.015	1.73	37
	(1.25)	(0.81)			
AWAY	0.945	0.505	.019	1.92	37
	(0.47)	(0.82)			
Philadelphia					
HOME	−1.84	0.496	.031	2.29	37
	(0.41)	(1.08)			
AWAY	−0.332	−0.099**	.001	1.77	38
	(0.19)	(2.26)			
Phoenix					
HOME	−0.685	1.46	.125	1.84	37
	(0.17)	(0.70)			
AWAY	−7.00	0.089	.001	1.65	39
	(2.17)	(1.49)			
Portland					
HOME	−10.1*	0.178	.002	2.29	38
	(1.88)	(1.22)			
AWAY	−2.41	0.182	.003	2.27	37
	(1.07)	(1.35)			

Table 4
(Continued)

Sample/Statistic	α ($|t|$)	β ($|t|$)	R^2	DW	n
San Antonio					
HOME	1.41	1.48	.111	2.12	37
	(0.33)	(0.68)			
AWAY	−5.71**	0.253*	.010	1.29a	38
	(2.37)	(1.75)			
San Diego					
HOME	−2.58	0.212	.004	1.96	38
	(1.45)	(1.44)			
AWAY	−12.4**	−0.387**	.010	1.79	38
	(2.33)	(2.11)			
Seattle					
HOME	0.261	1.11	.082	2.20	38
	(0.07)	(0.18)			
AWAY	−4.92	0.406	.010	1.98	38
	(1.53)	(0.88)			
Utah					
HOME	−3.21	0.788	.096	1.92	37
	(1.45)	(0.52)			
AWAY	0.619	0.881	.071	2.03	39
	(0.20)	(0.23)			
Washington					
HOME	0.120	1.22	.114	2.33	37
	(0.05)	(0.38)			
AWAY	−4.80	0.629	.026	2.40	40
	(1.24)	(0.59)			

Note: Absolute t-statistic is in parentheses for the tests. H_0: $\alpha = 0$, H_0: $\beta = 1$. A single (double) asterisk indicates significance at the .10 (0.05) level. The notation a indicates that the Durbin-Watson statistic is significant at the .05 level.

The empirical analysis so far has suggested that the EMH in the "semi-strong" or "strong" form cannot be rejected easily. However, as indicated earlier, the regression results cannot distinguish between the "semistrong" form where public expectations reflect all available information, and the "strong" form of the hypothesis where not even traders with inside information are able to capture above-normal gains. Regression analysis will yield the same results if the public, in aggregate, has expectations based on the true reduced form model of the game, or if there is at least one marginal trader to bring the estimated parameters of the model to the hypothesized values by capturing wealth transfers at the margins.

Table 5
Regression Analysis of Market Forecast (λ)—Home and Away, Casino Lines Only, 1983–84

Sample/Statistic	α ($|t|$)	β ($|t|$)	R^2	DW	n
Atlanta					
HOME	1.80	1.83	.304	1.90	20
	(0.60)	(1.27)			
AWAY	−2.32	0.945	.169	1.50	17
	(0.61)	(0.10)			
Boston					
HOME	6.71	1.62	.075	2.44	22
	(0.55)	(0.49)			
AWAY	3.32	0.098	.0003	1.93	17
	(0.59)	(0.66)			
Chicago					
HOME	4.67**	1.53	.433	2.33	19
	(2.47)	(1.25)			
AWAY	−13.01*	−0.807*	.034	2.51	19
	(1.72)	(1.74)			
Cleveland					
HOME	−2.99	−0.942**	.073	2.33	18
	(1.03)	(2.32)			
AWAY	3.69	1.28	.159	2.25	24
	(0.64)	(0.45)			
Dallas					
HOME	2.09	1.67	.285	2.28	21
	(0.62)	(1.11)			
AWAY	−3.95	0.268	.0062	1.83	21
	(0.90)	(0.94)			
Denver					
HOME	2.80	1.19	.134	1.98	20
	(0.76)	(0.27)			
AWAY	−0.394	1.17	.039	2.13	20
	(0.40)	(0.13)			
Detroit					
HOME	0.016	1.25	.136	1.61	21
	(0.003)	(0.35)			
AWAY	1.99	1.12	.253	2.63	17
	(0.91)	(0.24)			
Golden State					
HOME	−0.712	0.545	.057	2.39	22
	(0.35)	(0.92)			
AWAY	8.04	2.93	.263	2.52	15
	(0.81)	(1.42)			
Houston					
HOME	−1.87	−1.01**	.059	1.65	22
	(0.61)	(2.23)			
AWAY	9.12	2.35	.190	1.76	18
	(1.03)	(1.12)			

Table 5
(Continued)

Sample/Statistic	α ($|t|$)	β ($|t|$)	R^2	DW	n
Indiana					
HOME	1.34 (0.59)	0.473 (0.76)	.024	1.94	21
AWAY	−2.11 (0.18)	0.579 (0.32)	.014	1.67	16
Kansas City					
HOME	−0.295 (0.09)	0.739 (0.36)	.061	1.44	18
AWAY	5.81 (1.11)	1.82 (1.00)	.176	1.83	25
Los Angeles					
HOME	−9.89 (1.04)	−0.421 (1.38)	.010	1.86	19
AWAY	1.49 (0.94)	1.12 (0.25)	.238	2.24	19
Milwaukee					
HOME	−2.15 (0.54)	0.790 (0.39)	.102	1.74	21
AWAY	5.17 (1.49)	1.96 (1.06)	.216	1.81	19
New Jersey					
HOME	−0.130 (0.04)	0.538 (0.80)	.052	2.06	18
AWAY	−0.690 (0.27)	0.238 (1.38)	.009	2.22	22
New York					
HOME	−13.15* (1.98)	−0.658 (1.54)	.024	2.27	17
AWAY	6.17 (1.57)	1.42 (0.45)	.135	2.53	17
Philadelphia					
HOME	−4.01 (0.49)	0.261 (0.73)	.003	2.64	22
AWAY	−3.21 (0.93)	−0.897** (2.21)	.077	1.98	15
Phoenix					
HOME	−3.61 (0.59)	0.924 (0.08)	.055	1.73	20
AWAY	−5.41 (0.93)	0.205 (0.84)	.003	1.37	20

Table 5
(Continued)

Sample/Statistic	α ($|t|$)	β ($|t|$)	R^2	DW	n
Portland					
HOME	−2.23**	1.19	.052	2.21	21
	(2.11)	(0.16)			
AWAY	−4.95	0.081	.001	0.973a	15
	(1.59)	(1.22)			
San Antonio					
HOME	8.41	2.85*	.353	1.42	18
	(1.29)	(1.92)			
AWAY	−4.20	0.404	.018	1.27a	25
	(1.06)	(0.95)			
San Diego					
HOME	−1.08	0.559	.038	1.47	18
	(0.40)	(0.63)			
AWAY	−16.02**	−0.647**	.050	2.43	22
	(3.12)	(2.62)			
Seattle					
HOME	2.30	1.87	.308	2.08	22
	(0.62)	(1.39)			
AWAY	−7.76*	−0.494	.019	1.74	17
	(1.82)	(1.61)			
Utah					
HOME	−12.26**	−0.331	.018	1.68	12
	(2.45)	(1.70)			
AWAY	−1.31	0.687	.050	1.48	24
	(0.31)	(0.49)			
Washington					
HOME	2.56	0.936	.085	3.08a	17
	(0.67)	(0.08)			
AWAY	−3.02	0.702	.033	2.11	25
	(0.60)	(0.38)			

Note: Absolute t-statistic is in parentheses for the test. $H_0: \alpha = 0$, $H_0: \beta = 1$. A single (double) asterisk indicates significance at the .10 (0.05) level. The notation a indicates that the Durbin-Watson statistic is significant at the .05 level.

Hence, to distinguish between the "strong" and the "semistrong" forms of the EMH winnings, data on potential inside traders must determine whether bookmakers are able to win more than 4.54 percent of the handle or whether wagerers are able to win significantly more than −4.54 percent. Analysis of the efficiency of basketball lines suffers from the same problems as analyses of stock and bond markets, in that there are no data on individual trader-wagerer performance against the market-line.

Table 6
Quarterly Nevada Casino Sports Book Handle and Winnings 1975–83
(in thousands of dollars)

Quarter Ending	Handle	Win	%
3/31/75	4,452	44	0.9sb
6/30/75	3,415	271	7.9
9/30/75	7,407	594	8.0
12/31/75	23,935	1,700	7.1f
3/31/76	10,886	6	0.1sb
6/30/76	12,414	101	0.8
9/30/76	22,106	886	4.0
12/31/76	46,583	1,728	3.7f
3/31/77	13,485	713	5.3sb
6/30/77	17,387	558	3.2
9/30/77	26,479	1,045	3.9
12/31/77	70,372	3,988	5.7f
3/31/78	30,951	−236	−0.8sb
6/30/78	25,832	556	2.2
9/30/78	49,568	3,789	7.6
12/31/78	96,913	4,544	4.7f
3/30/79	49,301	−9,717	−19.7sb
6/30/79	32,663	702	2.1
9/30/79	71,418	3,755	5.3
12/31/79	120,227	7,398	6.2f
3/31/80	56,556	255	0.5sb
6/30/80	44,766	715	1.6
9/30/80	73,456	2,373	3.2
12/31/80	141,672	6,340	4.5f
3/31/81	75,394	−2,248	−3.0sb
6/30/81	69,253	−709	1.0
9/30/81	66,979	3,951	5.9
12/31/81	147,487	11,293	7.7f
3/31/82	98,575	−2,834	−2.9sb
6/30/82	73,002	1,493	2.0
9/30/82	87,002	3,780	4.3
12/31/82	156,587	5,138	3.3f
3/31/83	150,086	−556	−0.4sb
6/30/83	118,435	2,670	2.3
9/30/83	148,792	5,091	3.4
12/31/83	268,889	12,094	4.5f
Mean			2.6%
Standard Error			4.8%

Note: The notation f indicates football season; sb indicates NFL Superbowl
Source: Nevada State Gaming Control Board, *Gross Gaming Revenue Reports*.

In our case, however, we have data on the handle and winnings of Nevada sports books, presented in Table 6, which shows the actual winnings of one significant set of inside traders, bookmakers. Table 6 presents Nevada sports book handle, winnings, and winnings as a percent of the handle for the period 1975 to 1983.

These data suggest that the "strong" form of the hypothesis cannot be rejected with these data. Percentage winnings of bookmakers are not significantly different from either $H/22 = 4.54$ percent, or, for that matter, from zero. Hence, the hypothesis that bookmakers capture wealth transfers is suspect for a much more persuasive reason. Not only are there few potential marginal gains indicated by regression analyses that inside traders like bookmakers could take advantage of, Table 6 indicates that Nevada sports book winnings are not significantly different than zero.

Another interesting point that can be made with respect to Table 6 concerns the seasonal pattern of winnings. Note that basketball wagering occurs primarily in the first and second quarters of the year. However, the major event that generates a large handle for bookmakers in this period is the National Football League's Superbowl. From the seasonal pattern showing low sports book winnings in the first quarter following relatively high winnings in the fourth quarter, during the football season, it appears that bookmakers tend to lose either on the Superbowl, or on basketball wagering, or both.

In short, the results of our empirical analyses suggest two interesting points. First, as noted earlier, the market appears to be approximately efficient. Deviations from hypothesized values in the sample are fairly rare. Further, whatever implications that may be drawn from the results in favor of market inefficiency appear to be transitory. Second, it does not appear that legal Nevada bookmaking is a highly profitable venture, although this observation requires some qualification. Although bookmakers have only held out 2.6 percent of the handle, this may represent a tremendous return on investment for the fixed capital and costs of maintaining the book from the standpoint of a casino. In addition, these winnings against the public are understated by any possible illegal activity. In any event, the results cannot refute the hypothesis that these futures markets are efficient.

IV.   Conclusions

The results of the analyses just described provide a useful, if unconventional, test of efficient markets and rational expectations hypotheses on market behavior. The results cannot refute the Muthian hypothesis that expectations formulated by the public are based on the true reduced form model of the game. Because the evidence shows that, in aggregate, these expectations are unbiased and inside traders (i.e., bookmakers) do not earn above normal winnings, the results provide strong evidence of the efficient utilization of information by the market.

One aspect of these findings that should be qualified concerns the role of bookmakers as inside traders and the quality of information available on their winnings. First, as noted earlier, there may be other subsets of the public who are also inside traders in the sense that they have made greater investments in obtaining and analyzing available information. Our analysis cannot refute the existence of such traders and the possibility that they earn above-normal winnings because we have no data on this subset of traders, as we do for bookmakers in Nevada. However, we can point out that the analysis of lines and spreads yields very little additional information that would be useful to these traders. Therefore, if such traders do exist, the information they use must be either more detailed or more idiosyncratic than the methods and data used here.

Another aspect of the analysis that requires qualification concerns the nature of the data on sports book winnings. Winnings data will be affected by most known forms of illegal "skimming" activities, wherein actual winnings are diverted or losses increased. Although such activities have been known to occur in legal sports books, for these activities to affect our test involving these data, they would have to be extremely widespread, or involve very large amounts of money per book, or both.

For these activities to affect the mean win for the industry shown in Table 6 to the point of affecting our analysis, sports book skimming alone would have to amount to more than $29 million annually (based on 1983 and 1984 handles). We suppose that anything is possible, but this level of skimming out of one casino department would be extremely difficult to sustain without being detected in a closely audited regulatory environment. Our doubt is increased by the casual observation that most detected skimming does not involve sports book departments.

Finally, although our findings generally are supportive of the conventional wisdom that markets are efficient, we cannot reject other explanations of market behavior out of hand. Some of the earlier evidence could be viewed as supportive of the views expressed by Keynes noted at the outset, that financial markets are dominated by unstable psychological factors; that is, the "animal spirits" of investors. There are some indications that professional basketball (and, perhaps, all sports) conforms to some degree to the "beauty contest" model offered by Keynes. For example, in the 1983–84 season, the previous season's champion, Philadelphia, lost fairly consistently against the line in the first half of the season; that is, it was strongly overrated. However, in the second half of the season, Philadelphia played fairly even against the line.

More generally, cases noted earlier where deviations from hypothesized values occurred, usually involved either the best or worst teams in the league. Hence, in spite of the generally accurate forecasts provided by the line, the "beauty contest" characterization does have some credibility in these cases.

Appendix: Analyses of Regression Residuals

This appendix presents results of analyses of regression residuals from the equations estimated in Tables 3–5 in Tables A1 to A3, respectively. The discussion of Table 2, concerning the Theil inequality coefficient and the Durbin periodogram tests describes the contents of these tables. In addition, Table A4 presents a tabulation of the results for the purpose of explanation.

Table A1 provides analyses of residuals of the regressions shown in Table 3, for all cases, home and away, for the 1982–83 season. Table A2 presents the results for the regressions in Table 4, for all cases (including newspaper lines), home and away, for the 1983–84 season. Table A3

Table A1
Theil Inequality Coefficient (U) Analysis of Market Forecast (λ)—
Home and Away, 1982–83

Sample/Statistic	Bias	Dev. Unit	Resid.	Max. Dev.	n
Atlanta					
HOME	.0122	.0457	.9241	.1693	35
AWAY	.0224	.1455	.8321	.1420	36
Boston					
HOME	.0039	.0103	.9858	.1177	36
AWAY	.1284	.0926	.7790	.2255	33
Chicago					
HOME	.0023	.0011	.9965	.1428	36
AWAY	.0173	.0146	.9681	.1935	35
Cleveland					
HOME	.0031	.0484	.9484	.1517	34
AWAY	.0361	.0000	.9639	.2055	36
Dallas					
HOME	.0019	.0403	.9578	.1331	37
AWAY	.0090	.0046	.9864	.2899	37
Denver					
HOME	.0020	.0473	.9507	.1514	36
AWAY	.0133	.0009	.9859	.1387	34
Detroit					
HOME	.0376	.0421	.9203	.2090	36
AWAY	.0257	.0058	.9685	.1283	33
Golden State					
HOME	.0510	.0661	.8829	.1980	35
AWAY	.0006	.0430	.9564	.1486	36

Table A1
(Continued)

Sample/Statistic	Bias	Dev. Unit	Resid.	Max. Dev.	n
Houston					
HOME	.0429	.0247	.9323	.1704	35
AWAY	.1009	.0383	.8609	.1405	37
Indiana					
HOME	.0255	.1375	.8370	.0798	35
AWAY	.0022	.0564	.9414	.1726	34
Kansas City					
HOME	.0390	.0003	.9607	.1017	36
AWAY	.0066	.0002	.9932	.2037	33
Los Angeles					
HOME	.0344	.0266	.9390	.2084	34
AWAY	.0080	.0200	.9721	.1770	40
Milwaukee					
HOME	.0104	.0087	.9809	.1926	34
AWAY	.0061	.0073	.9866	.3155	33
New Jersey					
HOME	.0264	.0036	.9700	.1072	36
AWAY	.0015	.0353	.9632	.1735	34
New York					
HOME	.0940	.0279	.8782	.1767	32
AWAY	.1380	.0086	.8534	.1822	37
Philadelphia					
HOME	.0117	.0003	.9880	.0957	37
AWAY	.0057	.0119	.9824	.7522	38
Phoenix					
HOME	.0152	.0109	.9739	.1541	36
AWAY	.0909	.0185	.8906	.1146	33
Portland					
HOME	.0018	.1219	.8764	.2557	31
AWAY	.0232	.0232	.9536	.1251	38
San Antonio					
HOME	.0129	.0032	.9839	.0891	36
AWAY	.0422	.0341	.9237	.2199	35
San Diego					
HOME	.0930	.0001	.9069	.2436	34
AWAY	.0014	.0002	.9985	.2346	37
Seattle					
HOME	.0001	.0063	.9936	.1192	40
AWAY	.0017	.0005	.9978	.2261	31
Utah					
HOME	.0313	.0200	.9487	.0516	33
AWAY	.0085	.0177	.9738	.1375	36
Washington					
HOME	.0115	.1011	.8874	.2290	36
AWAY	.0068	.0166	.9766	.0826	34

Table A2
Theil Inequality Coefficient (U) Analysis of Market Forecast (λ)—All Cases, Home and Away, 1983–84

Sample/Statistic	Bias	Dev. Unit	Resid.	Max. Dev.	n
Atlanta					
HOME	.0065	.1044	.8891	.1886	38
AWAY	.0510	.0265	.9225	.1231	38
Boston					
HOME	.0195	.0154	.9652	.0682	37
AWAY	.0745	.0113	.9142	.1170	38
Chicago					
HOME	.0785	.0115	.9100	.3134	37
AWAY	.0091	.0148	.9760	.1279	40
Cleveland					
HOME	.0192	.0077	.9731	.2135	38
AWAY	.0000	.0019	.9981	.1492	35
Dallas					
HOME	.0309	.0001	.9690	.0854	39
AWAY	.0053	.0293	.9654	.1428	36
Denver					
HOME	.0000	.0007	.9993	.0824	40
AWAY	.0118	.0049	.9833	.0811	37
Detroit					
HOME	.0529	.0007	.9464	.1296	38
AWAY	.0277	.0001	.9726	.2657	36
Golden State					
HOME	.0258	.0315	.9427	.1073	38
AWAY	.0523	.0011	.9465	.0992	38
Houston					
HOME	.0116	.1124	.8759	.0907	38
AWAY	.0058	.1421	.8520	.2309	37
Indiana					
HOME	.0085	.0049	.9865	.2531	39
AWAY	.0053	.0121	.9826	.0836	38
Kansas City					
HOME	.0001	.0448	.9551	.1165	38
AWAY	.0000	.0359	.9641	.1128	38
Los Angeles					
HOME	.0370	.0530	.9100	.1657	37
AWAY	.0019	.0074	.9908	.2217	39
Milwaukee					
HOME	.0410	.0048	.9542	.2644	39
AWAY	.0065	.0000	.9935	.1767	39
New Jersey					
HOME	.0127	.0253	.9619	.0774	38
AWAY	.0009	.0099	.9892	.1119	37
New York					
HOME	.0346	.0176	.9478	.1804	37
AWAY	.0380	.0179	.9442	.0902	37

Table A2
(Continued)

Sample/Statistic	Bias	Dev. Unit	Resid.	Max. Dev.	n
Philadelphia					
HOME	.0492	.0304	.9203	.1233	37
AWAY	.0145	.1227	.8629	.1064	38
Phoenix					
HOME	.0639	.0132	.9229	.1984	37
AWAY	.0664	.0526	.8810	.2069	39
Portland					
HOME	.0907	.0357	.8736	.0935	38
AWAY	.0040	.0492	.9468	.1249	37
San Antonio					
HOME	.0068	.0127	.9804	.1839	37
AWAY	.0618	.0730	.8652	.3452	38
San Diego					
HOME	.0314	.0525	.9162	.1366	38
AWAY	.0290	.1069	.8641	.1563	38
Seattle					
HOME	.0010	.0009	.9981	.1268	38
AWAY	.0530	.0198	.9272	.1523	38
Utah					
HOME	.0556	.0072	.9372	.1400	37
AWAY	.0127	.0014	.9859	.0486	39
Washington					
HOME	.0028	.0041	.9931	.2303	37
AWAY	.0574	.0085	.9340	.1812	40

Table A3
Theil Inequality Coefficient (U) Analysis of Market Forecast (λ)—
Home and Away, Casino Lines Only, 1983–84

Sample/Statistic	Bias	Dev. Unit	Resid.	Max. Dev.	n
Atlanta					
HOME	.0116	.0818	.9066	.0756	20
AWAY	.0419	.0007	.9574	.2882	17
Boston					
HOME	.0063	.2606	.9822	.1998	22
AWAY	.0005	.0283	.9711	.7135	17
Chicago					
HOME	.2105	.0664	.7231	.1237	19
AWAY	.0036	.1505	.8458	.1222	19
Cleveland					
HOME	.0174	.2468	.7357	.1685	18
AWAY	.0286	.0086	.9628	.1556	24
Dallas					
HOME	.0257	.5850	.9159	.1706	21
AWAY	.0025	.0441	.9534	.1070	21

Table A3
(Continued)

Sample/Statistic	Bias	Dev. Unit	Resid.	Max. Dev.	n
Denver					
HOME	.0350	.0038	.9612	.1868	20
AWAY	.0105	.0009	.9887	.1915	20
Detroit					
HOME	.0217	.0063	.9720	.2479	21
AWAY	.0503	.0037	.9460	.2561	17
Golden State					
HOME	.0076	.0400	.9524	.1788	22
AWAY	.1725	.1111	.7164	.2134	15
Houston					
HOME	.0026	.1990	.7983	.1861	22
AWAY	.0014	.0716	.9270	.0633	18
Indiana					
HOME	.0096	.0289	.9615	.1285	21
AWAY	.0167	.0072	.9761	.1560	16
Kansas City					
HOME	.0035	.0081	.9884	.2087	18
AWAY	.0098	.0412	.9490	.1964	25
Los Angeles					
HOME	.0344	.0972	.8684	.1284	19
AWAY	.0606	.0034	.9360	.2178	19
Milwaukee					
HOME	.0077	.0079	.9844	.1580	21
AWAY	.0589	.0582	.8828	.2249	19
New Jersey					
HOME	.1212	.0339	.8449	.1718	18
AWAY	.0318	.0839	.8843	.1298	22
New York					
HOME	.0884	.1247	.7868	.1756	17
AWAY	.1726	.0110	.8164	.1367	17
Philadelphia					
HOME	.0315	.0251	.9434	.2450	22
AWAY	.1177	.2405	.6417	.1382	15
Phoenix					
HOME	.0692	.0004	.9304	.1784	20
AWAY	.0191	.0372	.9437	.2688	20
Portland					
HOME	.0609	.1464	.7927	.1367	21
AWAY	.0780	.0940	.8279	.2905	15
San Antonio					
HOME	.0716	.1732	.7551	.3045	18
AWAY	.0099	.0370	.9532	.3762	25
San Diego					
HOME	.0038	.0241	.9720	.1849	18
AWAY	.1361	.2205	.6434	.1357	22
Seattle					
HOME	.0577	.0829	.8594	.1488	22
AWAY	.0429	.1407	.8164	.0821	17

Table A3
(Continued)

Sample/Statistic	Bias	Dev. Unit	Resid.	Max. Dev.	n
Utah					
HOME	.1978	.1792	.6229	.476	12
AWAY	.0029	.0107	.9864	.2995	24
Washington					
HOME	.0767	.0004	.9229	.3708	17
AWAY	.0138	.0061	.9801	.0851	25

presents analyses of residuals from Table 5, for casino lines only, home and away, for the same season.

As noted earlier, none of the regressions from any of the equations presented yielded residuals that proved nonnormal using the Durbin periodogram test. Other equations, run during the course of the research, using different aggregation schemes, however, did yield values that could be rejected. These cases were encountered for samples combining home and away games, which provides a better aggregation scheme for testing for "streakish" behavior against the line.

As for the results of the Theil inequality coefficient analyses, the analyses provide additional information on the forecast bias of the line and serial correlation. The maximum bias component of the Theil inequality coefficient is 0.2105 for Chicago, at home, in Table A3 (casino lines only, 1983–84). Including this case, there are only seven cases in which the bias component of the Theil inequality coefficient (first column) is greater than 0.1.

To the extent that these analyses provide any indication of nonnormality, they tend to reinforce the theme of the effects of "unstable psychological factors" on the market noted in the concluding remarks. Of the seven cases summarized in Table A4, all but one (New York in the 1982–83 season), tended toward the top or bottom third of the league in terms of their overall records and final standings in the league.

Notes

1.   Sheffrin (1983) provides a summary of many of these studies.
2.   In addition, the results from Nevada casino lines must be consistent with illegal lines that can be obtained elsewhere. Otherwise, it would be possible to arbitrage between bookmakers, or what is known as "play the middle" in the vernacular of sports betting and which is similar to a

Table A4
Most Biased Forecasts

Season (Table)	Team	Bias	Record	Overall Standing
1982–83				
(A.1)	Chicago	0.1284	28–54	19
	Houston	0.1009	14–68	23
	New York	0.1380	44–38	12
1983–84				
(A.3)	Chicago	0.2105	27–55	22
	New York	0.1726	47–35	7
	San Diego	0.1361	30–52	19
	Utah	0.1978	45–37	8–9

"straddle" position in a commodities futures market. Playing the middle involves betting against a team where it is favored by more points and for it where it is favored by fewer points and, thereby, possibly win on both bets if the spread falls between the two lines. Or, if the spread is outside of the "middle," the bettor's wagers cancel. The possibility of "getting middled" provides further incentives to bookmakers to set an accurate line and, more to the point, not move it once it is set.

3.   Briefly, the reason we heavily discount the possibility of "fixing" NBA games has to do with the salary levels in the league. To assure a "fix" one would have to bribe or threaten a player who plays a majority of the game and, therefore, probably earns in excess of $500,000 per year and, possibly, more than $1 million. The size of the bribe required to induce this player to forgo this salary for the rest of his career if caught therefore would be very large. This, in turn, would require that an extremely large amount of money be bet on the game in question to cover the bribe and make a profit—possibly $10–20 million. It is very unlikely that any bookmaker would take such a large bet and, if one attempted to break up the bet into a more reasonable size of, say, $1000, the logistics of 10,000 to 20,000 bets between the time the line is posted (usually the morning or afternoon of the game in professional basketball) and game time would be prohibitive. Further, the level of activity on a single game clearly would be noticed by bookmakers and probably would lead them to call off all bets on the game. In the two years of gathering the data used here, two games were inexplicably scratched off the board. However, in both cases, the action was explained by an injury to a key player. Hence, although we recognize that "fixes" are not impossible to arrange, especially if threats rather than bribes are used, they are very unlikely, and therefore, the lines used here are probably not substantially affected by this kind of activity.

References

Ali, Mulchtar. 1977. "Probability and Utility Estimates for Racetrack Bettors." *Journal of Political Economy* 85 (August): 803–16.

Bassett, Gilbert W., Jr. 1981. "Point Spreads versus Odds." *Journal of Political Economy* 89 (August): 758–68.

Cargill, Thomas F., and Gordon C. Rausser. 1975. "Temporal Price Behavior in Commodity Futures Markets." *Journal of Finance* 30 (September): 1043–53.

Cootner, Paul. 1967. "Speculation and Hedging." *Food Research Institute Studies* 7 (June): 201–13.

Fama, Eugene F. 1970. "Efficient Capital Markets: A Review of Theory and Empirical Work." *Journal of Finance* 25:383–423.

Figlewski, Stephen. 1979. "Subjective Information and Market Efficiency in a Betting Market." *Journal of Political Economy* 87:75–88.

Frydman, Roman, Gerald P. O'Driscoll, Jr., and Andrew Schotter. 1982. "Rational Expectations of Government Policy: An Application of Newcomb's Problem." *Southern Economic Journal* 49 (October): 311–19.

Gruen, Arthur. 1976. "An Inquiry into the Economics of Race-Track Gambling." *Journal of Political Economy* 84 (1976): 1969–77.

Ignatin, George. 1984. "Sports Betting." *The Annals* 474 (July): 168–77.

Keynes, John M. 1964. *The General Theory of Employment, Interest, and Money.* New York: Harcourt, Brace, and World.

Losey, Robert L., and John C. Talbott, Jr. 1980. "Back on the Track with the Efficient Market Hypothesis." *Journal of Finance* 35 (September): 1029–43.

Merchant, Larry. 1973. *The National Football Lottery.* New York: Holt, Rinehart and Winston.

Muth, John F. 1961. "Rational Expectations and the Theory of Price Movements." *Econometrica* 29:315–35.

Nevada Gaming Control Commission. 1984. *Race Book and Sports Pool Summary* (May).

Reuter, Peter, and Jonathon Rubinstein. 1982. *Illegal Gambling in New York: A Case Study in the Operation, Structure, and Regulation of an Illegal Market.* U.S. Department of Justice, National Institute of Justice. Washington, D.C.: U.S. Government Printing Office, April.

Samuelson, Paul. 1965. "Proof that Properly Anticipated Prices Fluctuate Randomly." *Industrial Management Review* 6 (Spring): 41–49.

Sargent, Thomas J., and Neil Wallace. 1965. " 'Rational' Expectations, the Optimal Monetary Instrument, and the Optimal Money Supply Rule." *Journal of Political Economy* 83 (April): 241–54.

Schiller, Robert J. 1978. "The Use of Volatility Measures in Assessing Market Efficiency." *Journal of Finance* 36:291–304.

Sheffrin, Steven M. 1983. *Rational Expectations.* London: Cambridge University Press.

Smith, Vernon L. 1971. "Economic Theory of Wager Markets." *Western Economic Journal* 9 (September): 242–55.

Snyder, Wayne W. 1978. "Horse Racing: Testing the Efficient Market Model."
    Journal of Finance 33 (September): 1109–18.
Stevenson, Richard A., and Robert M. Bear. 1970. "Commodity Futures: Trends
    or Random Walks?" *Journal of Finance* 25 (March): 65–81.
Working, H. 1934. "A Random-Difference Series for Use in the Analysis of
    Time Series." *Journal of the American Statistical Association* 29
    (March): 11–24.

VII Sports and Labor Economics

Kenneth Lehn

Information Asymmetries in Baseball's Free Agent Market

During the past generation, economists have shown considerable interest in the operation of markets characterized by an asymmetric distribution of information among traders.[1] Normative inquiries into this subject generally have focused on the allocative effects of asymmetric information between buyers and sellers. Typically, these studies have posited the existence of inefficiencies when the allocation of resources diverges from that which would result if information was distributed uniformly among market participants. Positive inquiries in this area explicitly have recognized information costs as the source of these asymmetries. Instead of comparing actual market outcomes with outcomes in a world of costless information, these studies have investigated the extent to which information asymmetries can explain the existence of otherwise anomalous institutions.

Among the many studies in this area, few have been empirical.[2] In large part, this results from the scarcity of cases in which simultaneously the conditions for a natural experiment exist and the necessary data are available. As a result, little is known empirically about the effect of asymmetric information on the operation of markets.

One case which lends itself to empirical investigation is major league baseball's re-entry market, more commonly referred to as the free agent market. Prior to 1976, major league clubs had an exclusive and transferable right to renew the contracts of players on their rosters. Prompted by an arbitration ruling which declared this "reserve system" illegal, the major league players' association and the club owners entered into a collective bargaining agreement in 1976 which granted players the right to become free agents after six years of major league service. At the end of the 1976 season, then, players who were eligible to become free agents either signed new contracts, usually guaranteed multiyear contracts, with the club for which they had played in 1970, or they became free agents and signed contracts with new clubs. In each subsequent year, a new crop of players has become eligible to exercise their free agency option. They, too, either have signed new contracts with the clubs for which they had been playing, or they have become free agents and signed contracts with new clubs.

The abruptness with which the market for player services changed in 1976, combined with the way in which it changed, allows examination of issues related to the literature on information asymmetries. One issue concerns the extent to which information regarding a player's expected performance is distributed asymmetrically among clubs. Presumably, the club for which a player has performed has more information with which to estimate the player's future performance than do clubs that have not employed the player. This information may pertain to the player's ability, motivation, health, and so forth. If such an asymmetry exists, then, on average, the expected performance of free agents will be lower than the expected performance of eligible players who do not become free agents. Consequently, it is of interest to compare the post-contract performance of free agents with the post-contract performance of eligible players who sign contracts with the clubs for which they had been playing.

Empirical Evidence on Disability

To examine this issue empirically, contract data and performance data have been collected for 155 major league players.[3] These players represent all players who (a) were on the opening day roster of a major league club in 1980, (b) were free agents or would have been eligible to become free agents in the next free agent market, had they not signed a contract with the club for which they had been playing, and (c) had signed guaranteed contracts which were at least three years in length. To test for the existence of information asymmetries in the free agent market, an experiment is conducted on two groups of players—players who exercised their free agency option and eligible players who signed contracts with the clubs for which they had been playing.

Elsewhere, it has been shown that among free agents and players eligible to become free agents guaranteed multiyear player contracts have supplanted the traditional one-year player contracts which prevailed during the reserve system.[4] Evidence has been presented which strongly suggests that this contractual change, in large part, accounts for a 33 percent increase in the overall disability rate among major league players during the four seasons immediately following the creation of free agency.[5] Regarding a player's expected disability, the club for which a player has been playing is likely to have two types of information about the player which other clubs do not have.

One type of information concerns the player's motivation. Assuming that player disability is, in part, a function of the player's behavior, it is expected that guaranteed multiyear contracts increase the likelihood of player disability. In the sporting press, players and club physicians frequently cite the relationship between conditioning and disability. For example, one player, commenting on a specific conditioning program, stated that "Gus's program has had an enormous effect on my career. . . . His program has . . . allowed me to escape serious injury and has allowed me to perform even when I have been injured. Commitment to his program is something that requires hard work and dedication."[6] Since guaranteed multiyear contracts insure the players' income against future disability, these contracts (relative to one-year contracts) reduce the costs of disability that are borne by the players. If conditioning is not costless to the players, and if monitoring the players' condition is not costless to clubs, then a direct relationship between guaranteed multiyear contracts and player disability is expected. Furthermore, players with guaranteed multiyear contracts are more likely to reveal injuries than other players and they are less likely to rehabilitate as quickly as other players.

Ex ante, clubs do not have perfect information regarding the incentive effect of guaranteed multiyear contracts on individual players. Commenting on this, player Pete Rose stated that, "The main thing is knowing your player. Some players will give their best efforts every day whether signed to a one-year contract or a 100-year contract. Others don't."[7] In effect, the club for which a player has performed is likely to have "inside information" regarding this element of a player's makeup. If so, this asymmetry increases the difference between what a player expects to earn as a free agent and what he could earn by signing a contract with the club for which he has been playing, resulting in a self-selection of players into the free-agent market who are more likely to experience disability than their counterparts who sign contracts with the clubs for which they had been playing.

A second type of information asymmetry which is relevant here concerns information about the player's health. Independent of an incentive effect, there should be a self-selection of players into the free-agent market who are likely to experience higher disability rates in the future because of the way they have been worked in the past, or because of a physical problem which is difficult for other clubs to monitor. In this study, this type of information asymmetry is empirically indistinguishable from asymmetries in information about a player's motivation. Both types of asymmetries, however, suggest that the post-contract increase in disability will be greater among free agents who sign guaranteed multiyear contracts than it will among players who sign guaranteed multiyear contracts with the clubs for which they had been playing.

Table 1 presents evidence which is consistent with this hypothesis. For the 155 players in the sample, the total number of days spent on the disabled list was calculated in the three seasons before and in all seasons after signing their contracts. The average number of days spent on the disabled

Table I
Pre-Contract Disability, Post-Contract Disability, and Percentage Change in Disability for 155 Players

Group of Players	N	Average Age	Pre-Contract Disability	Post-Contract Disability	Percentage Change in Disability
All players	155	30.82	4.73	12.55	165.40
Not free agents	99	30.89	4.76	9.68	103.36
Free agents	56	30.68	4.67	17.23	268.95

Source: Contract data received from Major League Baseball Player Relations Committee, Inc.

Table 2
Pre-Contract Disability, Post-Contract Disability, and Percentage Change in Disability for 58 Pitchers and 97 Nonpitchers

Group of Players	N	Pre-Contract Disability	Post-Contract Disability	Percentage Change in Disability
Pitchers				
Not free agents	33	3.66	9.57	166.94
Free agents	25	5.12	28.07	448.24
Nonpitchers				
Not free agents	66	5.30	9.74	83.77
Free agents	31	4.31	9.83	128.08

Source: Contract data received from Major League Baseball Player Relations Committee, Inc.

list per man-season was then calculated for the three seasons before, and all seasons after signing these contracts. Among players who signed contracts with the club for which they had been playing, this average increased from 4.76 before signing the contract to 9.68 after signing the contract, an increase of 103.36 percent. Among free agents, the corresponding average increased from 4.67 to 17.23, an increase of 268.95 percent. For both sets of players the post-contract increase in disability is statistically significant at the 0.05 level.[8] The difference in post-contract disability between the two groups of players is also statistically significant at the 0.05 level.[9]

Disaggregating the figures by player position reveals that the difference in the increase in post-contract disability between free agents and non-free agents is almost exclusively a pitcher's phenomenon. Table 2 shows that among pitchers, average disability increased from 3.66 days to 9.57 days for non-free agents, an increase of 166.94 percent. For free agent pitchers, however, this average increased from 5.12 to 28.07, an increase of 448.24 percent. Among nonpitchers, average disability increased from 5.30 days to 9.74 days, an increase of 83.77 percent, for non-free agents. For free agents, the corresponding increase was from 4.31 days to 9.83 days, a 128.08 percent increase.

Empirical Evidence on Playing Performance

It also is of interest to compare the post-contract change in playing performance of free agents with the post-contract change in playing performance of eligible players who were not free agents. Elsewhere, it has been shown that for pitchers, innings pitched and runs earned are significant determinants of players' salaries.[10] It has also been shown that at bats, slugging average, and stolen bases are significant determinants of nonpitchers' salaries. Accordingly, these performance statistics will be used for purposes of the comparison.

Table 3 lists the average number of innings pitched and average earned run average in the pre-contract and post-contract period for free agent

Table 3
Pre-Contract Playing Performance, Post-Contract Playing Performance, and Percentage Change in Playing Performance for 58 Pitchers

	Pitchers		
Group of Pitchers	Pre-Contract Innings Pitched	Post-Contract Innings Pitched	Percentage Change in Post-Contract Innings Pitched
Not free agents	187.49	174.96	−6.69
Free agents	162.95	137.02	−15.92

Group of Pitchers	Pre-Contract Earned Run Avg.	Post-Contract Earned Run Avg.	Percentage Change in Post-Contract Earned Run Avg.
Not free agents	3.28	3.57	8.84
Free agents	3.47	3.70	6.63

Source: Contract data received from Major League Baseball Player Relations Committee, Inc.

Table 4
Pre-Contract Playing Performance, Post-Contract Playing Performance and Percentage Change in Playing Performance for 97 Nonpitchers

Group of Players	Pre-Contract at Bats	Post-Contract at Bats	Percentage Change in Post-Contract at Bats
Not free agents	454.82	407.92	−10.31
Free agents	408.90	379.78	−7.12

Group of Players	Pre-Contract Slugging Avg.	Post-Contract Slugging Avg.	Percentage Change in Post-Contract Slugging Avg.
Not free agents	.419	.422	.071
Free agents	.411	.413	.048

Group of Players	Pre-Contract Stolen Bases	Post-Contract Stolen Bases	Percentage Change in Post-Contract Stolen Bases
Not free agents	10.28	6.95	−31.39
Free agents	10.04	6.21	−38.15

Source: Contract data received from Major League Baseball Player Relations Committee, Inc.

pitchers and eligible pitchers who were not free agents. The percentage decrease in innings pitched was more than twice as large for the former group than it was for the latter group. In part, this result is accounted for by the greater amount of time spent on the disabled list by free agent pitchers. The earned run average of both sets of pitchers increased after signing guaranteed multiyear contracts. Contrary to the prediction here, this increase was slightly smaller among free agents than it was among eligible pitchers who signed contracts with the clubs for which they had been pitching.

Table 4 contains similar numbers for nonpitchers. As was found with the disability statistics, no significant difference exists in the change in post-contract performance between free agents and eligible players who were not free agents. Both sets of nonpitchers experienced a decline in post-contract at bats; this decline was slightly larger among non-free agents than among free agents. Both sets of players experienced a small and approximately equal increase in post-contract slugging average. Average stolen bases declined by 38.15 percent for free agents and 32.39 percent for non-free agents.

Summary

This paper has argued that there are theoretical grounds for believing that information regarding the expected performance of free-agent players is distributed asymmetrically between clubs which have employed the players and other clubs. Evidence has been presented which shows that the post-contract increase in disability is significantly higher among free-agent pitchers who sign guaranteed multiyear contracts than it is among eligible pitchers who have not become free agents.

In equilibrium, it is expected that clubs participating in the free-agent market will discount these informational asymmetries. Rather than viewing the period under observation as a period in which clubs were bidding "irrationally" for free agents, this period can be viewed as a period in which clubs, and players, were obtaining information about participation in a new market. Prior to 1976, a free-agent market had not existed. As participants in this market gather information, it is expected that they will adjust their behavior in future periods. Evidence of this phenomenon in baseball's free-agent market is found in Tables 5 and 6. The data in these tables show a downward trend in the number of five-year contracts received by free agents during the past few years.[11] Of particular note is that no free-agent pitcher has received a five-year contract since 1980. While these data

Table 5
Number of Players Signing 5-Year Contracts 1977–1982

	All Players		
Year	Number of Players Signing 5-Year Contracts	Number of Free Agents Signing 5-Year Contracts	Number of Other Players Signing 5-Year Contracts
1977	30	10	20
1978	16	7	9
1979	21	6	15
1980	27	7	20
1981	29	5	24
1982	14	1	13

Source: "Who Got 5-Year Contracts," *The Sporting News*, March 20, 1982.

Table 6
Number of Pitchers and Nonpitchers Signing 5-Year Contracts, 1977–1982

Year	Pitchers		
	Number of Pitchers Signing 5-Year Contracts	Number of Free Agent Pitchers Signing 5-Year Contracts	Number of Other Pitchers Signing 5-Year Contracts
1977	9	4	5
1978	6	3	3
1979	6	2	4
1980	10	5	5
1981	6	0	6
1982	4	0	4

Year	Nonpitchers		
	Number of Nonpitchers Signing 5-Year Contracts	Number of Free Agent Nonpitchers Signing 5-Year Contracts	Number of Other Nonpitchers Signing 5-Year Contracts
1977	21	6	15
1978	10	4	6
1979	15	4	11
1980	17	2	15
1981	23	5	18
1982	10	1	9

Source: "Who Got 5-Year Contracts," *The Sporting News*, March 20, 1982.

are not conclusive, they do suggest that over time clubs have become less enthusiastic about participating in the free agent market.

Notes

Generous financial support for this study was provided by the Washington University School of Business, the Center for the Study of American Business and the H. B. Earhart Foundation. Proprietary contract data used in this study were provided by the Major League Baseball Player Relations Committee. Helpful comments were received from Alexandra Benham, Lee Benham, Harold Demsetz, Nicholas Dopuch, C. Raymond Grebey, William Marshall, Lyn Pankoff, Laura Starks, Robert Virgil, Barry Weingast, and Jess Yawitz.

1. For a review of this literature, see Hirshleifer and Riley (1979).
2. For a recent empirical study, see Bond (1982).
3. Contract data were obtained from the Major League Baseball Player Relations Committee for all players on the opening day roster of a major league club in 1980.
4. See Lehn (1982).
5. Ibid.
6. Quote attributed to Bob Boone in Hoefling (1981).
7. *The Sporting News,* May 23, 1981.
8. A t-statistic was calculated to test the statistical significance of the difference in the average number of days spent on the disabled list before signing the contract and this average after signing the contract. The t-statistics corresponding to the difference in these means is 2.6 (with 519 degrees of freedom) for non-free agents and 3.8 (with 304 degrees of freedom) for free agents.
9. The t-statistic corresponding to the difference in post-contract disability for the two groups is 2.1 (with 361 degrees of freedom).
10. See Lehn (1981).
11. Similar data were not available on the recent trend in three-year contracts received by free agents.

References

Bond, Eric. 1982. "A Direct Test of the Lemons' Model: The Market for Used Pickup Trucks." *American Economics Review* 72 (September): 836–40.

Hirshleifer, Jack, and John G. Riley. 1979. "The Analytics of Uncertainty and Information—An Expository Survey." *Journal of Economic Literature* 17 (December): 1375–1421.

Hoefling, Gus. 1981. *Championship Conditioning Programs.*

Lehn, Kenneth. 1981. "Property Rights, Contracts and Player Performance in Major League Baseball." Ph.D. dissertation, Washington University.

———. 1982. "Property Rights, Risk Sharing and Player Disability in Major League Baseball." *Journal of Law and Economics* 25 (October): 343–66.

The Sporting News, May 23, 1981, March 20, 1982.

David N. Laband and Bernard F. Lentz

Family Traditions in Professional Baseball: An Economic Interpretation

The greatest influence in my life has been my father. He had the most effect in shaping my career and attitudes.

—Roy Smalley III

I. Introduction

In 1981, at least 18 active major league baseball players were the sons of former major league baseball players. A number of other players had fathers who played minor league baseball but never broke into the major leagues. American League Player of the Year honors for 1983 went to Cal Ripken, Jr., of the Baltimore Orioles, whose dad, Cal, Sr., was a former minor leaguer and then manager of the team. Many more former and current professional players and coaches have sons who now play in the farm systems of the major league teams.

Although it is impossible to track down all of the fathers of current major league players who played in the minor leagues, we can estimate the percentage of major league players in 1980 whose fathers were major or minor league players (Table 1).

In 1979, 1,147 players spent all or part of the season with at least one major league ball club. Forty-seven of these men were sons of former major league baseball players, as identified in *The Baseball Encyclopedia* (Reichler 1979). Throughout the history of baseball, there have been roughly 15.7 times as many minor league players as those who made it to the major leagues (188,000 versus 12,000).[1] If we assume that ratio to hold for sons and their fathers, then an additional 15.7 times 47 = 738 players would be the sons of minor leaguers. Altogether, this means that as many as 785 out of 1,147 major league players may have followed in their fathers' footsteps.

In this paper we present an economic theory of occupational following among professional baseball players. We argue that sons are beneficiaries of an exceedingly valuable human capital transfer from their fathers, which motivates them to voluntarily choose baseball as their own career. In Section II we discuss the role played by human capital transfers in motivating sons of professional baseball players to subsequently compete in their fa-

Table I
Estimating the Percentage of Major League Ballplayers
Whose Fathers Played Baseball in the Majors or Minors

Total major league players	12,000
Total minor league players (excludes players who moved to the majors)	188,000
Ratio of minor leaguers to major leaguers	15.7
Total major league players— 1980	1,147
Number of sons of former major league players	47
Number of sons (estimated) of former minor league players (15.7 × 47)	738
Percentage of players who are sons of major or minor league players	785/1147 = 68.4%

Source: The Sporting News, *Official 1981 Baseball Register*; J. Reichler, ed., *The Baseball Encyclopedia* (1979).

thers' sport and provide a Beckerian model of the father's transfer calculus. This leads us to investigate, in Section III, the impact of such human capital transfers on the career success of second-generation ballplayers compared to that of first-generation ballplayers. Our findings suggest that there are no significant differences between first- and second-generation baseball players, in terms of career performance, *once they receive a professional contract*. On the other hand, followers are more likely than nonfollowers to acquire major league–caliber playing skills, and we find that the *real* advantage to following is reflected in the initial entry figures: Second-generation ballplayers are *fifty times* more likely to make it to the big leagues than are first-generation players. Concluding comments are offered in Section IV.

II.   Like Father, Like Son: A Legacy of Baseball

Many factors influence a youngster's decision to play baseball (or any sport). Exposure to the stars and associated role-model formation, genetics, and skill acquisition all are important elements in the process. Ignoring the reasons why a youngster, particularly the son of a former baseball star, first becomes interested in baseball, the question of interest is, What factors determine how successful he will be as a player? This leads us immediately to address the issue of the importance of nonhuman capital transfers versus the importance of learned skills.

The Role of Genetics

There can be no doubt that good "breeding" is as important in the formation of pro-caliber baseball players as in horseracing. Professional athletes pass along physical characteristics that may enable their children to become excellent athletes, too. Speed, visual acuity, reflexes, agility—all these physical traits may form part of the legacy inherited by the son of a former standout ballplayer.

However, as we have demonstrated elsewhere (Laband and Lentz 1983a, 1983b), the transfer of physical capital, alone, is not the determining factor with respect to why the recipient-son subsequently follows in his father's occupational footsteps. Transferred human capital may augment considerably the value of physical capital (characteristics) inherited by sons of former professional baseball players, raising the expected net return from following in their fathers' footsteps.

The Pressure to Succeed

A second legacy inherited by sons who follow in their sportstar fathers' footsteps is name recognition by fans and other intimates of the game. Fans, other players, sportscasters, even coaches, at every level of competition, make performance comparisons between father and son. Almost without fail, junior will be taunted along the way for not being as good as his father. Moreover, he will probably hear, more than once, that he will *never* be as good as his father was.

The additional pressure this comparison puts on sons of former standout sports figures can make it only more difficult for them to achieve the kind of success realized by their famous fathers. If and when the son learns how to cope with it, however, that pressure can change from being a liability to an asset. One of the things that every professional athlete must learn to conquer (i.e., deal with efficiently, in the economic sense) is pressure. The earlier he or she learns how to cope with it, the better. Thus, sons who follow in their fathers' footsteps, by being exposed to heavy pressure early on in their own careers, may develop the means to shrug off or otherwise deal efficiently with the pressure-cooker environment of professional sports competition. In an indirect fashion, this ultimately will permit them to perform at a consistently higher level than most of their peers.

Given the intensity of the competition *and* the added pressure on the son who follows, it is remarkable that so many sons of former baseball greats make it to the major leagues. A good case can be made for the importance of human capital transfers in (a) motivating sons to follow in their fathers' baseball tradition, and (b) the apparent success of second-generation ballplayers.

Human Capital Skills

Fathers who make it to the major leagues, especially if they are good enough to last for a few years, pick up a lot of tips about how to be a better ballplayer. These tricks of the trade might involve anything from batting stance and fielding tips to how to pace yourself during the 162-game season. These tips, available to sons at a young age, are a valuable addition to his baseball lore. The earlier in his career a player learns these vital aspects of his chosen sport the greater is his opportunity to understand their potential significance and refine his own abilities. He can work on a throwing or batting style until it becomes an almost unconscious action. Other players may not pick up some of these tips until they reach college or even later. Then they struggle to master these new skills. Sons of former players acquire major league training right from the beginning. Continual practice and refinement of these skills while growing up makes them accomplished and fluid performers.

Two issues are of critical importance to understanding the relationship between human capital transfers and occupational following in baseball (or in any occupation). First, the informational aspect of the game of baseball is apparent. Skills required for success in baseball are learned, by and large, rather than inherited. Coaches value highly a player who has a good mental grasp of the sport in which he or she participates, including all of its complexities, because such knowledge implies better performance from that individual, ceteris paribus, than from a player who does not have as complete a mental grasp of the sport. Different sets of circumstances require different responses from the athletes. A one-out, bases-loaded hit to the first baseman, for example, elicits a different response from the first and second basemen (not to mention all of the baserunners) than does a two-out, bases-loaded hit to the same spot. This savvy, or knowledge of the game, is difficult to come by; it is specific human capital, and one must invest in its acquisition.

Second, the nature of his father's occupation is such that the son has access to it from an early age. By virtue of their heritage, sons of ex-professionals almost always grow up surrounded by their father's sport. Retired players become scouts or coaches for college or professional teams. Junior is allowed to tag along to spring training, summer camps, and free-agent try-out camps. His father probably socializes with his colleagues—coaches, players, and former teammates. The son can get into the games, the practices, even the locker rooms.[2]

The practical effect of growing up in the environment that surrounds his father's chosen sport is to provide the son with access to a wealth of information about the sport. He grows up surrounded by sporting aficionados—players, coaches, fans, scouts, reporters, broadcasters, and, of course, his father. From these various sources, the son "absorbs" tidbits of knowledge about the game played by his father. This is the real advantage of growing up with baseball (or whatever sport) "in the blood." As a by-product of such growing up, a son is able to learn many general and specific aspects of the game. Once he has decided upon a specific position to play, his access to pro-caliber players, on a one-to-one basis, serves as a superb means of obtaining useful playing tips from some of the (by definition) premier performers in the world.

On the other hand, sons of plumbers, engineers, and all non-baseball-oriented workers find it much more costly to obtain the same quality education in the game of baseball. They must pay to attend summer camps. Quality of instruction in junior leagues and in high school or college is probably lower than the quality education that sons of professionals are able to obtain. Moreover, the followers pick up pro-caliber playing tips at such an early age that they have years to refine their abilities, whereas first-generation players probably do not learn comparable tips until years later.

Children who follow in their athlete-father's footsteps thus have a two-fold advantage over sons of electricians, engineers, and economists. First, the son who grows up in a world peopled by members of his father's sport, in general, has a longer and more intimate acquaintance with that sport, by age eighteen, than does the average boy. Second, the *quality* of information and instruction he acquires is likely to be much higher than the quality of information acquired by a nonfollower, ceteris paribus. Because the son of a former baseball great acquires this career-specific human capital at such an early age, at such relatively low cost to himself, anticipated returns from choosing his father's career as his own may well be higher than they would be from choosing any other occupation, for which he would have to undergo several years of formal education or training, with all of the implied out-of-pocket and opportunity costs.

The Formal Model

There has been a tendency to treat intergenerational transfers of human capital as bequests from parents to children (Ishikawa 1975; Becker and Tomes 1976; and Tomes 1981). Using this type of model, we can, following Becker (1962), characterize the individual, in this case a father with no son, as attempting to maximize the net discounted present value of his earnings (W). Let z represent the number of years that the individual invests in his own formal schooling (or other human capital acquisition). C_t is the annual, out-of-pocket cost of training, and Y_{nt} is his annual opportunity wage. If he makes the investment (I), he works for $T - z$ years and receives annual earnings of Y_{It}:

$$W = \int_0^z (-Y_{nt} - C_t)e^{-rt}\, dt + \int_z^T (Y_{It} - Y_{nt})e^{-rt}\, dt \tag{1}$$

The father of a son who follows in his father's occupational footsteps is assumed to maximize the net present discounted value of the earnings of both himself and his son (W_F). For $E - z$ years, the father is able to earn Y_{It} per year. From E to $E + z$ he is personally transmitting career-specific human capital to his son. When that transfer is complete, he again starts earning Y_{It} until he retires (year T). As he invests time (from E to $E + z$) in transferring human capital to his son, he forgoes some portion (α) of his earnings. During this same time period, the son forgoes earnings of $Y_{n(t-E)}$ per year and incurs a direct cost of acquiring that information which is a fraction (β) per year *less* than the cost of formal schooling. For the rest of his working life, $\tau - (E + z)$, the son earns $Y_{I(t-E)}$ per year.

$$
\begin{aligned}
W_F = {} & \int_0^z (-Y_{nt} - C_t)e^{-rt}\, dt + \int_z^E (Y_{It} - Y_{nt})e^{-rt}\, dt \\
& + \int_E^{E+z} [(1 - \alpha)Y_{nt}]e^{-rt}\, dt + \int_{E+z}^T (Y_{It} - Y_{nt})e^{-rt}\, dt \\
& + \int_E^{E+z} [-Y_{n(t-E)} - (1 - \beta)C_{t-E}]e^{-rt}\, dt \\
& + \int_{E+z}^\tau [Y_{I(t-E)} - Y_{n(t-E)}]e^{-rt}\, dt
\end{aligned} \tag{2}
$$

The father of a son who follows, but receives an indirect (i.e., formal schooling) transfer of human capital, or whose son does not follow, also attempts to maximize the net present value of both his own and his son's earnings (W_{NF}):

$$
\begin{aligned}
W_{NF} = {} & \int_0^z (-Y_{nt} - C_t)e^{-rt}\, dt + \int_z^T (Y_{It} - Y_{nt})e^{-rt}\, dt \\
& + \int_E^{E+k} [Y_{n(t-E)}]e^{-rt}\, dt + \int_{E+k}^{E+k+z} [-Y_{n(t-E)} - C_{(t-E-k)}]e^{-rt}\, dt \\
& + \int_{E+k+z}^\tau [Y_{I(t-E-k)} - Y_{n(t-E)}]e^{-rt}\, dt
\end{aligned} \tag{3}
$$

The son begins formal acquisition of human capital skills k years after the recipient of direct transfers begins his acquisition. He pays full cost for the education and forgoes income while getting schooling. After his formal training is completed, he earns $Y_{l(t-E)}$ annually for $[(\tau - (E + k + z)]$ years.

Removing elements common to (2) and (3) yields

Follower:

$$
\int_{E}^{E+z} [-Y_{n(t-E)} - (1 - \beta)C_{(t-E)}]e^{-rt}\, dt
$$
$$
+ \int_{E+z}^{E+z+k} [Y_{l(t-E)} - Y_{n(t-E)}]e^{rt}\, dt
$$
$$
+ \int_{E+z+k}^{\tau} [Y_{l(t-E)}]e^{-rt}\, dt \tag{2'}
$$
$$
+ \int_{E}^{E+z} (-\alpha Y_{lt})e^{-rt}\, dt
$$

Nonfollower:

$$
\int_{E}^{E+k} Y_{n(t-E)}e^{-rt}\, dt + \int_{E+k}^{E+z+k} [-Y_{n(t-E)} - C_{(t-E-k)}]e^{-rt}\, dt
$$
$$
+ \int_{E+z+k}^{\tau} Y_{l(t-E-k)}e^{-rt}\, dt \tag{3'}
$$

The first term of (2') represents the follower-son's opportunity and direct costs of training under his father. The second term is the present value of earnings while he is out of training but the nonfollower is still in training (from $E + z$ to $E + z + k$). The third term is the present value of his earnings for the rest of his life: With normal age or experience income patterns this will exceed $Y_{l(t-E-k)}$, the nonfollower's income, at least in the early first half of his career. The final term is the present value of the father's time spent training his son.

For equation (3') the first term represents the nonfollowing son's after-school and summer earnings while the follower is training and before he (the nonfollower) starts school. The second term represents the opportunity and direct costs of schooling for the son, noting that *his* opportunity earnings will likely exceed those of a follower while the follower is in training, because the nonfollower has k years of market experience. The final term is the son's earnings over the rest of his career. Note that when the nonfollower starts his career, the follower already has k years of experience and, hence, is more likely to have a higher income.

As k approaches zero, that is, when followers and nonfollowers begin acquisition of their career-specific human capital at the same age, the father's decision to train his son directly depends on whether $(2') - (3')$ is greater or less than zero. At $k = 0$ the father faces

$$\int_{E}^{E+z} \beta C_{t-E}\, e^{-rt}\, dt + \int_{E}^{E+z} -\alpha Y_{It}\, e^{-rt}\, dt \gtreqless 0 \qquad (4)$$

where the first term represents the present value of the cost-savings of training his son directly, and the second term is the present value of lost earnings suffered by the father during the training period. Direct transfer of human capital from father to son occurs when (4) is strictly greater than zero.

Not surprisingly, α and β are crucial elements in the decision to undertake direct transfers of human capital; α is the proportion of current earnings forgone by the father during the transfer period. It is affected by the degree of interface between the home and the workplace, technological characteristics of the occupation engaged in, and the marginal tax rate on Y_{It}. The term β represents the proportion of costs that are saved by acquiring the career-specific human capital directly as opposed to indirectly. The β will depend upon the degree to which a son gets along with his father, the father's knowledge of his son's abilities, and so on.

No more explicit evidence of the importance of the father's role in this process can be found than in the frequency with which sons end up playing the *exact same* position on the field as their fathers before them. Of the 121 second-generation major league players listed in *The Baseball Encyclopedia* (Reichler 1979), over 38 percent (46/121) played the exact same position as their fathers. Furthermore, an additional 17 percent (21/121) played positions that were closely related to the positions played by their fathers. For example, the father might have played shortstop whereas the son plays third base; sons who become catchers can learn a lot about how to help out their pitchers from their pitcher-fathers. All in all, nearly six out of every ten sons of former players who made it to the major leagues did so in a position in which they could gain valuable tips from their fathers.

III.   Career Success of Followers

We turn our attention now to the question of performance of followers versus nonfollowers. The theory presented in the previous section implies that second-generation baseball players might be significantly better on-field performers than first-generation players. Interestingly enough, player statistics across several dimensions of baseball "performance" reveal no such differences between the two groups for major league ballplayers in 1980, see Table 2.

Table 2
Statistics of First and Second Generation Players

	First Generation	Second Generation
Infielders:		
Batting average	.254	.254
Fielding average	.966	.966
Games played	572	529
Age when first in major league	22.64	22.31
Outfielders:		
Batting average	.255	.263
Fielding average	.979	.981
Games played	597	956
Age when first in major league	22.27	23.50
Catchers:		
Batting average	.228	.252
Fielding average	.979	.986
Games played	462	370
Age when first in major league	22.31	22.58
Pitchers:		
Earned run average	4.13	3.81
Age when first in major league	21.84	22.00

Source: The Sporting News, *Official 1981 Baseball Register*; Reichler, *The Baseball Encyclopedia* (1979).

Defensively, there is virtually no difference between the two groups. Fielding averages for infielders, outfielders, and catchers are the same for sons of former players and for their nonfollower peers. Among the catchers, followers appear to have a slightly higher batting average than nonfollowers. Other than that difference, batting averages are remarkably similar between the two groups. There also is relatively little difference in the age at which a player first breaks in with a major league team. On the whole, pitchers break in at a younger (average) age than players in the other three categories. Among outfielders, sons of former players hit the big leagues a full year *later,* on average, than did their nonfollower colleagues. Otherwise, there is no appreciable difference between the two groups. Second-generation pitchers have a slightly lower earned run average than first generation pitchers, but the difference is not great. There is some variability in the number of games played. The average second-generation outfielder plays over 350 games more than a first-generation outfielder—over two full seasons' worth of games. Of course, this category includes Carl Yazstremski, who is pulling up the average for followers. If you exclude Yaz, the average number of games played is pretty close among the outfielders. First-generation players seem to have the edge in games played by catchers and infielders, although the differences are far fewer than among the outfielders.

It may be that follower-nonfollower differences are most observable at point-of-entry (age 18) among major league players. Accordingly, we analyzed several categories of offensive and defensive playing statistics for minor league catchers in 1980. The data were available from *The Official 1981 Baseball Register,* an annual publication of *The Sporting News.* Table 3 reports results of ordinary least squares regression (OLS) of several player characteristics on batting average (offensive) and fielding average (defensive). Across both categories, the estimations reported show a positive, but statistically insignificant impact of following on one's playing statistics. We note that college attendance exerts a strong, positive influence on both the offensive and defensive categories, and that number of games played has a positive impact on fielding average of catchers. Both regressions cover only catchers in their first year of professional baseball, to control for experience effects. A number of additional regressions were estimated but are not reported here. The dependent variables analyzed included: at bats, runs, hits, triples, doubles, RBI's, put-outs, assists, and errors. Across all of these estimations, the *FATHER* coefficient signed in at the expected (positive) direction, but lacks statistical significance. Because number of games played was a strong determinant of fielding average, we looked at the impact of following on games played and again found no significant differences between the two groups of players. Finally, we looked at the influence of following on level of minor league entry. With level of entry weighted by the probability of breaking in at each level (at initial entry), we again found a strong impact of college attendance, but a statistically insignificant follower impact.[3]

The performance comparisons analyzed up to this point both suffer from a sample selectivity problem that mitigates against our finding statistically significant differences between first- and second-generation ballplayers. We have argued that, at age 17 or 18, sons of former baseball greats, *on average,* are better ballplayers than players without a family tradition in baseball. However, examination of the playing performance of minor or major league players constitutes an analysis at the margin, because (presumably) all potential pro prospects have been selected via the draft. The unsuccessful component of all aspiring baseball players has been omitted from the sample.

Table 3
OLS Regression Results for Minor League Catchers in Their First Year, 1980
(t-statistics in parentheses)

| Variable | Betas | |
	Batting Average	Fielding Average
Constant	215.24	793.15
	(13.66)[a]	(21.20)[a]
GAMES PLAYED	0.124	1.74
	(0.47)	(2.80)[a]
ATTENDED COLLEGE	55.59	81.25
	(3.94)[a]	(2.42)[b]
COLLEGE GRAD	−14.49	16.14
	(−0.60)	(0.28)
FATHER PLAYED	14.53	51.01
	(0.64)	(0.95)
	N = 125	N = 125
	R^2 = .130	R^2 = .128
	SE = 73.25	SE = 173.93

[a]Significant at .01 level.
[b]Significant at .05 level.

The real, measurable advantage of following shows up in terms of the probability of making it to the big leagues in the first place. By providing their sons with a valuable, baseball education, fathers pave the way for their sons to compete at the highest level. Given the intensity of the competition facing youngsters who try to break into the pro ranks, the mere fact that we observe so many sons of former players is indicative of the value of the transferred human capital. Followers who make it up to the top are not better players than the nonfollowers who make it up; on the other hand, second-generation players have a much higher probability of breaking into the cartel. This type of comparison (of the probability of breaking into the big leagues) does not suffer from the sample selectivity problem noted earlier and permits us to evaluate the relative performance of the *average* first-generation player versus the *average* second-generation player.

Table 4 details the appropriate chi-square test of the probability of a player making it to the major leagues, given that he is either the son of a former major leaguer or a first-generation player. There were 47 second-generation major leaguers playing in 1980 and 1,100 first-generation players. The 1980 *Census of Population* records 29,073,447 men between the

Table 4
Chi-Square Statistic for the Probability of Making It
to the Major Leagues in 1980

	Father in Major Leagues	Father Never in Major Leagues
Son in major league	47	1,100
Son not in major league	23,953	29,048,347
Total	24,000	29,049,447

Probability that son of a former major leaguer makes it to majors is derived as 47/24,000 = .0019583.
Probability that son of a non-major leaguer makes it to majors is derived as 1,100/29,049,447 = .0000379.
The chi-square test that the former exceeds the latter is $\chi^2 = 2193.48$

ages of 20 and 34, the prime baseball-playing years. If each of the 12,000 former major leaguers (up to 1980) had two sons playing ball in 1980, an obvious exaggeration, but one that works against our finding of differences, some of $24,000 - 47 = 23,953$ individuals would be sons of former players who did not make it to the major leagues. Thus, the probability of a second-generation player making it to the majors equals $47/24,000 = .0019583$, whereas the probability of a first generation player breaking into the big leagues is only $1100/29,049,447 = .0000379$. The chi-square test that the former is greater than the latter is statistically significant at better than the .01 level ($\chi^2 = 2193.48$).

IV.   Concluding Comments

In this paper we have proposed an economic theory of occupational following among professional baseball players, based on a Beckerian model of human capital transfers within the family. The high observed incidence of family traditions in baseball is motivated in part, we argue, by low-cost (to the son) transfers of career-related human capital from father to son. The degree of access of the son to his father's workplace is a primary factor in the cost difference between the follower and the nonfollower, in acquiring a baseball education. The value of the transferred human capital is revealed dramatically by two comparisons: the probability that a player will make it to the major leagues and the degree to which sons follow exactly into their fathers' playing positions. Our findings suggest that second-generation players are roughly fifty times more likely to break into the major leagues than first-generation players, and that nearly 60 percent of second-generation players follow into their father's playing position, or into a closely related one.

Notes

We are indebted to Cal Ripken, Jr., for valuable insights and encouragement. Remaining errors, of course, are our own responsibility.
1. Vass 1982, 5. The 12,000 figure is from *The Baseball Encyclopedia;* the 188,000 figure was supplied by the Baseball Hall of Fame via telephone conversation.
2. Pete Rose's son was clearly visible in the dugout with his famous father during the 1983 World Series between Baltimore and Philadelphia.
3. These results are available upon request.

References

Becker, G. S. 1962. "Investment in Human Capital: A Theoretical Analysis." *Journal of Political Economy* 70 (October): 9–49.

Becker, G. S., and N. Tomes. 1976. "Child Endowments and the Quantity and Quality of Children." *Journal of Political Economy* 84 (August): 5143–62.

Ishikawa, T. 1975. "Family Structures and Family Values in the Theory of Income Distribution." *Journal of Political Economy* 83 (October): 987–1008.

Laband, D. N., and B. F. Lentz. 1983a. "Like Father, Like Son: Toward an Economic Theory of Occupational Following." *Southern Economic Journal* 50, no. 2 (October): 474–93.

———. 1983b. "Occupational Inheritance in Agriculture." *American Journal of Agricultural Economics* 65, no. 2 (May): 380–400.

Reichler, J. L., ed. 1979. *The Baseball Encyclopedia.* 4th ed. New York: Macmillan Publishing Company.

The Sporting News. 1981. *Official 1981 Baseball Register.* St. Louis: The Sporting News.

Tomes, N. 1981. "The Family, Inheritance, and the Intergenerational Transmission of Inequality." *Journal of Political Economy* 89 (October): 928–58.

Vass, G. 1982. "They Follow in the Footsteps of Their Fathers." *Baseball Digest* (February): 9–20.

Rex L. Cottle

Economics of the Professional Golfers' Association Tour

In the last three decades, the Professional Golfers' Association Tour (PGAT) has achieved prominence among professional sports and, along with the others, has become immune to antitrust legislation. Two recent incidents have aroused public interest in the economic structure, as well as the legal structure, of the PGAT. First, the PGAT commissioner imposed restrictions on touring pros bypassing American tour events to participate in foreign events. Second, a two-tiered tour that would effectively reduce the number of veteran players eligible for competing on the tour was proposed by the PGAT commissioner and subsequently rejected.

Up to now, the focus of the economic research on professional sports (e.g., Neale 1964; Jones 1969; and Rottenberg 1956) has dealt exclusively with team sports rather than individual sports. As a result of the cartel structure of individual sports, where individual athletes collude to sell their joint services to independent tournaments and then compete among themselves for a share of the "wage fund," or purse, the theories developed to explain team sports behavior are not transitive to sports played by individual competitors.

A number of studies (e.g., Ward 1958; Steinherr 1977) have explored various aspects of labor-managed firms. Ideas from these studies apply to the synergistic collusion of professional golfers and the tour's unusual wage fund distribution. By treating the PGAT as a cartel with the express purpose of restricting competition for players and of controlling complementary inputs (cosponsoring tournaments and television rights), its peculiar market characteristics will be analyzed and conjecture given on its future economic stability. While many of the testable hypotheses derived from this study are applicable to other nonteam sports as well as other collusive market arrangements, this paper concentrates solely on professional golfers.

The first part of this paper lays out the PGAT's institutional structure. A theoretical model explaining the economic behavior of the PGAT is developed in the second part of the paper and is followed by an analysis of some present and future problems confronting this athletic cartel.

Institutional Structure of the PGAT

The Professional Golfers' Association (PGA) was organized in 1918 for the express purpose of eliminating the selling of player services by independent brokers and improving the marketability of golfing events. The tour's evolution, from a sparse tournament schedule throughout the first half of this century to its present sequence of forty-eight tournaments, can be attributed largely to the support provided by the PGA and equipment manufacturers on the one hand and by resort hotels, chambers of commerce, and major corporations on the other. During the past thirty years, the real value of the total purses in sanctioned PGAT events has increased more than elevenfold, while the number of events has not quite doubled.

In its formative years, the PGA underwrote several tournaments in order to solidify the players' schedules. Similarly, equipment manufacturers backed the tour because of the benefits they derived from viewers watching professional golfers plying the tools of their trade. The chambers of commerce have continually supported local tournaments, not only because of the gate receipts generated by a golfing event, but also because of the indirect benefits of national advertising. California, Florida and, to a lesser extent, Hawaii have capitalized on their climates, encouraging tourism by televising tournaments during the winter months to entice snowbound northerners to vacation in the sunshine.

The PGAT came into being in 1968 as a means of bringing about détente between touring professionals and the more numerous, but staid, club professionals. For thirty years, these two factions feuded over who should run PGA tournaments. With the formation of the Tournament Players' Division of the PGA (later to be called the PGAT), touring professionals were finally allowed to manage the tour as they saw fit. In addition to administering the eligibility of professional golfers, the commissioner of the PGAT was given the responsibility for scheduling, televising, marketing and sanctioning all tour events.

With the exception of a few exemptions to the local sponsor, local PGA section and, for open competition, PGAT cosponsored events are restricted to PGA members only. Currently, a player may receive his "tour card," or membership in the PGAT, by completing successfully the PGAT's qualifying school or by earning a minimum amount in PGAT events annually with neither a set standard of performance for "awarding" memberships, nor a minimum quota of acceptance. The PGAT determines the number of tour cards granted at each school based on an "unpublicized" set of criteria.

For example, of 447 applicants to the qualifying school in 1974, 19 received credentials. Upon qualifying, a player is accorded a playing card on a probationary basis, which gives him the right to compete for the non-exempt positions remaining in a tour event. Historically, this licensing of touring professionals has effectively restricted entry into the golfing industry.

In cosponsoring a tournament, the PGAT agrees to provide a "representative field" of players in exchange for the prize money and television royalties. With only one minor exception (designated tournaments), the PGAT has no control over which tour golfers will constitute the representative field. Furthermore, domestic tournaments are prohibited from paying appearance money to individual golfers as a means of enticing them to play in their event. Several foreign tournaments have recently circumvented this ruling in an attempt to lure star golfers away from PGAT events. Ross (1977, 4) claims that "appearance money . . . can run from $5,000 to $50,000 . . . [with] expenses paid and . . . whatever prize money he wins."

A Monday qualifying round provides nonexempt golfers (that did not play in the entire preceding tour event) an opportunity to compete for the few remaining positions in a tournament. In order to appease partially those golfers not participating in the cosponsored tournament, the PGAT has organized satellite tournaments for them. In recent years, the number of satellite tournaments has been declining, with only one satellite event in 1980.

Exempt players, those pros who do not have to qualify on the Monday prior to the actual tournament, are free to enter whichever tournaments they wish. Such freedom is unique to individual sports, unlike indentured athletes in team sports. Furthermore, the allocation of tournament privileges is administered by the PGAT and not by the cosponsoring tournament. Demotions and requalifying of golfers are sanctioned by the rules of the PGAT.[1]

Television coverage of cosponsored events is controlled by the PGAT. After deducting all operational expenses of the PGAT, the remaining revenue from the sale of television rights is apportioned among tour events according to their purse size and whether or not the events were actually televised.

Economic Structure of the PGAT

Adam Smith's ([1776] 1937, 128) famous quote, "People of the same trade seldom meet together, even for merriment and diversion, but the conversation ends in a conspiracy against the public, or in some contrivance to raise prices," can also be applied to those people whose merriment and diversion are part of their trade. While golf is a favorite pastime for millions of people around the world, it is the vocation, as well as avocation, of professional golfers.

Like OPEC nations and union members, professional golfers formed a cartel arrangement as a collusive means of selling their services as a monopolist rather than as independent agents. An unusual feature of the professional golfers' cartel is that the PGAT has become the centralized contractual agent for the pooled players, with compensation to its membership being allocated according to the player's relative standing in the field at the end of the event, not according to the player's marginal revenue product to the tournament. Such a dichotomy precludes both the bilateral contracting of individual golfers with the various tournaments and the central agent contracting for individual players' services with a specific tournament. Consequently, the result of players pooling their skills and bargaining as a monopoly is a unique market, one in which the centralized contracting agent agrees to supply a representative field of players to various sequentially arranged tournaments. Each tournament competes for an unidentified mixture of players by providing prize money with no control over its distribution.

The professional golfer supplies a flow of services and absorbs the cost of developing the human capital necessary to compete as well as operating costs of participating on the tour (e.g., transportation, food, lodging, entry fees, opportunity cost of competing, and tools of the trade) just like the traditional firm in economic analysis. Many players form partnerships in order to obtain the necessary financial support to operate on the tour. The pro-partner specializes in production and the "backer" puts up the financing with winnings shared on a prorated basis. Each golfer acts as an economic agent within the structural framework of the PGAT industry.

Conceptually, the PGAT is homologous in an economic sense to any cartel arrangement in that an individual's self-interest is restricted only by the interest of the cartel. Though entry into the cartel is not free, it must be in the golfer's best interest to remain in the cartel or he would leave it.

Since the PGAT is, in effect, a monopolist, the theory of derived demand implies that it is in the golfers' best interest if competitive conditions are maintained in the supply of complementary factors of production. While control over the number of golfers is vital for monopoly power, the profitable exploitation of such a market power dictates that the PGAT sells its collective service to only a limited number of tournaments. This is done by sanctioning or cosponsoring all tournaments in which its members can win official prize money.

In order to sustain its monopolistic power, the PGAT must be able to detect and deter cheating by its members. Most cartels utilize government regulations as enforcement devices to prevent members from chiseling.

However, the PGAT has been able to police successfully its members through various controls (e.g., violators will be suspended from tournament competition for a period of time) rather than rely on outside enforcement. Since the news media covers most of the activities of touring pros, the policing costs of the PGAT cartel are minimal. Though the government has not up to now brought the PGAT under antitrust regulation, it has not prevented similar associations from forming. For example, under current tour regulations, a player wanting to compete in a conflicting event must obtain permission from both the sponsor of the tour event and the commissioner of the PGAT. Violators are usually fined and some are even suspended temporarily from competing in PGA cosponsored events. The mobility of golfers is thus circumscribed, not by the lack of outside opportunity, but by the limited supply of PGAT-sanctioned tournaments.

For simplicity, let a tournament's derived demand for golfers and the corresponding marginal revenue (marginal prize money) be denoted in Figure 1 by D and MR, respectively.[2] Let golfing units, g, be a common unit of measure for professional golfers. Golfing units are a function of the number of golfers and their quality. The better players possess more golfing units than the lesser players. Let MC denote the marginal cost of another golfing unit to compete, inclusive of opportunity cost. Assume both golfers and tournament directors are risk averse.

If the PGAT is a textbook monopolist, it will maximize net revenues accruing to its members by charging the tournament in question a price of OA

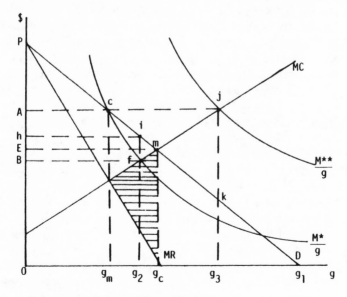

Figure 1. A tournament's demand for golf units

per player and supplying Og_m golf units for prize money totaling $OAcg_m$. In order for the PGAT to behave in such a manner, it would have to pay each player's cost of competing plus distribute the net proceeds among cartel members in a mutually beneficial manner. As is usually true at the monopoly price ($P > MC$), there are more cartel members wanting to play than is optimal from the cartel's perspective. Thus, the potential of chiseling exists with the inevitable consequence of destroying the cartel. If a competitive situation were to exist among pro golfers, the price would be forced down to OE and the tournament would demand a larger number of golf units, Og_c. The shaded area represents the net revenue loss to pro golfers as a result of competition.

As is readily apparent from the previous section, the PGAT does not have control over individual golfers nor does a tournament purchase an individual player's services. Through licensing and controlling the size of the field, the PGAT can limit the golfing units to g_m in order to maximize the total wage fund and create some means of compensating the ($g_c - g_m$) golfers for not competing.

The individual golfer's decision to participate is not based upon a contracted wage offer by tournaments, but by whether his expected return from competing covers his cost of competing. Let a golf unit's expected return be denoted by $E = E(M, g)$, $\partial E/\partial M > 0$, $\partial E/\partial g < 0$, where M is the size of the purse and g is the number of golf units. As the size of the purse increases, *ceteris paribus,* a golfer would expect to earn a larger return from participating. As the number of golf units competing in a tournament increases, the chance of finishing in any given position in the final queue is reduced, and, consequently, a golfer's expected return from competing decreases. For graphical clarity, define $E = M/g$ (refer again to Figure 1). Once the purse size, M^*, is negotiated, the cost to the tournament of one more player entering the event is practically zero. It would be in the tournament's best interest to attract g, golf units. However, with a purse size of M^*, only g_2 golfers would rationally choose to compete. As a result, the tournament would receive $OPig_2$ in total revenue. After paying M^*, ($OBfg_2$) to the PGAT, the tournament would net $BPif$.

The PGAT can maximize the wage fund (purse) for selling player services to a tournament on a pseudo-individual basis by making an all-or-nothing offer greater than M^*.[3] If the PGAT offers the event (shown in Figure 1) an all-or-nothing purse of M^{**}, then as long as the total revenue, $OPKg_3$, generated by g_3 golfers participating is greater than M^{**}, $OAjg_3$, by at least enough to allow a competitive return to the tournament, the tournament would pay the lump-sum purse of M^{**}.

The PGAT guarantees a representative field in return for a purse. To ensure that it can fulfill such an arrangement without possessing property rights to individual players, the PGAT has two discretionary options. First the PGAT could negotiate a large purse, which would raise the expected return of golfers relative to their costs to compete, thus ensuring an excess supply of players for each event. Second, the PGAT could restrict the number of tournaments, which would reduce the number of opportunities for pro golfers to earn income and, simultaneously, increase the number of golfers willing to participate in any one event. The PGAT minimizes its transaction cost by using the response of both tournaments and golfers to a change in the purse size to guarantee a representative field. This supports Cheung's (1977, 520) argument, "While transactions costs determine behavior, they are also determined by behavior. Thus . . . the arrangement under which economic activities are carried out is itself a matter of choice, consistent with constrained maximization."

Economic literature is full of monopoly pricing strategies. Most of these studies, however, fail to consider how implementing any of these strategies affects the market equilibrium. Not only does the PGAT use lump-sum pricing, but it has been able to discriminate between the tournaments for its services because the following market conditions exist: (1) the PGAT has sufficient monopolistic power to control the supply of pros in each tour event; (2) demand elasticities differ appreciably, since tournaments are heterogeneous as to demographic characteristics, geographical location, and economic base of the drawing area; (3) the PGAT is able to segment the various markets by sequential scheduling of tour events and, in turn, prevent direct competition between tournaments for golfers; and (4) resale of player services is impossible because of the nature of the service provided.

A discriminating all-or-nothing pricing scheme, which usurps all economic profits from each tournament on the tour, would maximize the long-run return to the PGA. Each tournament would still be content to earn a competitive return on its investment and not seek alternative sources of generating charitable donations.

The legality of a multi-lump-sum pricing policy has been challenged in other industries but has never been questioned in the golf industry. That does not preclude future antitrust action by the U.S. Department of Justice. For such a policy to be implemented, knowledge about the various tournaments' derived demand is essential. Given that the PGAT can negotiate separately with each buyer and that an excessive number of buyers exist, the PGAT is in a superior position to behave as such a discriminating monopolist.

Problems Confronting the PGAT
Foreign Competition

To prevent golfers from contracting separately with individual tournaments and to ensure cartel stability, the PGAT has banned appearance money from all tour events. Regular tour events are thus left with only three schemes to alter the mixture of pros in its field. First, a tournament may up the ante by offering more prize money and, in so doing, raise a golfer's expected returns and possibly attract the marginally noncommitted players. Along with the larger purse comes the fringe benefit that the tournament will receive preferential treatment in tour scheduling. By improving its position in the schedule, a tournament is in a better position to attract more of the leading golfers. For example, because of the traveling complications to Great Britain, American tournaments that circumscribe the British Open have not drawn as many top pros as they would have if situated in a more favorable slot in the schedule. To eliminate this problem, the American event immediately following the British Open has been recently declared a designated tournament requiring all top players to compete.

Second, the tournament can partially subsidize a touring pro's cost of competing by offering such amenities as reduced rates on lodging, free limousine service, free babysitting service, reduced prices on meals for the golfer's family and countless other cost-saving perquisites.

Third, as a tournament receives more prestige in the golfing world (e.g., the Masters), it provides an opportunity for the winning pro golfer to earn extra income as a result of national publicity (i.e., endorsements, exhibitions, corporation golf). A player's expected nongolf earnings from a major tournament are thus considerably greater than for any regular tour event, so more players are willing to compete in a major tournament than regular tour events with a comparable purse. To a lesser extent, tournaments higher in the hierarchy of the regular tour are able to attract more players with the equivalent prize money than the less publicized tournaments. In this vein, the PGAT recently redesigned the format of the World Series of Golf and added the Tournament Players' Championship in an attempt to elevate them above regular tour events and into the major events category.

From a tournament's perspective, each acceptable form of player enticement is a gamble. There is no assurance that the added expense will be effective in attracting the noncommitted golfers that the tournament is seeking. For that matter, the general response by the players to one of these schemes may be so great that several noted nonexempt players may not make it through Monday qualifying. As a result, the tournament's gate receipts may actually decline. These forms of attracting individual pros are analogous to a poker player continuing to bet on his hand with the hope of enticing a specific card from the remaining cards in the deck at a cost of discarding a better one.

Foreign tournaments have recently circumvented the PGAT regulation on contracting with individual golfers by offering appearance money to leading U.S. pros in addition to whatever they might win. By offering prize money plus appearance money, a foreign tournament can, in effect, hire an individual professional by supplementing his expected income enough to cover the marginal cost of playing rather than increasing the lump-sum offer to the collective field of players. This reduces the uncertainty of the field's quality and increases its profits by paying a smaller total amount to the pros than under lump-sum pricing of the PGAT.

This can be easily shown by considering a tournament, represented in Figure 2, offering a total purse of M^*. The tournament would actually attract g_2 playing units. In order to entice, say, g_3 golfing units, the tournament must increase the purse size to M^{**}. By allowing two-part pricing—a minimum purse of M^* plus appearance fees—the tournament could purchase g_3 golfing units for as little as $M^* + QRN$. As participation increases, the expected return per playing unit falls, necessitating financial enticement to $(g_3 - g_4)$ units. With two-part pricing, g_3 units will participate for a cost of $OSQRg_3$ ($< M^{**}$) and generate a profit of $SPRQ$ ($> JPR$).[4]

Two-part pricing is thus a very effective means of purchasing player participation and still retaining a competitive atmosphere. At the extreme, a single tournament's two-part pricing scheme would convert the tournament into a golfing exhibition by paying each player the value of his marginal product to the tournament, $OVRg_3$, and maximize tournament profits, VPR. Given the enormous volume of private exhibitions performed an-

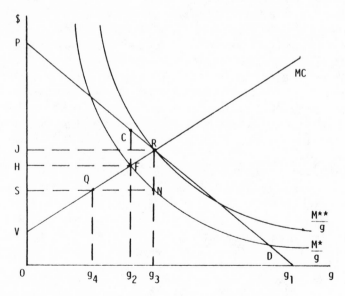

Figure 2. A tournament's demand for golfing units with prize money and appearance money

nually by touring professionals and the profits generated, exhibitions might become a potential threat to the PGA's dominance of the golfing market in the near future.

Two-part pricing assumes that the pricing scheme is independent of a player's marginal revenue product. If the player's productivity is affected by the disincentive of appearance money, then the tournament must weigh the marginal reduction in revenue versus the cost savings resulting from the two-part pricing.

From the PGAT's point of view, a return to competitive pricing would lower profits accruing to the cartel, increase its output, and generate more tournaments. Thus, the heart of the issue concerning the recent threats by the PGAT commissioner about restricting foreign participation of members is nothing more than the usual cartel conflict between the self-interests of its members and the cartel's interest.

Pooling of golfing units outside regular tour events poses the greatest threat to the PGAT. In retaliation, the PGAT is challenging foreign tournaments. First, coterminous with the contracting of a representative field of players, a regular tour event now purchases the conditional rights to all touring professionals for that week. Not all cartel members will choose to participate in every event, but any pro wishing to compete elsewhere must receive approval from both the conflicting tour event and the commissioner. Competition for top golfers, however, has forced tournaments to soften their control of nonparticipating pros for fear of reprisal by pros bypassing its event in future years. Second, the PGAT is currently developing plans to modify the present tour schedule to allow its members to participate more in foreign tournaments during the off-season. Such a plan would force foreign tournaments to arrange their schedules around the PGAT schedule. Third, a PGAT World Tour following the conclusion of the regular tour has raised the very real possibility that foreign tournaments may be facing direct competition from the PGAT in their own countries. Either of the latter proposals would raise the cost of predatory behavior by foreign tournaments and lessen their impact on domestic events.

The cost to the PGAT for policing violators of tournament agreements is minimal, since it is the job of the press and news media to cover all major sporting events that attract professional golfers. However, the cost to the violator is high. He would lose not only direct income by being suspended from playing in regular tour events but also indirect income from not being covered by television, newspapers, and radio. Such coverage enables pros to attract and retain lucrative endorsements.

Individual versus Collective Interests

Two potential conflicts exist between a golfer's best interest and the PGAT's best interest. First, the PGAT, in effect, ties in the lesser known players with the superstars when offering a representative field to a tournament. Successful tie-in sales require the monopolist to tie lesser valued "products" with one whose price elasticity of demand is low and is already being purchased. To ensure profitability, the PGAT has used different means to enforce the tie-in with established stars (i.e., Arnold Palmer and Jack Nicklaus) so as to maximize the collective income. This is currently being accomplished by requiring all players to compete annually in a minimum number of tournaments in order to retain their playing cards and by designating certain tournaments in which all the top players must compete.

A crisis developed in 1977 that vividly illustrates the divergence of individual and group incentives. At that time, the Tournament Policy Board of the PGAT withdrew lifetime exemptions from prior winners of the PGA Championship and the U.S. Open Championship (both major events on the tour), giving younger players more opportunity to play in regular tour events and thus jeopardizing the tenure of veteran players on the tour. Since the exemption status is nontransferable, its current value to the veteran is the present value of the marginal income he derives, both on and off the tour, resulting from the opportunities attributable to this status. Though this request was later rescinded and a format for a senior tour subsequently developed, the incident depicts the legal danger to the present structure of the PGAT and hints at its potential self-destruction.

The PGAT has emerged as a source of "brand-name capital," which is of considerable value to young players. Success on the PGAT, thereby, is the yardstick by which golfers are compared. Much like a young associate lawyer who does the work for name lawyers as a means of investing in his future, young golfers must go through a tour school prior to competing with the stars of the tour. Twenty years ago, a first-year professional was prevented from receiving winnings earned during the first six months of tournament competition. Though it can no longer be classified as indebted servitude, golfers today must put forth a sizable investment of time "served" in order to be given the opportunity to acquire the brand-name capital. The difference between the control by the collective body of golfers and lawyers over new entrants into their industries is quite small. Both require schooling that they directly control. Once licensed, new members are allowed to practice their trade. The major difference lies in the timing of their investment. New golfers must invest before being licensed, lawyers afterward.

Second, the staging of a golf tournament is an example of Alchian-Demsetz's (1972) "team production," which exists when (1) different resources are combined, (2) the product is not the sum of the separate outputs of the cooperating resources, and (3) not all resources are controlled by any one person. Alchian and Demsetz (1972, 779) stress that "if the economic organization meters poorly, with rewards and productivity only loosely correlated, then productivity will be smaller; but if the economic organization meters well productivity will be greater."

A golfer who improves his appeal to the viewers in some way other than winning tournament prizes and therefore attracts a larger gate will ultimately affect the size of M. Since he would receive only a portion of the change in M, he may be expected to shirk some of his responsibility to the PGAT. Rather than improving his appeal at the gate, either by his showmanship or colorful play, a golfer tends to concentrate his efforts on improving his relative standing in the final queue. The incentive to shirk the showmanship activities is thus positively correlated with the size of the purse. Frank Beard (1972), a touring professional golfer, claims that if either Jack Nicklaus or Lee Trevino would appear for three consecutive years in some lesser known event, its purse would double. Even if this assertion were true, a superstar's expected net return from competing would amount to only a fraction of the additional revenue accruing either to the tournament or to the PGAT. What incentives, other than advertising endorsements, do veteran players such as Arnold Palmer have in continuing to compete and lose money?

Since the PGAT imposes a limit on the number of competitors in any tour event, a Monday qualifying round is used to determine which nonexempt golfers can enter the actual tournament. Qualifying is based, once again, upon a player's position in the Monday qualifying queue and not upon his value to the tournament. This method for allocating the limited number of nonexempt positions widens the dichotomy between the reward system and the productivity of players to the tournament and reinforces the player's desire to improve his position in the queue while shirking more from his efforts at increasing the purse by attracting larger galleries.

The long-run effects of shirking and the eventual balking at further subsidizing the younger players at the expense of the older golfers, leads one to question the stability of the PGAT cartel. By ignoring their obligation to attract crowds, and by concentrating on their own game, the individual incentives of the players will eventually destroy the collective product of the PGAT. Such tunnel vision is the historical reason why cartels have a short life expectancy.

What would happen if the top players decided to break off from the PGAT? Could the PGAT survive without them or would they have to submit to allowing appearance money as a way of retaining the superstars, even if their best golf is history? What will happen to the PGAT if incentives to attract audiences are not provided to the up-and-coming stars of tomorrow? The news media have characterized the "young lions" as "walking robots void of personality." That is because of the present individual incentives to improve standing rather than to appeal to the viewers. Pro golf is entertainment and not just "shot making." As the shirking increases, the productivity of the PGAT will decline, ultimately leading to its demise. Unless the PGAT can find a way to correct the present rewards dichotomy, the PGAT as we now know it is in severe jeopardy.

Conclusions

This paper offers an economic analysis of the PGAT with the intention of assessing the stability of the present market structure. Not only is the PGAT a monopoly supplier of professional golfers, but also it effectively extracts most of the consumer surplus from the cosponsoring tournaments while still allowing considerable freedom to its collusive agents. Players may choose to enter any event they wish, but not all players can compete in any one tournament. The excess supply of golfers combined with the limited number of events provides the PGAT with total market control, even to the extent that it negotiates TV contracts independently of the cosponsors.

Economic research into professional sports has focused on questions surrounding team sports and not on sports played by individual competitors. In general, all sports have been given a privileged status as to antitrust sanctions based upon their unique market arrangement. If one views professional golf like any other form of show business, the uniqueness of the cartel vanishes and the obvious questions of restraint of trade reappear.

Like any other cartel, the PGAT has been continually confronted with competition from outside its ranks and from internal dissent. So far, the PGAT has been strong enough to meet these challenges. But given the incentives that players have to shirk their responsibility and the growing strife between the veteran and young golfers, the PGAT will face ever-growing challenges in the near future. And unless the PGAT can develop a means of paying golfers the value of their participation on the tour, the PGAT will inevitably dissolve.

Notes

I wish to thank Dean Beman, Hugh H. Macauley Jr., Richard B. McKenzie, and Bruce Yandle for insightful criticisms of earlier drafts of this paper. The responsibility for errors and any other ambiguities is, of course, my own.

1. In *Deesen v. Professional Golfers' Association of America* [138 F 2d 165 (9th Cir. 1966), cert. denied 385 U.S. 846 (1966), rehearing denied 385 U.S. 1932], the court found that eligibility standards were required by the industry structure and, thus, gave the PGA the right to enforce these requirements.
2. The derived demand for golfers is a function of their ability to produce gate receipts and not necessarily the execution of golf shots, even though

the latter is positively correlated with the former. Arnold Palmer attracts more fans to the tournament today than almost any other player, even though he is not the golfer he was in his prime. Furthermore, the profit motive still dominates a tournament's behavior. Profits are simply guised as charitable donations. It is in the sponsors' best philanthropic interest to make as much money as possible for the worthy causes it supports.

3. Let C = total cost of golfers competing and $\bar{D}(g)$ be the inverse marginal revenue product function of golfers net of a tournament's operating costs. The PGAT's constrained maximization of the wage fund would be accomplished by maximizing the La Grangian $H = M - C + \lambda \left[\int_0^R \bar{D}(g)dg - M \right]$ with the first-order conditions of the constrained maximization resulting in $\bar{D}(g) = \partial C/\partial g = MC$ and $M = \int_0^R \bar{D}(g)dg$. Thus the PGAT would allow the competitive number of units to participate, but would charge a lump-sum purse equal to the total net revenue generated from the golfers, ignoring wealth effects.

4. If golfers strongly prefer risk, then two-part pricing may actually cost the firm more than under lump-sum pricing. However, the number of golfing exhibitions and corporate golfing events have markedly decreased in the last ten years, which implies golfers' aversion to risk without substantially large expected gains.

References

Alchian, A., and H. Demsetz. 1972. "Production, Information Costs, and Economic Organization." *American Economic Review* 62 (December): 777–95.

Barkow, A. 1974. *Golf's Golden Grind: The History of the Tour.* New York: Harcourt, Brace, Jovanovich.

Beard, F. 1972. "Let's Help the Sponsors Who Really Need Help." *Golf Digest* (November): 118–20.

Cheung, S. 1977. "Why Are Better Seats 'Underpriced'?" *Economic Inquiry* 15 (October): 513–22.

El-Hodiri, M., and J. Quirk. 1971. "An Economic Model of a Professional Sports League." *Journal of Political Economy* 79 (December): 1302–19.

Jones, J. 1969. "The Economics of the National Hockey League." *Canadian Journal of Economics* 2 (February): 1–20.

Leibowitz, A., and R. Tollison. 1980. "Free Riding, Shirking, and Team Production in Legal Partnerships." *Economic Inquiry* 18 (July): 380–94.

Neale, W. 1964. "The Peculiar Economics of Professional Sports." *Quarterly Journal of Economics* 78 (February): 1–14.

Noll, R. 1974. *Government and the Sports Business.* Washington, D.C.: Brookings Institution.

Ross, J. 1977. "Tournament News." *Golf Magazine* (October): 4–6.

Rottenberg, S. 1956. "The Baseball Players' Labor Market." *Journal of Political Economy* 64 (June): 242–58.

Scully, G. 1974. "Pay and Performance in Major League Baseball." *American Economic Review* 64 (December): 915–30.

Smith, Adam. [1776] 1937. *An Inquiry into the Nature and Causes of the Wealth of Nations.* New York: Modern Library.

Steinherr, W. 1977. "On the Efficiency of Profit Sharing and Labor Participation in Management." *Bell Journal of Economics* 8 (Autumn): 545–55.

Ward, B. 1958. "The Firm in Illyria: Market Syndicalism." *American Economic Review* 48 (September): 566–89.

VIII Sports and Income Distribution

Robert E. McCormick and Robert D. Tollison

Crime and Income Distribution in a Basketball Economy

In this paper we report the results of a study of the relation between criminal activity and the distribution of income in a controlled environment. Our controlled experiment consists of a time series of college basketball games; we analyze the play of the Atlantic Coast Conference (ACC) Basketball Tournament from 1954 to 1982. Our analogy is this: Play on the basketball court generates a game-by-game, player-by-player distribution of points scored. In terms of the circular flow identity, this distribution of output is equivalent to a distribution of income.[1] We also have an accurate game-by-game proxy of the amount of crime on the court given by the number of personal fouls called by the officials. Hence, it is a relatively simple matter to investigate the link, if any, between the distribution of income, as points, and the extent of crime, as fouls, on the basketball court.

To the best of our knowledge Ehrlich's 1973 paper is the major source of evidence that crime is a function of the income distribution. Specifically, one of his findings is that a more *unequal* income distribution begets more crime. As he notes, however, the empirical richness of this result is confounded by the collinearity of income inequality and urbanization. The purpose of this paper is to pursue Ehrlich's finding on an income distribution which is not subject to the collinearity problem, and to determine if there is a feedback effect of crime on the distribution of income.

Specifically, in Section I, we compare the distribution of points scored per player in the basketball data and the contemporaneous data on the distribution of income in the United States. In Section II, we present an empirical model of crime and the distribution of income employing the basketball data.

I.   Empirical Income Distributions

The burden of the argument here is to show that a basketball economy mirrors the economy in general, which is to say that economic principles are useful in explaining and predicting behavior on the basketball court. To the extent that a basketball game resembles an economy, observations there may be useful in drawing inferences about a broader and more general setting.

It is our strongly held belief that basketball games are no less the real world than any other business activity. Basketball players spend enormous time acquiring and honing their skills. Many are rewarded with extremely large incomes, and it is a fact of the game that players who score many points, who provide many assists, who gather many rebounds, or who excel at defense are rewarded the most. It is also true that expulsion from the game occurs after five fouls in the college game and after six fouls in professional basketball. Consequently, coaches and players are continuously alert to the number of fouls accumulated by any player. Sportscasters routinely report interim statistics, say at half-time, giving equal weight to points scored, rebounds, and fouls committed. All this means, to us at least, that players fully realize the consequences to themselves and their teams of committing fouls. In other words, players who foul too much sit on the bench a lot, and players who sit on the bench a lot do not get paid as well. Crime on the basketball court reduces a player's income.

We subjected this argument to empirical scrutiny. Data are available on individual player performances in several categories. We obtained annual data from 1978 through 1984 for each member of Clemson University's basketball team. Then we estimated the amount of time (in minutes) that each member played per season as a function of: free-throw shooting percentage, field-goal shooting percentage, rebounds per minute, total points per minute, steals per minute, blocked shots per minute, assists per minute, turnovers per minute, and fouls committed per minute. All told we have 101 observations. We estimated the time series equation two separate ways. First, we estimated the model with different parameters for each of three positions on the team: guard, forward, and center. That is, we estimated the relationship for each position separately pooling the error terms. Second, we estimated the parameters pooling all players regardless of position. In either case, there is a negative and statistically significant relation between playing time and fouls committed per minute. Summary statistics are reported in Table 1. The conclusion is inescapable. The more fouls a player commits, the less he plays. In turn, this strongly suggests that his income from basketball is reduced. In other words, on the basketball court at least and holding other things constant, crime does not pay.

More importantly, this is evidence that inferences drawn from observing a basketball game in operation may have broader application. We offer two other types of evidence to bolster this proposition. In an earlier paper we found evidence, using the same data that underlie this paper, that basketball games are played by economic actors, and that economic theory is

Table I
Parameter Estimates of Time Played Equation

		Parameter	t-ratio
Separate estimation*	Guards' fouls	−4,069.4	−3.27
	Centers' fouls	−9,078.4	−2.67
	Forwards' fouls	−1,855.7	−1.78
F-ratio = 3.01	r^2 = .592	n = 84	
Combined estimation*	All fouls	−2,125.0	−3.64
F-ratio = 6.19	r^2 = .429	n = 84	

*Other parameter estimates were deleted from the table for brevity, but they are available on request.

useful in explaining the behavior of players, coaches, and officials during a game (McCormick and Tollison 1984). Specifically, players foul less when there is a greater chance of being caught; the stock of human capital of participants, including coaches, players, and referees, affects the outcome of a game; and players respond to relative prices in the person of their opponent's abilities.

In addition, the empirical distribution of points scored in a basketball game bears close resemblance to the actual distribution of income in the U.S. economy. From Smith Barriers's *The ACC Basketball Tournament Classic,* we collected the game-by-game, player-by-player distribution of scoring for each tournament game. These data correspond to the box scores of games reported in newspapers. The ACC Tournament is played annually in early March, and, throughout the history of the conference, there have been seven or eight member teams. It is a single-elimination tournament, and each tournament has six or seven games depending on the number of teams in the league at the time. All teams participate in the tournament, except in 1961, when the University of North Carolina did not play because they were guilty of playing an ineligible player. For these reasons we have a total of 194 games over the entire time period.

Table 2 reports the tournament-by-tournament, individual distribution of points scored. For each game we ranked the proportion of the total score produced by each player and formed quintiles from lowest to highest. The data are reported in summary form for economy in presentation. The game-by-game data are available on request.[2] The comparable data on the U.S. distribution of family income over the same period are also given in the table.

Inspection of the table reveals that the data grouped by quintiles are re-

Table 2
Basketball and U.S. Income Proportions by Fifths

Year	Basketball Quintiles					U.S. Quintiles				
	1st	2nd	3rd	4th	5th	1st	2nd	3rd	4th	5th
1954	4.8	9.8	15.3	23.6	46.5	4.8	11.1	16.4	22.5	45.2
1955	5.3	11.0	16.5	25.9	41.2	4.8	11.3	16.4	22.3	45.2
1956	5.0	10.1	16.3	24.7	43.9	4.8	11.3	16.3	22.3	45.3
1957	5.9	11.6	17.4	24.2	41.2	4.7	11.1	16.3	22.4	45.5
1958	5.7	9.8	15.9	26.9	41.8	5.0	12.0	18.0	24.0	41.0
1959	4.0	9.7	17.4	27.2	41.7	4.6	10.9	16.3	22.6	45.6
1960	5.5	9.9	18.3	25.7	40.6	4.6	10.9	16.4	22.7	45.4
1961	4.7	10.5	16.9	25.8	42.1	4.6	11.0	16.4	22.6	45.4
1962	4.9	7.8	15.7	24.8	46.8	4.6	10.9	16.3	22.7	45.5
1963	5.6	11.1	19.0	26.5	37.7	5.1	12.0	17.6	23.9	41.4
1964	4.3	9.6	16.9	25.7	43.4	5.2	12.0	17.7	24.0	41.1
1965	4.6	9.6	16.6	26.6	42.7	5.3	12.1	17.7	23.7	41.3
1966	4.2	10.4	18.1	27.9	39.4	5.4	12.4	17.7	23.8	41.7
1967	4.6	11.1	17.4	25.1	41.8	5.4	12.2	17.5	23.7	41.2
1968	5.1	11.0	18.0	26.9	50.7	5.7	12.4	17.7	23.7	41.6
1969	5.1	10.1	17.4	26.2	41.1	5.6	12.3	17.6	23.5	41.0
1970	5.2	11.3	16.5	25.1	41.9	5.5	12.0	17.4	23.5	41.6
1971	6.4	11.2	17.8	26.9	37.7	5.5	11.9	17.4	23.7	41.6
1972	4.7	10.2	17.3	27.0	40.9	5.4	11.9	17.5	23.9	41.4
1973	5.4	10.6	17.7	27.0	39.3	5.5	11.9	17.5	24.0	41.1
1974	4.9	9.6	16.1	26.8	42.7	5.4	12.0	17.6	24.1	41.0
1975	3.6	8.6	17.2	27.1	43.5	5.4	11.8	17.6	24.1	41.1
1976	5.7	9.2	16.8	26.2	42.2	5.4	11.8	17.6	24.1	41.1
1977	5.0	8.8	15.1	27.8	43.3	5.2	11.6	17.5	24.2	41.5
1978	5.3	10.4	15.8	26.4	41.1	5.2	11.6	17.5	24.1	41.5
1979	5.1	10.5	20.0	27.7	50.4	5.3	11.6	17.5	24.1	41.6
1980	5.1	8.2	15.5	26.2	45.0					
1981	4.7	9.2	16.3	24.9	44.9	5.0	11.3	17.4	24.4	41.9
1982	7.1	11.6	16.1	25.0	40.1	4.7	11.2	17.1	24.3	42.7

Sources: S. Barrier, *The ACC Basketball Tournament Classic* (Greensboro, N.C.: Metro Sports, 1981); and U.S. Bureau of Census, *Statistical Abstract of the United States* (Washington, D.C.: Government Printing Office, various editions).

markably similar. This similarity suggests that the forces driving income distribution in general are also at work in the case of basketball.[3] This result, coupled with our earlier work on basketball and crime, provides a strong basis for the analysis of crime and income distribution using basketball games as controlled experiments. All told, the bulk of the evidence presented here convinces us that a basketball game is a mirror of life and that it is appropriate to draw general inferences about society and a large-scale market economy from observing the behavior of actors in a college basketball game. At the very least, we have found no evidence to the contrary. The ball is in the skeptic's court to demonstrate otherwise.

II. Crime and Income Distribution

We contend that rules violations in a basketball game are parallel to criminal activity in general. Basketball rules violations include such things as walking, being three seconds in the lane, double dribbling, being out of bounds, and personal and technical fouls. In our data, we can observe one of these rules violations—the number of personal fouls called by the officials in a game.

When it comes to discussing crime, it is important to note that the more easily measured aspect of crime, the number of arrests, and the more difficult aspect, the actual number of crimes, are *not* the same thing. Failure to make this distinction can be fundamentally misleading. Low arrest rates can be associated with high crime rates, and vice versa. Although the number of arrests and the real crime level do not have to be monotone transformations of each other, our earlier analysis of the ACC data leads us to believe that they are in this case. That is, a higher number of fouls called is positively correlated with a higher number of actual fouls committed on the court. This means that the number of fouls called in a game proxy the amount of crime committed on the court.

In order to investigate whether crime has any impact on the distribution of income, it is important to control for other causal factors. These include such standard variables as age, training, ability, experience, and so forth. To control for these factors in the basketball data, we used the following variables:

EXP   the difference in coaching experience of the winning and losing teams measured by the number of years as coach at the respective school,

PLAYEXP   the difference in the number of lettermen on the winning and losing teams,

HITEDIFF   the difference in the heights of the players on the winning and losing teams measured by the heights of the three tallest centers on the team,

FREEDIFF   the actual difference in the free-throw shooting percentages between the two teams,

FGDIFF   the actual difference in the field-goal shooting percentages between the two teams,

DIFF   the difference in the final score of the game,

SCORE   the total score of the two teams,

SCORERS   the total number of players who scored in the game, and

FOULS   the total number of personal fouls called in the game.[4]

Table 3
OLS Estimates of Income Equation

Independent Variable	Parameter Estimate	Hirschman–Herfindahl Index		
		F-ratio	3.23	
		Prob > F	.0013	
		R-square	.1462	
		Standard Error	t-Ratio	Prob > |t|
INTERCEPT	0.07685	0.006424	11.9638	.0001
HITEDIFF	−0.000306	0.000527	−0.5808	.5622
EXP	−0.000103	0.000116	−0.8852	.3773
PLAYEXP	−0.000001	0.00031	−0.0033	.9974
SCORE	−0.0000237	0.0000319	−0.7432	.4584
SCORERS	−0.0005596	0.0003584	−1.5611	.1203
FOULS	−0.000111	0.0000473	−2.3477	.0200
FREEDIFF	−0.0121	0.0053552	−2.2595	.0251
FGDIFF	−0.005084	0.010186	−0.4991	.6183
DIFF	0.00036	0.000134	2.6894	.0079

Independent Variable	Parameter Estimate	Entropy Index		
		F-ratio	29.19	
		Prob > F	.0001	
		R-square	.6071	
		Standard Error	t-Ratio	Prob > |t|
INTERCEPT	1.006	0.05037	19.9668	.0001
HITEDIFF	0.00532	0.00413	1.2872	.1998
EXP	0.00097	0.00091	1.0569	.2921
PLAYEXP	0.00104	0.00244	0.4267	.6701
SCORE	−0.00049	0.00025	−1.9664	.0509
SCORERS	0.0095	0.00281	3.3701	.0009
FOULS	0.000975	0.00037	2.6309	.0093
FREEDIFF	0.0747	0.042	1.7788	.0771
FGDIFF	0.042	0.0799	0.5259	.5997
DIFF	0.00867	0.00105	8.2543	.0001

We describe the distribution of player scoring in each game with four summary statistics: the entropy index, the Hirschman-Herfindahl index, and the one- and two-player concentration ratios. Table 3 reports the ordinary-least-squares estimates of the regression of the four summary statistics on the independent variables listed above. Our approach is in the tradition of others who have studied the empirical determinants of the individual distribution of income. We make no pretense of having a

Table 3
(Continued)

		One-Firm Concentration Ratio		
		F-ratio	2.15	
		Prob > F	.0276	
		R-square	.1023	
Independent Variable	Parameter Estimate	Standard Error	t-Ratio	Prob > |t|
INTERCEPT	0.1867	0.0203	9.1776	.0001
HITEDIFF	−0.000293	0.00167	−0.1754	.8609
EXP	−0.000414	0.000369	−1.1209	.2639
PLAYEXP	0.000204	0.000984	0.2076	.8358
SCORE	0.000026	0.000101	0.2534	.8002
SCORERS	−0.000246	0.00114	−0.2169	.8285
FOULS	−0.000352	0.00015	−2.3534	.0197
FREEDIFF	−0.0432	0.017	−2.5474	.0117
FGDIFF	−0.037	0.032262	−1.1470	.2530
DIFF	−0.000227	0.000424	0.5364	.5924

		Two-Firm Concentration Ratio		
		F-ratio	1.65	
		Prob > F	.1031	
		R-square	.0805	
Independent Variable	Parameter Estimate	Standard Error	t-Ratio	Prob > |t|
INTERCEPT	0.31244	0.0269	11.6136	.0001
HITEDIFF	−0.00128	0.0022	−0.5804	.5624
EXP	−0.000519	0.0005	−1.0645	.2886
PLAYEXP	0.00065	0.0013	0.4994	.6181
SCORE	−0.000027	0.00013	−0.2003	.8415
SCORERS	−0.0002	0.0015	−0.1323	.8949
FOULS	−0.0004	0.0002	−2.0410	.0428
FREEDIFF	−0.0459	0.0224	−2.0467	.0422
FGDIFF	−0.0393	0.0427	−0.9216	.3581
DIFF	0.000326	0.00056	0.5814	.5618

theory that predicts whether crime increases or decreases the dispersion of income.

The results uniformly suggest that more crime on the basketball court is associated with a more equal distribution of player outputs.[5] The coefficient on *FOULS* in the one- and two-firm concentration ratio specifications is negative and significant at the 5 percent level. In the entropy specification the coefficient is positive and significant at the 1 percent level. The

Table 4
3SLS Estimates of Foul and Income Equations

Variable	Foul Equation			
	Parameter Estimate	Standard Error	Approx. t-Ratio	Prob > |t|
INTERCEPT	−9,041.36	868.21	−10.4138	.0001
HITEDIFF	0.733	0.591	1.2404	.2169
EXP	0.0973	0.1336	0.7282	.4678
PLAYEXP	−0.346	0.3549	−0.9760	.3308
OFFEXPAV	−0.1641	0.2337	−0.7022	.4837
ATTEND	0.000198	0.000569	0.3480	.7284
YEAR	4.6527	0.4434	10.4928	.0001
WFTPCT	−17.965	9.0394	−1.9874	.0489
LFTPCT	−11.24	6.8225	−1.6475	.1017
WFGPCT	−73.95	16.4643	−4.4914	.0001
LFGPCT	−53.211	12.277	−4.3343	.0001
SHOOT	21.981	4.2507	5.1712	.0001
CHARGE	26.503	5.4624	4.8519	.0001
OFFICIAL	−23.994	3.984	−6.0221	.0001
SCORE	0.369	0.042065	8.78	.0001
H-H INDEX	−128.4002	90.6	−1.4172	.1587

Variable	Hirschman–Herfindahl Index Equation			
	Parameter Estimate	Standard Error	Approx. t-Ratio	Prob > |t|
INTERCEPT	0.0728	0.006622	10.9929	.0001
HITEDIFF	−0.000676	0.0005354	−1.2624	.2088
EXP	−0.000164	0.00012	−1.3656	.1742
PLAYEXP	0.000057	0.000325	0.1756	.8608
SCORE	−0.0000277	0.0000312	−0.8883	.3759
SCORERS	−0.00026	0.0003686	−0.7148	.4759
FOULS	−0.00011	0.0000477	−2.3086	.0224
FREEDIFF	−0.0122	0.005328	−2.2935	.0233
FGDIFF	−0.00254	0.01	−0.2460	.8061
DIFF	0.000246	0.0001349	1.8231	.0704

coefficient on *FOULS* in the Hirschman-Herfindahl equation is negative and significant at the 5 percent level.[6] All of these results are in accord with the idea that crime and the distribution of income are not independent; income is more equal where crime is higher or vice versa.[7]

We are now in a position to link our findings to those of Ehrlich. In his model the dispersion of income affects the level of crime. In our regressions the level of crime affects the dispersion of income. Taken together,

Table 4
(Continued)

| Variable | Foul Equation | | | |
	Parameter Estimate	Standard Error	Approx. t-Ratio	Prob > |t|
INTERCEPT	−9,075.2	866.762	−10.4702	.0001
HITEDIFF	0.764607	0.590182	1.2955	.1973
EXP	0.103605	0.133493	0.7761	.4390
PLAYEXP	−0.342724	0.355933	−0.9629	.3373
OFFEXPAV	−0.165586	0.233917	−0.7079	.4802
ATTEND	0.00020	0.00057	0.3560	.7224
YEAR	4.669	0.4428	10.5442	.0001
WFTPCT	−18.17	9.167136	−1.9820	.0495
LFTPCT	−11.232	6.808116	−1.6499	.1012
WFGPCT	−76.05	16.3842	−4.6416	.0001
LFGPCT	−51.68	12.39017	−4.1710	.0001
SHOOT	21.813	4.2528	5.1290	.0001
CHARGE	26.71	5.4646	4.888	.0001
OFFICIAL	−24.123	3.987	−6.0511	.0001
SCORE	0.3744	0.041675	8.98	.0001
ONE-FIRM CR	−35.363	29.27	−1.2081	.2291

| Variable | One-Firm Concentration Ratio Equation | | | |
	Parameter Estimate	Standard Error	Approx. t-Ratio	Prob > |t|
INTERCEPT	0.17385	0.02104	8.2627	.0001
HITEDIFF	−0.0011738	0.001702	−0.6898	.4914
EXP	−0.0004157	0.0003826	−1.0864	.2791
PLAYEXP	0.00075983	0.0010335	0.7352	.4634
SCORE	0.000009	0.0001	0.0908	.9277
SCORERS	0.00068868	0.00117066	0.5883	.5573
FOULS	−0.0003583	0.00015158	−2.3639	.0194
FREEDIFF	−0.03969	0.01693	−2.3436	.0205
FGDIFF	−0.02997	0.03282	−0.9133	.3626
DIFF	−0.0001378	0.00042855	−0.3216	.7482

these results suggest that crime and the distribution of income are jointly determined. To investigate this possibility, we estimated the various basketball income distribution equations simultaneously with a model of fouls from our earlier paper, including the measures of income dispersion as explanatory variables. Three-stage–least-squares estimates of both equations are reported in Table 4. The other independent variables not previously defined are:

Table 4
(Continued)

| Variable | Foul Equation | | | |
	Parameter Estimate	Standard Error	Approx. t-Ratio	Prob > |t|
INTERCEPT	−9,110.88	868.6741	−10.4883	.0001
HITEDIFF	0.75063	0.59322	1.2654	.2079
EXP	0.10419	0.13371	0.7792	.4372
PLAYEXP	−0.35185	0.3555	−0.9898	.3240
OFFEXPAV	−0.16537	0.2343	−0.7058	.4815
ATTEND	0.0002096	0.000569	0.3681	.7133
YEAR	4.687	0.44369	10.5638	.0001
WFTPCT	−17.75	9.08866	−1.9531	.0528
LFTPCT	−11.594	6.837	−1.6958	.0922
WFGPCT	−75.997	16.3947	−4.6355	.0001
LFGPCT	−52.505	12.3398	4.2550	.0001
SHOOT	21.9399	4.2581	5.1525	.0001
CHARGE	26.7339	5.4707	4.8867	.0001
OFFICIAL	−24.195	3.9916	−6.0616	.0001
SCORE	0.374450	0.0418	8.96	.0001
TWO-FIRM CR	−19.6597	20.92	−0.9398	.3490

| Variable | Two-Firm Concentration Ratio Equation | | | |
	Parameter Estimate	Standard Error	Approx. t-Ratio	Prob > |t|
INTERCEPT	0.29997	0.029	10.3412	.0001
HITEDIFF	−0.0031785	0.00234	−1.3558	.1773
EXP	−0.00075	0.000527	−1.4292	.1551
PLAYEXP	0.000938	0.00142	0.6588	.5111
SCORE	0.000081	0.000137	−0.5928	.5542
SCORERS	0.0009473	0.0016149	0.5866	.5584
FOULS	−0.000379	0.000209	−1.8129	.0719
FREEDIFF	−0.0536	0.0233	−2.2984	.0230
FGDIFF	−0.0351	0.0452	−0.7767	.4386
DIFF	0.00000152	0.000591	0.0026	.9979

WFGPCT	field-goal shooting percentage of the winning team,
LFGPCT	field-goal shooting percentage of the losing team,
WFTPCT	free-throw shooting percentage of the winning team,
LFTPCT	free-throw shooting percentage of the losing team,
SHOOT	a dummy variable for a rules change in 1973,
CHARGE	a dummy variable for a rules change in 1963,

Table 4
(Continued)

Variable	Foul Equation			
	Parameter Estimate	Standard Error	Approx. t-Ratio	Prob > |t|
INTERCEPT	−9,199.25	856.73	−10.7376	.0001
HITEDIFF	0.44	0.6009	0.7322	.4653
EXP	0.05597	0.1335	0.4194	.6756
PLAYEXP	−0.4937	0.355	−1.3892	.1670
OFFEXPAV	−0.1492	0.23	−0.6476	.5183
ATTEND	0.000125	0.00056	0.2229	.8239
YEAR	4.715	0.437595	10.78	.0001
WFTPCT	−20.773	9.013	−2.3047	.0227
LFTPCT	−6.5699	7.0626	−0.9302	.3539
WFGPCT	−83.386	16.334	−5.1051	.0001
LFGPCT	−38.415	13.478	−2.8502	.0050
SHOOT	21.5692	4.1976	5.1385	.0001
CHARGE	27.8869	5.406	5.1586	.0001
OFFICIAL	−25.242	3.995	−6.3188	.0001
SCORE	0.364	0.041619	8.75	.0001
ENTROPY INDEX	22.807	8.4368	2.7033	.0077

Variable	Entropy Equation			
	Parameter Estimate	Standard Error	Approx. t-Ratio	Prob > |t|
INTERCEPT	1.025	0.0549	18.68	.0001
HITEDIFF	0.00841	0.0044468	1.8913	.0606
EXP	0.0014783	0.0009998	1.4786	.1414
PLAYEXP	0.001166	0.0027	0.4318	.6665
SCORE	−0.0004717	0.0002594	−1.8181	.0711
SCORERS	0.007196	0.003047	2.3616	.0195
FOULS	0.0012039	0.0003952	3.0460	.0028
FREEDIFF	0.0834	0.0442	1.8840	.0616
FGDIFF	0.0188	0.0857	0.2193	.8267
DIFF	0.009373	0.001117	8.3880	.0001

OFFEXP   average number of tournament games officiated by the crew,

OFFICIAL   the number of officials who called the game, 2 or 3.

The results provide an interesting contrast to Ehrlich's findings. First, modeling fouls endogenously does not significantly alter the single-equation results on income distribution reported in Table 3. Second, the dispersion of income significantly affects the number of fouls in two of the four specifications. In the other two specifications the coefficient is close to significance. Third, the basketball data cast a different light on Ehrlich's finding that income inequality is associated with more crime. We observe that a more equal distribution of income is associated with more crime. Entropy is positively associated with more fouls, while one- and two-firm concentration ratios and the Hirschman–Herfindahl index are negatively related. This is the opposite of what Ehrlich found, which suggests that his concern about multicollinearity may have been well-founded, and contradicts the widely held view that crime is the result of a skewed income distribution.[8]

Notes

We are indebted to the Clemson University Athletic Department, especially Bob Bradley, for help on this project and to Michael Maloney for helpful comments. We also received constructive remarks from two referees.

1.   In a narrow sense, points are income on the basketball court. Nothing else counts except the score. In this sense the identity is complete. In a broader context, some players get paid for skills other than scoring, a point we acknowledge. However, the strict, narrow analogy is what we have in mind. As such, it does not matter that points scored do not perfectly map into outside income. Points scored in a game *are* basketball income and that is our analogy. It remains to be seen whether the analogy is appropriate.

2.   Three points should be noted about the basketball data. As we have already noted, basketball embodies a team production process in which points scored are not the only relevant activity. Rebounds and assists, for example, are also important. However, we contend that players' income is, for the most part, a monotone transformation of points scored. Consequently, we use points produced as a convenient proxy for individual contributions to team production. Second, in forming the quintiles, unless the number of players scoring in the game was evenly divided into fifths, it was necessary to allocate the points scored by some players across two quintiles. Third, we only include players who scored in a game. This means that players with no point production were deleted from the sample. Including these players has no substantive impact on the results we report.

3.   See Stigler (1966), for a discussion of the determinants of income dispersion. For a demonstration that the income distribution from a controlled environment has the same functional form as the national income distribution, see R. C. Battalio et al., "Income Distribution in Two Experimental Economies," *Journal of Political Economy* 85 (1977): 1259.

4.   Subject to the caveats about North Carolina in 1961, data on these inde-

pendent variables were obtained from Office of the Commissioner and the Service Bureau, *Atlantic Coast Conference Yearbook*, ACC (1954–1983) and from Barrier (1981, n. 4). We are missing some data for 1955 and 1962, and for this reason games in these years are omitted in our regression analyses. The data are available from the authors.

5. The results are not sensitive to model specification. For example, deleting the experience variables does not significantly change the estimate of the coefficient on *FOULS*.

6. The income distribution is not very sensitive to changes in the level of crime. The elasticities (evaluated at the means), one-firm, two-firm, entropy, and H–H, are -0.11, -0.07, 0.04, and -0.09, respectively.

7. We note that the distribution of income in basketball contains victim compensation. The fouled team is awarded possession of the ball, or the fouled player gets a free-throw.

8. The other results in both Tables 3 and 4 are largely consistent with previous work on the distribution of income, which the reader can verify by inspecting the tables.

References

Barrier, S. 1981. *The ACC Basketball Tournament Classic*. Greensboro, N.C.: Metro Sports.

Battalio, R. C., et al. 1977. "Income Distribution in Two Experimental Economies." *Journal of Political Economy* 85:1259.

Ehrlich, I. 1973. "Participation in Illegitimate Activities: A Theoretical and Empirical Investigation." *Journal of Political Economy* 81:521.

McCormick, R. E., and R. D. Tollison. 1984. "Crime on the Court." *Journal of Political Economy* 92:223.

Office of the Commissioner and the Service Bureau. 1954–1983. *Atlantic Coast Conference Yearbook*.

Stigler, G. J. 1966. *The Theory of Price*. 3rd ed. New York: Macmillan.

IX Conclusion

Brian L. Goff and Robert D. Tollison

Sportometrics: Present and Future

I.   The Present

Sports behavior offers examples of almost every type of economic activity. The contributions presented in the preceding chapters bolster this conclusion. We have seen applications ranging from the criminal justice area to the testing of expectational efficiency in markets, to the outcomes of varied organizational rules, to the measurement of managerial efficiency. Sports research is not simply an article on baseball here and an article about football there. The applications to specific sports are linked by the same types of interests that define conventional economics.

Economics teaches that individuals rationally respond to incentives. Sports research shows that individuals behave no differently on Olympic tracks, Major League Baseball diamonds, or college basketball courts. Olympic sprinters squeeze better times out in the face of bigger payoffs; injuries are not just random events; ownership structure plays a significant role in injury rates. All economists know that management helps to determine final productivity and value. The sporting world is no different. Managers contribute differential amounts to winning. The athletic environment, though, allows us to observe these relative contributions in an explicit team production setting. Basic industrial organization theory tells us that monopolistic and competitive models produce similar outcomes only with special assumptions about costs. Sports research shows that monopolistic versus competitive structure matters in sports. Differences in the structure of competition in high school basketball have important implications for later player performance in the NBA. Through research in this field, we have also learned about the links between organizations and sporting activities. Athletic contests do not occur on an island separated from other institutions. Nobel prizes, research institutes, and productive faculty members are not the only draws for college treasuries. High performance levels on the playing fields affect university contributions and enrollments. From a normative perspective gambling may have its positive and negative aspects. However, the well-developed betting markets surrounding sports aid economic research, especially in testing theories about expectations. The jury is still out, but sports betting has permitted some of the best tests to date of the efficient markets model.

In total, the contributions in this book present a compelling case for the importance of sportometrics research. Rarely can such diverse subject matters be scrutinized with data drawn from one industry.

II.   The Future

It is presumptuous to suggest research topics to other people. The first rule of science is that anything goes, which means that freedom and scientific inquiry go hand in hand. Competition among scientists will sort the wheat from the chaff. So in discussing possible future projects, we are only seeking to round out the volume on a positive note. Others will have better ideas, but the surface has only been scratched. We shall be brief.

1. One such topic involves serial correlation in time series. In sports (and in other settings) serial correlation is the same thing as "momentum." What is the nature of momentum in the play of a game? Does it exist or is it merely a dramatization of random swings in events and emotions? If momentum exists in the serial correlation of scoring in a game, does it have different magnitudes of importance depending on the sport involved?

2. The economics of marathon-type road racing presents another promising area. During endurance events like marathons, strategizing is possible. This closely parallels the behavior of firms in concentrated industries. Does strategizing seem to occur in marathons? If it does, what effects does it have on outcome versus the outcome of perfectly competitive situations like sprints? What would a perfectly competitive distribution of running times look like? Does Nash-equilibrium behavior characterize runner behavior?

3. The governance framework of sports allows for analogies to constitutional economics. The proprietary nature of sports organizations increases the importance of research in this field. The constitutions that govern professional sports leagues evolve in a value-maximizing environment. How are they different from constitutions for governments that evolve in a nonwealth-maximizing environment?

4. A related topic is the effect on injuries of attenuated property rights. This research would look at injury rates in high school versus college versus professional sports, where there are obvious differences in property rights to human capital.

5. Also, the explicit team nature of sports permits many general hypotheses concerning production with team elements to be discussed. One is the effect of team production on managerial pay. Other things equal, do managers in areas where team elements are higher receive greater compensation? This research would build on the Clement-McCormick paper.

6. Does the Alchian-Allen theorem on shipping the good apples out apply to sports? For example, do football teams pass more (at the margin) in inclement weather as this theorem suggests they will?[1]

7. What happened to the number of hit batters before and after the helmet rule in Major League Baseball?

Obviously, these are suggestions of topics that interest us. There are without a doubt hundreds of other good possibilities. Sportometrics has a future.

Notes

1.   We are indebted to Robert E. McCormick for this point.

Contributors

BENNY D. BOWERS, University of North Carolina at Charlotte
THOMAS F. CARGILL, University of Nevada at Reno
R. CLEMENT, Clemson University
REX L. COTTLE, University of Mississippi
JOHN L. DOBRA, University of Nevada at Reno
ARTHUR A. FLEISHER III, Metropolitan State College
JOHN M. GANDAR, University of North Carolina at Charlotte
BRIAN L. GOFF, Western Kentucky University
RICHARD S. HIGGINS, Howrey and Simon
CLIFF J. HUANG, Vanderbilt University
DAVID N. LABAND, Clemson University
KENNETH LEHN, Securities and Exchange Commission and Washington
   University
BERNARD F. LENTZ, Ursinus College
ROBERT E. MCCORMICK, Clemson University
ROBERT A. MEYER, University of California, Berkeley
PHILIP K. PORTER, University of South Florida
GERALD W. SCULLY, University of Texas at Dallas
WILLIAM F. SHUGHART II, University of Mississippi
JOHN J. SIEGFRIED, Vanderbilt University
MAURICE TINSLEY, Datagraphics, Inc.
ROBERT D. TOLLISON, George Mason University
THOMAS ZAK, U.S. Naval Academy
RICHARD A. ZUBER, University of North Carolina at Charlotte

Index

Sportometrics was composed into type on a Linotron 202 digital photo-typesetter in ten point Times Roman with two points of spacing between the lines. Gill Sans was selected for display. The book was designed by Cameron Poulter, composed by G&S Typesetters, Inc., printed offset by Thomson-Shore, Inc., and bound by John H. Dekker and Sons, Inc. The paper on which this book is printed carries acid-free characteristics for an effective life of at least three hundred years.

TEXAS A&M UNIVERSITY PRESS : COLLEGE STATION